The Ways of the Word

THE WAYS OF THE WORD

Episodes in Verbal Attention

GARRETT STEWART

CORNELL UNIVERSITY PRESS
ITHACA AND LONDON

Copyright © 2021 by Cornell University

All rights reserved. Except for brief quotations in a review, this book, or parts thereof, must not be reproduced in any form without permission in writing from the publisher. For information, address Cornell University Press, Sage House, 512 East State Street, Ithaca, New York 14850. Visit our website at cornellpress.cornell.edu.

First published 2021 by Cornell University Press

Library of Congress Cataloging-in-Publication Data

Names: Stewart, Garrett, author.
Title: The ways of the word : episodes in verbal attention / Garrett Stewart.
Description: Ithaca [New York] : Cornell University Press, 2021. | Includes bibliographical references and index.
Identifiers: LCCN 2021020723 (print) | LCCN 2021020724 (ebook) | ISBN 9781501761393 (hardcover) | ISBN 9781501761409 (paperback) | ISBN 9781501761423 (pdf) | ISBN 9781501761416 (epub)
Subjects: LCSH: English language—Style. | Word (Linguistics) | English literature—19th century—History and criticism. | English literature—20th century—History and criticism. | American literature—19th century—History and criticism. | American literature—20th century—History and criticism.
Classification: LCC PE1421 .S676 2021 (print) | LCC PE1421 (ebook) | DDC 808/.042—dc23
LC record available at https://lccn.loc.gov/2021020723
LC ebook record available at https://lccn.loc.gov/2021020724

Contents

Scanned: Introduction in Overview   1

Part I. Paged: Wording in Place

1. Lexical Timelines, Phrasal Timings   27
2. The Tensed Word   58

Part II. Staged: Text Out Loud

3. Reading-en-Scène   89

Part III. Screened: Toward a Cinematics of the Sentence

4. Threading the Read   117

5. Fframe-Advance   158
Tracked: An Epilogue on Aftertones   199

Notes   229
Index   235

… Ways of the Word

Scanned

Introduction in Overview

The word's ways are not the world's ways. Except when they are constructing a fictive world. The word's ways are not natural, at least in the ventures, and wagers, of literary writing. If some swaths of words are found more or less at the vernacular ready, they are just as quickly reshaped, no sooner given than remade. Remade to order. Neither in their turns of phrase, nor their sway over us, are the word's ways of elicited literary response as much discovered as contrived.

Their artifice is their art, not only in the occasional neologism, but in their local verbal ecology: an aesthetic maintenance from sentence to sentence, edging forward from word *to/ward word*. A reader's reflexes may be inclined to ward off any glancing phonetic echoes and overlaps, as italicized there, that may result—or leave them be, let them happen, taking place within their own lexical displacements. In the latter case, touchstones of stylistic notice are often *touchtones*: grace notes playing— in a phonetically compressed echo or otherwise—across wording's variable syllabic register. Such stray tones may sound within the broader instrumentation of syntactic harmony or dissonance in literary writing, with lexical spans as well as phonetic clusters at times bent out of shape, pulverized, and redistributed. And in the phrasal membrane of a resulting literary tympanum, that summoned drum of the inner ear in reading, it is, as the epilogue will summarize it, one destination of this study to isolate and name—and by a typifying sound play in its own denomination—the literary moment of *epiphony*.

By "literary," I mean first of all to stress an etymological, not canonical, sense. This book's verbal attention is to the "lettered" text, where syllables and their words depend on an internal and serial structure analogous to the inclusive build of syntax in the temporality of reading. The provocations to such episodic verbal attention are drawn not just from narrative fiction but also from poetry. The effort is to course-correct two familiar critical tendencies: in prose fiction, where language loses ground to plot, even though language *is* that ground; in verse, where the richness of wording may be over-ridden on the rails of meter and lineation. My alternate story about "the ways of the word" calls out internal fashionings—as well as grammatical fastenings across the platform of lettered enunciation—that include, and also underlie, the normal rhetorical preoccupations of stylistic analysis.

Certain simple and preliminary assumptions, then, can guide one's lexical instinct in checking out (rather than dreaming to chart) some selective ramifications of the word over two centuries of literary writing, classic to contemporary, in poetry as well as prose, from Dickinson and Dickens to Don DeLillo, Whitman through Wharton, Woolf, and Wolfe down to Colson Whitehead, Tennyson to Thomas Pynchon, Melville to Toni Morrison, Forster and Fitzgerald to Jonathan Franzen, Poe to Richard Powers. The language in play across such writing produces "style" not just in—but *as*—the behavioral modification of words by syntax, even while the structure of wording is often rethought from within. Words: filed in technical stylistics under the rubric "diction" or "vocabulary" before being subdivided, in whatever order, by tone (in the restricted sense of low or elevated register), scale (syllable count), lineage (origin and derivation), phonetic stress (sound shapes), figurative quotient (metaphoric or literal). Wordings: felt in immediate literary motion as the triggers of verbal sensation and its sense—the word's ways of driving associations home.

En route, words work overtime in literary prose, both in their strenuous expended energies and over the course of syntactic time. Words in this way both structure and disrupt meaning, build and disconcert it by turns. Even momentary stumbling blocks can become alternate routes to sense. In the latest novel by the last-mentioned writer above, for instance, Powers's Pulitzer Prize–winning *The Overstory* (2018), a lexical understory concerns the introvert girl, lover of reading and trees, whose inscription in "booklike bark" sends roots into the deep etymology of *book* in the *beech* on which runes were once carved.[1] Yet when belatedly learning to talk, she is cursed with a sludgelike enunciation whose description at first calls up "slurry" as an adjective in a phrase that skirts oxymoron (*hard ooze*) when we are forced back on its noun form instead: "When her own speech started to flow at last"—with the dead metaphor of flow immediately materialized in the gurgle and clot of further wording—"it hid her thoughts behind a slurry hard for the uninitiated to comprehend" (113). The unsaid modifier *slurred* (deferring to the specialized noun form for "muck") feels echoed momentarily (in its "urred" nucleus) when we learn, two sentences on, that "h*er* fath*er* alone un*der*stands h*er* woodlands w*or*ld, as he always un*der*stands h*er* ev*er*y thickened w*or*d" (113): a breadth of comprehension sustained across the phonetic span—and evoked underbrush thicket—of *wood/world/word*.

Let such a modest phonic buildup, such "thickening," stand as emblematic. In one corner of my mind, an alternate subtitle for this volume from the start: "Episodes in Literary Concentration," that last abstract noun intended in a comparable double sense to its settled-upon alternative. As with the *attention* manifest in the shapings of prose—in the exactions of its own tensile energy, well in advance of being bestowed on it by close reading—the notion of literary *concentration* would also evoke its own response. Density breeds intensity in the work of reading. Or might well do so in a given case. There is no definitive way to range or categorize such moments, of course, only to sample some of their daunting variety of devices and enticements. The effort to do so here has resulted in a book that might once have been called "practical criticism"—except that its main praxis is appreciation rather than interpretation: no thesis in the usual sense, no organizing themes, no remobilized theory, just a motivated series of focal points tactically subdivided for comparison. *The Ways of the Word* does not advance any defiant position paper. Its only polemic is to exist at all in an academic climate where verbal issues of this sort are so seldom kept in sight (or earshot)—and whose mainstream weathervanes, to say nothing of methodological barometers, are tooled for other disciplinary crosscurrents than those of wording's high- or low-pressure fronts.

Yet certain facts about literary production, about writing as such, hence about wording, remain demonstrable—and very much worth recovering. Even when deliberately indeterminate, vocabulary sets the tenor of a sentence, drawing from a dictionary archive that is ideally revitalized in the process. Tapping the lexicon of a given linguistic inheritance, a writer's mental thesaurus is on call to narrow or sharpen a notion toward its most *pointed* form. Clarity is a matter of paring down, even as the mot juste can then be loosed into the fuller music of grammatical amplification, where surplus linguistic inference may remain in play beyond the task of exactitude. It is in this manner that words make the sense of a sentence. They contour the sensory medium of a given prose sequence—the aural and graphic traces of inscription—while generating a semantic yield from its succession. When craftily channeled, the sensorial grows tutorial, guiding our reception of what it brings to mind—as true for the *grandes allées* of ceremonial procession as for detours into the back alleys of the lowbrow. So-called Cockney punning, for instance, flummoxes a character in Dickens's *Our Mutual Friend* when, advised to seek counsel in the law courts of Doctors Commons, he wonders why he needs a physician named Scommons. Appreciative reading is advised to keep well within hailing distance of such phonetic play.

On points that may seem, so far, quite obvious, you are hearing here from the author of several academic studies of literary language meant to pursue such issues at their fullest theoretical scope. *The Ways of the Word* offers, instead, an approach held at a deliberate distance from the full panoply of technical vocabulary—linguistic, rhetorical, and theoretical alike.[2] Verbal intuition alone—including its upending at times by phrasal surprise or unexpected tangles—can get us to wording's inner linings without having to drive a categorical, let alone theoretical, wedge at every turn (of phrase). This amounts to no "resistance to theory," let alone mounts any. It is about reading in practice—and the practice of writing potentially learned from it. The anchor of the study's paired last chapters is (accordingly) an undergraduate syllabus for a course in creative writing, a transmedial venture that compares screen montage to the kinetics of syntax: analysis and prose writing together.

Through it all, fascination remains axiomatic. What should grab and hold us straight off, riveting us no less in prose fiction than in poetry, is the vital action of language in its generative complexity: a complexity that could never be exhausted by categorization, but that can best be evidenced by certain enlivening distinctions. I've therefore chaptered this verbal energy according to a tripartite structure meant to rotate into notice some leading features of its inventive drive. This involves writing at first paged (emplaced as script) for typical print reception; writing next staged in anomalous recitation (the theatrical "production" of a novelistic text—the text itself, its prose lines, not its storyline); writing then screened in the mind's audiovisual projection room for its latent cinematic analogues. These are merely convenient administrative divisions; the through line is an inquiry into the vibrant linguistic charge of words at work. What makes writing tick, and at how many coordinated levels, as a time-based medium? How to sound this out, in exactly more *senses* than one? How to keep up a close, almost tactile, contact with wording's shaping grip, its potent hold. Hold, clench, "shaping grip"—and sometimes (as right there) a latent internal *rip* whose impact may ripple into adjacent lexemes in a wording where verbal units are mobilized and regrouped as gradient modules.

Such are the word's ways, singled out and doubled down on, when weighed in the balance—in the stylistic equilibrium they themselves install and sustain. Sophisticated descriptive terminology, however commonplace or arcane, is certainly available—but not always immediately availing. Let's take (up) words *on their own terms* first. Kick off your shoes even while rolling up your sleeves, since it's mostly when one relaxes into language that its way with us gets fully engaged, even gently wrestled with, our attention always confident that literature's fictional force is bound—bound punctually forward—to win out. But relaxation in this sense retains its own vigil, as well as whatever an innate (or learned) verbal sensitivity may bring to the table and the sentence. So a few ground rules (very few) for what lies ahead. To be taken for granted in later engagements, what follows is the book's essential dictum—etymologically, that is, the already "said" in any instance of the verbalized: namely, the recognition that wording is the manifestation of grammar in syntax as well as of phonemes (the sound bites of alphabetic speech) in morphemes (the formative units of word meaning). Regarding the armatures of the verbal that will be met with ahead, there are, first, grammatical rules (possibilities for meaning): the static, because stabilizing, base for any potential shapes of phrase. At this level, wording is the grammatically sanctioned activation of the lexicon in syntactic form. Second, and closer in, wording is also more narrowly shaped by syllables: the consolidation of phonemes into morphemes, or sometimes their refusal to stay put there. Such refusal—a deviance, a freedom—is one mark of the literary moment at its most distilled.

Ground rules are one thing, but with this book's movement in and out of linguistic generalization and its literary instances, what about the principle of selection? Some readers will come to these chapters well enough disposed to "verbal concentration," the manifold pleasures of such "attention," but end up wishing the study had concentrated on other writings, other textures of writing, instead of—or in addition to—those brought forward in the course of its chapters. Inevitable. Yet the test cases offered here—for the mechanical "test" and tension of phrased words in syntax's pliable twining of sense, the functional slack and give and snap of the word's grammatical patterning at its most dramatic—are neither arbitrary nor in some blanket way meant as representative. They are simply exemplary in the best sense, each of its own linguistic intelligence to begin with. Even before poetry comes into conversation with prose in these pages, no thorough literary-historical scope is, nor could reasonably be, intended, either by selection or by expository overview. Mined from a rich but intermittent vein of mostly modern and contemporary writing in English, and tapping some predecessor moments in the fictional and verse canon, the effort is a matter of breadth rather than coverage. The intent is not to anatomize stylistic options but to put the faceting of literary phrase under a fine-ground and multifocal lens of attention, polished further by each new scrutiny. The risk, of course, is that the variegated display may seem vagrant, the argument wayward. But it is a risk mitigated by the fact that the real argument of these readings is the mental and sensory feel of immersion itself, not a sorted-out dispersion of verbal devices. There is certainly no proposed cross section of contemporary fictional writing offered here, no tabulation of leading habits, just a sampling of that radiant aptitude of language to which certain intensities, rather than codifiable types, of verbal infusion don't so much give way to as make *a way for*. Radiant, rare—and, regarding their principle of selection, to put it most simply and idiomatically, *choice*: primed for delectation.

But more than that, too. I like to think there's a kind of fail-safe in the unavoidable spottiness of the spotlit samples. The minute that readers might wish to insist on favored authors of their own doing similar things, or revealingly different ones, with the potentialities of prose—doing them, for instance, with compounded sound chains in the nexus of diction and syntax (from Hemingway to Cormac McCarthy, say, rather than just the cited moments from Faulkner et al.), with a departure into invented words and violated idioms (late Joyce in *Finnegans Wake*, Anthony Burgess in *Clockwork Orange*, rather than just Don DeLillo, Colson Whitehead, et al.), with hybrid cosmopolitan vocabularies from patois to postcolonial palimpsest (V. S. Naipaul to Amitav Gosh, rather than just Salman Rushdie, Zadie Smith, et al.), with the soundings of ethnic vernaculars (Sandra Cisneros, Louise Erdrich, rather than Toni Morrison et al.), or with the colonization of English fiction from another language base (Chinua Achebe or Jack Kerouac, rather than Conrad, Nabokov, and Brodsky)— the minute that some text (you name it; who but you?) seems missing from the selected bibliography, or some telling counter-case springs to mind, still a shared recognition is at work. You'll almost be able to hear the welcome of this open book: yes, that's exactly, a perfect comparison; or if not quite, then perhaps better yet, that one, in a related mode of verbal determination. The way the roster of examples to follow, as stands, is likely to prod additions, even corrective ones, is therefore a way of genuinely extending this book's turf—rather than necessitating some further defense of its hardly random but inevitably "partial" sampling. All I can say for now: see if you don't agree.

Verbal determination, then: built of words that are also constructs in themselves. There is an old game named *verbarium,* in which players are challenged to make as many words as possible from a batch of letters dealt to them. We can think of all literary writing as a massive and inexhaustible *verbarium,* a field of play where the alphabet (*alphabed*, as James Joyce called it) is the seedbed of a wording often cross-pollinated in process. For instance, as flagged in passing above, *word to word* can sound into *toward*, or *border r/aid* can spell its own cross-lexical encroachment. Such double-edged words beckon, at their very edges, as the degree zero of syntactic instigation: a scripted but invisible shift along the prose sequence generated from within an apparently fixed single lexeme.

Keeping one's eye on—and ear tuned to—the word within the microdrama of syntactic sequence, and sometimes the word's own inner theater of family history, is not always easy. Even a reader interested in style may be otherwise predisposed. I confess that my professional approach to the word as the essential stylistic quantum has involved something of a lesson belatedly learned. Twice, for recent publications, I've drawn what I thought was the short end of the commissioned stick, first for an anthology on Victorian poetry, then for another on narrative prose: chapters, respectively, "Diction" and "Words." I would have preferred the already assigned topics "Syntax" and "Sentences." But I soon found myself grateful for an unexpected boon. My bias, by both prejudice and training, had previously inclined me to favor the combinatory pulse of syntax over against the charge or charm of the single word swept up in it. *Diction, Words*: yes, the indisputable building blocks, even occasional gemstones, of literary artifacts, but not really (I thought) the heart of their drive and vitality, promising only static generalization and categorization. *Syntax*, on the other hand, had the allure of unrest and momentum, the spring of words into life.

While this former bias of my stylistic analyses scarcely mandates a root and branch retraction, the alternate emphasis of this study's opening chapter, "Lexical Timelines, Phrasal Timings," offers a kind of appreciative redress. It does so in part by tracing the roots and branches of words themselves, their etymological stems and suffixes. And whether or not surcharged with its own etymology, a lexeme can sometimes be heard to jump-start a stalled syntax from within its own syllabic flow—or flooding. Or spur a noisy lunge forward, backfires and all. The fatal good luck of his wife's knife thrust in going straight to the heart of the villain in Joseph Conrad's *The Secret Agent*, back from a "hazardous adventure" a few pages before, depends on the not-so-secret agency of syllabic contingency. Erupted in the echoic summary clause, "H*a*z*a*rd h*as su*ch accur*a*cies," this new sense of *chance* (rather than *risk*) elicits from "accuracies" the even more sibilant undertone of fateful 'accidents.'[3] Words don't just have weight in themselves but are a self-sparked field of phonic and inferential association, firing at times on more than one syntactic cylinder in a meaning cumulative, mutable, and often urgently renewed from syllable to syllable under lateral intensities from other bunched lettering.

In *Reading Voices* (1990), amid a thick cross-fire of theoretical debate at the time, I audited the aural effect of words even in silent reading, including the drift of phonemic sounds across word boundaries, in prose and verse alike.[4] Reading voices: a clause, not a phrase—registering a vocality not come upon in reading but accomplished by it. In this voicing, the drift-effects I wished to call out first struck me as essentially disruptive *syntactic* toggles in the toppling forward of sense: aggravations of phrasal expectation given to double take. I have come to realize that these are just as clearly lexical events: the word in the process—and sometimes lateral excess—of phrasing, intimately joined with other facets of wording's internal shape, history, and disposition. Even part III ahead, on the "cinematic sentence," hews as well to the single word's constitution by alphabetic matter in a clustered syllabic seriality that, in its own right, bears close comparison with the motorized frame-advance of screen machination, whether filmic or digital. But this is a closeness that stops well short, certainly, of fully conflating the automated roll (and differential transform) of optic traces in the discerned syntax of image on screen and the pause and reverse buttons of silent reading. Then, too, any further comparison between optical substrate and sublexical momentum (between single image frames and alphabetic increments) is no less of note when the verbal enchainments involved are more suggestively audial than visual, in wording as well as in representation, as in the "susp*en*se before Big B*en* strikes" in a rhapsodic passage from Virginia Woolf's *Mrs. Dalloway*, a kind of intimate counter-onomatopoeia anticipating the pending communal "boom."

No need, then, to isolate for exclusive or even predominant celebration the grand syntacticians of the literary sentence, from Dickens, Melville, and Meredith through James to Woolf and Faulkner (though all make appearances in these pages). And certainly no need to demote words to prefabricated machine parts in the work of syntactic engineering. Words have *built-in* ways of advancing, even charting, the trajectory of a sentence. My aim is to show how word forms, word formations, phonetic and semantic alike, operate with inertial momentum and linguistic (rather than narrative) velocity—across different force fields—to sound out, spell out, a wide range of submerged intensities, ironic or otherwise, in processual flux. If we let ourselves be beguiled or engrossed—or *spellbound*—by some skewed internal drift of wording, a whole resonant depth of suggestion may be opened to us.

Idiometrics

Etymology, usage, abused assumptions, repurposed turns of idiom: all are entailed in the thick of any engagement with—and gauging of—that abiding model of norm and deviance so often responsible for throwing literary effect into relief. In the idiometrics (my nonidiomatic coinage) of phrasal recalibration, the expectations of syntax may be short-circuited by an underlying grammatical logic. No better example of sabotaged idioms—as the very prototype of wording's wrench to complacency—than when, in a meditative "Foreword" to her first novel, *The Bluest Eye* (1970), Toni Morrison reflects on her bland vernacular acquaintance, as a young girl, with such substantive (if only in the sense of noun-like) phrases as "the pretty, the lovely, the ugly, the nice."[5] She admits to having used the adjective *beautiful* as well—before the memorable moment of discovery she has set out to recount. Deploying *beautiful* as a detached grammatical object, with no quotation marks around it, she writes that the recalled scene of confession and unrest "was the first time I knew beautiful. Had imagined it for myself." This knowing yields the objective, unexpected grammar of an action verb: "Beauty was not simply something to behold; it was something one could do" (x). Something one could configure for *oneself*. As this very sentence in its own low-keyed way does—when moving past the routine and sidelined alliteration of "Beauty . . . behold" to the slanted assonance (and dental alliteration) that answers, in a suspended chiasm, the syllabic core of "b*eau*ty" with "*do*."

Language, too, is not something just to understand, but to do. Or redo, through the torque of just such fresh predication, where idioms can be reignited in new modes of detonation. It is in this spirit, after the preceding assonance of "kn*ew* b*eau*tiful," that a wording like "Had imagined it for myself" is less a trailing parallel fragment than an autonomous node of assertion in the indirect object of that preposition phrase. In *Jazz* (1992), Morrison redefines clichés of passion by prepositional wording alone, in an inversion of vernacular wording: "Don't ever think I fell for you, or fell over you. I didn't fall in love, I rose in it. I saw you and made up my mind. My mind."[6] With the mind elevated to its own independence by desire, in the passing overtone of verticality in "made *up*," the only "fall" here is that one-word tumble down the rabbit hole of idiomatic profusion, where even a cross-lexical reemphasis gets spelled, or spilled, out in the pitching forward of *lover* from within the explicit denial of "fel*l over*."

The obvious, let alone blatant, in erotic depiction is often to be avoided in the inventions of literary writing by explicitly dodged prototypes of this sort, tweaked idioms. Fueling a late turn in the romance plot of *The Age of Innocence* (1920), Edith Wharton has Newland Archer say to Ellen Olenska—as if in the italics of a foreign, or at least an estranged, tongue— "*each time you happen to me all over again.*" She doesn't just 'happen to meet him,' or 'happen upon him.' Neither helping verb with infinitive nor its equivalent idiom for contingent encounter, instead the wording "happen to me" evokes an event in itself rather than the mere marker of a happenstance. In this romantic predication—as measured by an implicit idiometrics—the overridden norm of usage shadows Archer's next response as well, after Ellen admits to knowing what he means: "Does it—*do* I *too: to you?*" Not 'Does it happen to you too?' (in an already normalized variant of the previous wording)—as he seems about to fish for confirmation—but instead a befuddled stuttering uptake where the second person *ou* barely snaps free, in this spume of *oo* sounds, from the echoic infinitive and adverbial buildup set loose across *t—do/too/to(y)ou*. Here we trace the above-mentioned edginess of word borders in a rather extreme case. Not only does the idiomatic force of *happen* find itself alienated from its normal sense in this passage, but even the gaps between words become more than accidentally eventful—and precisely in the nervous erotic blending of first and second person.

So too in Morrison's *Beloved* (1986), when Denver has no idea how or where to seek help. The single preposition *away* (because redundant in context, and strikingly unidiomatic) is activated into a kind of mimetic suction between words when an "itchy burning in her throat made her swallow all her *saliva away*. She didn't know which *way* to go."⁷ Building on the open-throated internal rhyme in "sw*all*ow *all*," as it prods in turn the overexplicit modification ("saliva away"), the cross-lexical tension appears all by itself to release the uncertain "way" of the next sentence. Words seem to know, and show, their own way. Wording is always happening *to* readers, not just for them, all over again. Alienated, I repeat, from its normal sense. And so refurbished from just this internal remove, refreshed from within. In this respect, revisiting in chapter 1 a classic account of linguistic enervation—and the lowered intellectual and political guard it represents—should give immediate stress to such renovated laxity at the outset. Returning, that is, to *the* canonical essay on bad wording, George Orwell's postwar "Politics and the English Language," opens an intriguing channel into a new century's efforts at both parody and reparation.

Heard Roads to Harrow

Ghosting this new subhead is the idiom "row to hoe," not 'road to hoe'—as I had misheard it for years. Quite recently, regarding the way phonemes, such dentals among them, can nibble away at each other in aural transmission, there is the aside in Sigrid Nunez's novel *The Friend* where "a friend of mine . . . told me that, for years, he thought the expression was *It's a doggy-dog world* and was never quite sure what it meant."[8] Understandably. One often hears the phonetic row not taken, the path between. Such mishaps of audition—such phonic misshapings—are symptomatic. The ways of the word, in their marshaled rows or roadways for the transport of ideas, are not always highways, straight throughways, freeways, let alone unambiguously signposted detours. Sometimes they tunnel underground, with the tolls one might expect. Tolls on attention—and this even when apparently "above ground" in their routings, where sudden lane changes and off-ramps in the ways of the word, as well as arresting intersections, make travel as challenging as it is engaging in the most congested intensities of narrative writing. At such crossings, bottlenecks, and the rest, literary syntax can divide one word's orientation from the logic of its linked counterpart, springing new conceptual bondings and compounds under the shearing force of frictional adjacency alone. One signal instance of such serial displacement—in its disjunctive way with words—comes from none other than an unexpected case of highway signage, its own syllabic components suffering from rear-end collision in the punning press of expression.

To clarify the verbal upset involved, I need to set the scene—as well as its professional context. A few years back, I was in a shuttle to the airport on the way to an international conference in Sydney on "The Idea of Prose Style"—a gathering meant to buck the tendency to marginalize prose in the attentions of stylistic analysis. It was as if the barbed rubric at the University of New South Wales were "The Very Idea of Prose Style!"—

a mockery to be laid definitively to rest, once and for all, by one session and keynote address after another. All this in the offing, I was no doubt hyperattuned that morning to the ways of wording, their syllabic couplings and skids. My eye (and then ear) were jolted to attention when the airport shuttle passed under a giant LED freeway sign, newly installed, that cautioned *Asleep at the wheel ends in a wake*. Given its serial irony, the lettering might have been doled out in the format of a moving electronic sign, comprehension teased forth from one word on the way—and overlay—to the next in line across their disruptive graphic/phonemic (*graphonic*) track.

Warning aside in this unstable (and semigrammatical) clause, one kind of smash-up and disintegration had already taken place beneath the surface of digital script. The basic antithesis of *asleep/awake* didn't hold firm, as *a sleep* inevitably spun loose—nominalizing the adjectival risk—to match the Joycean mortal pun on *a wake*. Given this dizzy ricochet between syllabic accidents and fractures above the lanes of traffic that morning, in a verbal diversion dangerously distracting in its own right, I'm glad I wasn't driving. To brake now over this word-breaking semantic play is not just to vivisect the dead-serious mortuary hook of these attention-grabbing snags of diction but to help render them exemplary in their very exaggeration—as of course I went on to do when folding this example into my Sydney lecture. Even when words in fiction don't split their casements in such fissure and overspill, they are never found operating free of their immediate affiliates—and counter-forces—in the file of syntax, at whatever speed of comprehension. As with the lexical whiplash of that twin highway-patrol pun, the gearing of words to syntax is just where the rubber meets the road.

But then, of course, syntax is all words. To say so is to call up a perennial double axis in our thinking about linguistic performance. On one hand: word versus thing in the referential axis, perpendicular to the page, opening (out or back) upon the imagined space of the depicted in the mind of reading. On the other, horizontal rather than orthogonal (or virtual): word versus syntax. Yet both axes are likely to jackknife and collapse, both dichotomies implode, in the moment of their codependence. Words are in themselves things in their own complex materiality, with grammar realized by just such things in the ordering of its syntax. *The Ways of the Word* is devoted to words in the heft and density of their objecthood—not forgetting that there are things in the world beyond words, the designated objects of discursive formats, that everywhere outstrip the level of the syllable and its lexical bondings. And further distinctions persist. My attention is on defining less what words *are* than what—as alphabetic, phonetic, and etymological composites—words do in the stew of syntax (there it goes again, churned anew, in "word*s do*"!). To shift metaphors, what results from such episodes of attention is a revised estimation of syntax per se, backbone of all prose power. As its articulating vertebrae, words (it can't be overemphasized) exert an internal flexion as well—as they take place, take part, in the posture and gait of literary motions, including its sudden limps and productive stumbles.

To pose this book's developing question in a bifold grammar: How are words doubly *brought to shape*, built from within while being made to bear on, brought to give shape to, the linear syntax that mobilizes them? In the business of writing, amateur or professional, what etymological as well as artisanal precedents might there be for the expert fashioning of words in the foundry of prose discourse? If wordmongers are cousin to ironmongers in the indiscriminate dispensing of their wares, what transforms certain related occupations to a skill, a craft? For the wordsmith, what are the instruments? And what the pressure points? What pounds words into shape against what base? If we call the plane of grammar the base—the resistance against which words get shaped and fitted for operational slotting—then the formative pressure, the blow, the coup, must be delivered by the pen- or key-stroke, if not always master stroke, of something we call *style*. But style, of course, has already been shaping syntax into its own determining form. If this sounds circular, it is because of the malleability of the process at both interpenetrating scales: a give-and-take between diction and syntax, tooled word and sentence. In the workshop of expressive intent, the instrumental middle term pursued here is *wording*. Say again for now (in the identical sounding of its plural form): the mots justes—in other words, a most just and carefully fashioned wording—as it locates exactly the point, one stroke at a time, where the hammer strikes the anvil at the forge of invention.

Getting a—First—Word in—Edgewise

The splintering (or double grafting) of idiom, as instanced in the above subhead, is a symptom of the word's dual labors of inauguration in many a text. In an introductory spirit, we can profitably look back to some classic fictional launches across the nineteenth-century heyday of narrative prose. If the split idioms announcing this subsection seem to rub each other the wrong way, this effect comports well enough with the mode of the prose under investigation, where diction is rimmed—and edged forward at times—by contradictory drifts in the grammar of sentence and plot alike. Famously, Charles Dickens's quasi-autobiographical novel, *David Copperfield* (1850), opens with two tightly interknit sentences in which a single word—the word of words for realist prose fiction, "life" itself—undergoes a graded transformation so deep-going (in the genre and the dictionary alike) that it operates more as an ontological crux than as a giddy pun: "Whether I shall turn out to be the hero of my own life, or whether that station will be held by anybody else, these pages must show." After the scrupulous shift in modals from the first-personal "shall" to some alternate third-personal "will," only then the inverted grammar's arriving subject in *these* pages: themselves increments in the genre of a literary rather than a biographical *life*. Here too, in "must show," is the narratological imperative for *life* in a single, double-meant lexeme—and predicate: *must* as *cannot but* and *are charged to* at once, a natural result under construction from the start. So, too, as immediately follows, the doubling of *life* as biological and biographical: "To begin my life with the beginning of my life, I record that I was born (as I have been informed and believe) on a Friday, at twelve o'clock at night. It was remarked that the clock began to strike, and I began to cry, simultaneously." Birth registry notwithstanding, to trigger the near simultaneity of *i* sounds in "strike," "cry," and "si . . .," it just had to be a Fr*i*day n*i*ght for this coeval launch, this outset and onset of biology and biography together in the homonym "m*y* l*i*fe"—all reverberant with an "I" sounded many times over.

Launching that Dickensian sentence, the double take required of "begin my life with the beginning of my life" is both abrupt and textually encompassing in its way of wording. Even in paler, more mincing and fussy modes of initiation, there can be minor starts and startlements in a novel's precipitating words. One of the most notable openings in Victorian fiction zeroes in on the syllabic makeup and etymological associations of a word as markedly isolated as the thing it names. About his first encounter with Heathcliff in *Wuthering Heights* (1847), the feckless narrator, Lockwood, begins: "I have just returned from a visit to my landlord—the *solitary* neighbour that I shall be *troubled* with." Both *solitary* and *troubled* weasel out of standard idiom—*only* neighbor to be *bothered by*—to imply, in Lockwood's drastic "solitude," a more profound and ultimately quite "troubling" proximity to the narrative matter as yet on hold. Still unruffled by any of this, Lockwood continues in words releasing further unwitting ironies as he congratulates himself on having "fixed on a situation" that is "so completely removed from the stir of society." Stasis rather than selection is insinuated by *fixed*, even as *situation* quietly seethes with a sense of pending event, indeed crisis, as well as locale. Lockwood plows on in delusion: "A perfect misanthropist's heaven: and Mr. Heathcliff and I are such a suitable pair to divide the desolation between us," with the capping alliteration "divide the desolation" seemingly designed to stress the four-syllabled hyperbolic abstraction that turns isolation to a primal gloom.

Another classic tale of haunted passion, as *Wuthering Heights* will of course become, begins, half a century later, with a comparable ambiguity of phrasing that triggers more thematic anticipation than the reader is quite ready to process. At the opening of Henry James's *The Turn of the Screw* (1898), the strange personification involved in mentioning, in transitive grammar, the "house that had gathered us for this occasion" is preceded by a more vernacular sense of agency ascribed to narrative itself: "The story had held us, round the fire, sufficiently breathless." The straddling word *held* gathers the self-contained idiom *held us round* into the suspense of *held us . . . breathless*. This is a house-hold with a vengeance. But these relays are nothing compared to the twisted phrasing of the "story" alluded to, about a ghost-seeing and its failed debunking in a similar house, haunted not just by narrative but by actual specters. A boy afraid of what he has seen has roused his mother: "Waking her [the mother] not to dissipate his dread and soothe him to sleep again but to encounter also herself, before she had succeeded in doing so, the same sight that had shocked him." Two previous senses of *held* (contained, gathered) give way here to an oblique grammatical doubleness even in the reflexive pronoun: *encounter for herself; discover herself*. This effect is a perfect momentary anticipation of the coming story's protagonist, the troubled Governess, who, in seeing ghosts, sees only herself as well, her own projected neuroses.

In the lateral suspensions of a periodic sentence—often rendered tortuous in its dilation by James—this one story's inaugural grammar pries open its whole narrative occasion, prematurely hinted edgewise along the postponements, the microsuspense, of an equivocal syntax. Nor is it far-fetched to compare "to encounter herself" (in the very space of the specter) with a cinematic superimposition of mother and ghost in this flashback story—before fade-in again to the narrative setting at the present-tense fireside. James's kinetics are nothing if not protocinematic, at small scale and large, in syntactic double exposure as well as in narrative segue. The full force of this prelude is still pending in James's narrative. All we have to go by at the start, as with any narrative first time through, are the words that get it going and mark the mode of approach. No surprise in James that this approach is via a tricky sentence: difficult to understand on first go—or, more to the point, difficult not to misunderstand. Latin gave us a word for this, *subtle*, to which usage I'll come in a moment with a certain corrective slant. For now we can see how meaning depends on norms of grammar more foundational even than just idiomatic. The ways of the word are under inbuilt lexical pressure, with fissuring results—so that the reflexive pronoun *herself* hinges on a sense of eye-witness versus I-reckoning in this preliminary haunting.

From these novel-opening instances arises a principle: syntax *via* words—a truism best tested by verbal ambivalence. And from such a principle arises the analytic mission of this book: to let wording speak as much as possible for itself. Without any specialist nomenclature, we receive uniqueness and nuance in the very moment of its being wondered at. Impact comes from the page up, not set in frame by some top-down abstraction. With words working directly upon us, no technical parlance gets in the way of phrasing. Or put it that subtleties are found, not applied. Before *subtle* passed, in its etymological career, from Latin origin into wide Romance language application as "intricate" and "difficult to understand," its original sense was delicate, "fine-spun." In verbal terms, the threads of such spinning help display, at close enough range, the internal weave, the true texture, of an intricate wording, doing so without the application of some specialized methodological lens. *The Ways of the Word* concentrates in this way on the immediate gratifications of verbal analysis—with any theory or method kept mostly implicit in the exercise of this pleasure principle. A pleasure scarcely dead-ended or entirely self-serving, but ready at any moment to turn heuristic, exploratory, analytic.

Mattering to Meaning

In the spirit of this pleasure, one readily settles into the thought that it is only the words we have to go by, to go on. Reading, we may say, is an ongoing decision about how words might matter to meaning. Beginnings are only exemplary in this regard because so exclusively verbal, before any expectations regarding plot or psychology can let us think we are seeing *through*—or beyond—words to some extralinguistic action. Beyond its beginning, of course, any text, start to finish, is determined by the word's ways, its paths and strategies, idioms included, with all fictional space and its trans/actions released by cognitive triggers from linguistic script. No one sensibly denies this. But what about perceptual instigations released by the inward dimensions of wording, from its syllabic postures to the ligatures of their grammatical combinations? What *about* them, that is, when they don't seem in any way to be what the text is about?

Style as content? By what double-ledger notations are certain minuscule effects to be accounted for, or say reinvested, in the event of sense? A recent keen-eared student of mine, good at spotting the kind of inflected linguistic densities executed by prose texts, still admitted to thinking of such thickenings as "speed bumps" in the path of reading. Worth pausing over, but not easy to estimate as part of any thematic map. Even the most alert and intrigued students—if new to any toolkit one might call method in the registration of such sublexical and transphrasal effects, anything from the pulse of syllables to the backdrafts of grammar—can be pertinently upset in figuring out how to make them, so to say, *figure*. It's one thing for a student to case out such effects in literary prose, but another thing altogether to make an interpretive case *for* them, let alone to activate them in one's own writing.

I speak deliberately of students: students of reading, of writing, enrolled or not, and whenever the twain do meet. We are all still taking lessons from the word's literary ways—and means. In the actual classroom, with either literary analysis or creative practice on the line, or sometimes both in tandem (part III), there is often the question of targeted strategic effects behind literary technique. What does it *mean*, the internal echo across a syntactic span, the peripheral ambivalence of a punctuated grammatical shift, the paradoxical overlay of two tenses in the arc of a single phrase, the cross-word sibilant slip? If we're willing to go there at all, where do these verbal eccentricities take us? Speed bumps: not a bad characterization, certainly. If some of these imply unmarked road signs in the ways of the word, this latent utility hardly drains away their inherent interest. Word-ways, first and foremost, are entirely what they are at material or verbal base: just intrinsically interesting.

In the subvocal zone of phonic grasp, rasp, or inferred ligature, one may well sense at times some underlying harmonic pattern, some outré or muted belling or bullying of syllables, crowded half out loud into more pattern than semantics can demand or manage. So how do we imagine a registration of this as a node of decipherment in a genuine reading act? To classroom questions about how to move from a transient phonemic wrinkle through narrative phenomenology to hermeneutics—from a swift linguistic quirk to the slow work of an overall reading—there's only, at best, an ad hoc answer. This is the way it seems to work (out) here. And the question itself may be premature. When asked—about certain internal densities, even when turned to palpable echoic niceties—what exactly is it that they mean, my response has typically been to rephrase the question. It's not what they mean, but how they matter. What they mean is that you are reading—and not even just really reading, in some valorized academic sense. What they mean, if noticed at all, is that you are not just watching language—but making the full audiovisual materiality of it work for you. Even at the subvocal level, you are on alert and on call at once, silently voicing into the open the very texture of text, "fine-spun" nuances included. This matters in prose fiction simply (and often not so simply) because it is there: not there for the necessary tasking of further interpretation, further meaning, some concerted thematization, but there in the way meaning is fundamentally made.

Mattering to meaning, then: not a direct transfer or pipeline (A to B) but a progressive negotiation in the reading of literary fiction. And whenever students in creative writing courses wax eagerly tactical on this score, the way some of the most creative students in critical studies often do ("What's the point?" The *interpretable* point? And hence the lesson to be learned?), one can at least say that, in opening the release valve of such linguistic intricacies into the pace of *their own prose*, these students would be neither indulging private pleasures, nor seeding hidden treasures, but simply letting verbal texture have its say, its woven way. Which is why this volume is dedicated to readings *in*, rather than readings *of*, fiction.

"How to Read"

We may look back at this point to a text whose title is nothing if not openly instructional—if hardly classroom targeted. Even if we were tracing the routes of the word only through what we might call wholly (but arbitrarily) enjambed and stanza-free page-block lineation, through prose alone rather than prosody, there is certainly no reason to ignore the thoughts of a poet on the matter. Quite the opposite. And such thoughts are especially apt when asserting that prose, not verse, is the most important field of verbal invention—the true aesthetic breakthrough—in the modern era, Stendhal to Flaubert to James and beyond. This is the historical backdrop for Ezra Pound's "How to Read" (1931), as suggestive as it is polemical, where we are told, among many other things, that poetry will never read the same after the post-Romantic innovations of prose.[9] It is in view of this that chapter 5 takes up Pound's famous resistance to Tennysonian sonority for comparison with filmic treatments of the Victorian poet's narrative verse.

Pound's "How to Read" essay ranges the broad spectrum of literary effects over three dovetailed categories: the ear, the eye, and, inclusively, wording's materially specific form of action in linguistic shape. In the ordinary course of reading, whether prose or poetry, all categories operate at once, since it is inescapably "language" itself (not some abstracted formal quality) that is "charged or energized" in the manifestation of either the mellifluous or the visual. Pound gives a fuller explanation of these major intensifications, in the order of their cultural evolution. Melopoeia is the defining *strain* (tendency and music both) of the bardic tradition, words heard before and apart from meaning. Phanopoeia (without etymological highlighting on Pound's part, from the Greek for *phaino/pheno*: "shining," "made visible") is the image-generating capacity of language. Logopoeia is the turning of the Word (not sacred but self-sufficient) upon itself to probe linguistic impulses beyond those of strict designation. You could array these tendencies, in their most concentrated and overt forms, as *onomatopoeia* (sound echoing sense), *ekphrasis* (words depicting a visual object), and *paranomasia* (words acting punningly, playfully, upon themselves). More broadly, Pound has isolated—from within the total orchestration of writing under the aspect of poetics—the euphony, imagery, and letteral density of both prose and verse.

We might summarize further, then, that for a poetics of prose, the functional units and operable scale of the three modes entail the syllabic chord changes of a quasi-musical *phrasing*, the verbal *portrayal* of visual things beyond words, and the stretch and bend, the fold and give, of the narrative *inscription* itself under laws of lexicon and grammar. *The Ways of the Word* deploys this third echelon of poetics to compass the other two. The concentrated logocentric effect of time-based wording pursed in part I passes through, in part II, an unexpected melopoetic transformation on stage: the alternating verbal music and cacophony of *The Great Gatsby* being given an actual airing in the auditorium, a full postbardic recitation. The two categories converge again in part III's comparison of screen rhetoric and the tacit cinematographics of literary phrasing, both made manifest as forms of *phanopoetic* montage. It is no accident that the Greek root *pheno* (or *phaino*) gave its name to one predecessor of cinema's incremental motion, the phenakistoscope: the spinning plate or disk (planar version of the drum-shaped zoetrope) that oscillated its allotted, slotted images (like the skidding overlap of lettering just there, there and gone) into the sped differentials of motion or gesture. The audiovisual kinesis "screened for" in this way, in chapters 4 and 5, is not limited to the shimmering optic "phaino" of the framed image. The word art of logopoeia is also a mode of discursive kinesis: the sentence in action. Even Pound's favored imagism is at base a verbalism, a subtle (again "finespun") logopoeia of phrasal filaments.

The spirit of everything to come in our attention to the clocked rhythms and detected way stations of the word involves a response to logopoeia that hardly closes it off from echo or image, sound or conjured sighting, in some exclusively inward worrying of its word forms. This *wordedness* of poetry or prose, if sketchily estimated by Pound's discussion, is a delimitable category simply to the extent that it "employs words not only for their direct meaning, but it takes count in a special way of habits of usage, of the context we expect to find with the word, its usual concomitants, of its known acceptances, and of ironical play" (25). *"Takes count"/calls to account/ counts out*—ultimately counts *on*: with this broad linguistic net cast, logopoeia is manifest in the sinews of prose by every feature of its operation, from the circuit of etymology through the upset of standard lexical expectations to the oscillations of idiom, grammar, and the ironic tensions of these interwoven norms. It is in just this respect that logopoetics "holds" (another of

Pound's loaded verbs: *carries* or *sustains* as well as *locates*) "the aesthetic content which is peculiarly the domain of verbal manifestation, and cannot possibly be contained in plastic or in music" (25). Nor, less than the other two categories, is it susceptible to translation. An alliterative harmony, for instance, is capable of occasional transposition from one language to another, and a visual image, already the product of optic translation into language, travels easily, plays widely. But for the poetics of the word in a given language, there are no other words than that language's own.

The non-referential "charge" this involves, tapping the structural basis of meaning rather than its particular result in message, is what Pound calls—in "energized" and responsible play—"the dance of the intellect among words" (25). Depending on the specific linguistic topography of a verbal reserve in one language or another, this notion locates those features of "style" that cannot operate in any real divorce from sound or image. Again: the art of wording itself that "holds the aesthetic content"—holds it in place and up to view. But what kind of pas de deux is this logocentric dance of the *intellect* in practice? Polyglot Pound may well have been looking back to the root meaning (Latin this time, rather than Greek) of *inter+legere* (to pick out among, as words; *to read* per se). Let's readily grant that the *legend* (same etymological ancestry) of Pound's linguistic "intellect" is inseparable from word recognition: logopoetics as the disclosed *logic* of wording per se, surcharged from within. In this vein, "meaning" tracks the near accidents of its own sedimented activation: alternatives functionally overwritten, the lexical or syntactic competition dodged or coopted, the flow sustained by layering *and* undercurrent. Hence our topic, our exploratory terrain, our surveyed topography—including the tropes to which it compels us in prospecting the lay of the land, as well as its subterranean currents and subsidiary increments. Three years after "How to Read," Pound's *The ABC of Reading* (1934) sounds again the keynotes of a primer: this time for the foundationally alphabetic, rather than musical or visually mimetic, character of poetry. It's an open invitation, for any reader, to approach prosody or prose with a letter-alert eye and ear.

Readers in Prospect

So where does this leave you, or leverage your attention, as we move first to paired chapters on the many facets of wording in its role as a time-based medium: ranging from the linguistic history of the word unit itself in etymological time, subject to numerous revivals and atavisms alike, to the tense of its predications in the layerings of narrative? Only examples can answer. Same, too, when discussion shifts to a middle chapter—a medial (and intermediate) interlude of sorts—about the once-removed work of reading a novel aloud on stage: a distancing yet ultimately verbally intimate gesture (the dramatization of *The Great Gatsby* itself, text not story, under the hero's born name *Gatz*). What light, or footlight, is shed there on the paged reading flipped through in the coming two chapters? How do our initial "episodes of attention" get crystallized in an actual theatrical attendance? And what brighter beam yet, in the third and more speculative phase of discussion, might illuminate the inherent kinetic flickers, tracking shots, montage cuts, and focus pulls of a quasi-cinematic prose projected in double bill with some actual movie moments? Again, minimizing theory in the grip of literary technique, everything depends on exemplification.

And focus. Given an attention "on alert and on call at once," as I had characterized the reader's stance above, what the past participial headword of part I means to evoke is the "paged" condition of *reading* as well as writing. This entails the executed ways of the word not just as they hit the imprint sheet, not just as script. What such ways of the made phrase simultaneously pace off for us are the means by which it is the reader, too, who—in the other sense of the verb—is sometimes *paged* by words. In chapter 2, something of a rhetorical limit case appears in a blast of Whitman's most self-assertive reader apostrophes: a stanza from "Crossing Brooklyn Ferry" that summons us, *via* enunciation alone—and with the full etymological force of that Latin shorthand for "way" forward—to audibilize internally the elapsing of syllables into syntax. With Whitman's versified *voyage à deux* between text and reader in mind—forbidding all *adieux* between the poet and his transmitted script, given the intoned potency of its temporal as well as spatial impact in future receipt—*via* is an adverb that would name there the true way of the word, the marker of mediation per se. The page pages us. Both meaning and its music are our response, our page/d stance, our Poundian dance.

In the testing of such response, and with my own readers in prospect, the way forward should be nowhere near as mysterious in its demarcations as the evidence is various. In what follows, words become—if not exactly the marquee stars of page, stage, and inner perceptual screen—at least the starred and glossed flashpoints of a literary, a letteral, drama otherwise too often missed or minimized (in commentary more than, I like to think, in actual reading). Their every tacit asterisk—by way of internally italicized citations—yields here to annotation: earmarked for enunciation in the build of sense. The full spread of comparison, then: page, stage, screen; serial script, extended theatrical recitation, mobile techniques of focus and transition in the prose equivalents of filmic sequence; deciphered ink, then audited voice, and finally the discerned shifts, collisions, and displacements in the planar relay not just of phrased image but of phrasing at large. The purpose: testing the granularity of language—in various ratios and intensities of stylistic perception—through a triangulation with theatrical incarnation and filmic mobility alike, which is to say with both dramatic verbal enactment and the inner screening of wording's edited reel.

That's the plan of these pages, hospitable to unscheduled surprises whenever the choice of text can help arrange them. And with a keen sense of potential readers in the wings, brandishing prompt texts of their own in instancing a subtly different work of words. Again, a no-lose situation: a self-fulfilling adequacy of attention. This author's only sensible response: if you can't find exactly the descriptive terms you're looking for in my exemplified accounts of verbal energy, and are at the same time finding more interesting stylistic examples in your own reading, then you're looking in all the right places, wherever they may be in the replete spectrum of classic or contemporary verbal invention. As the first paired chapters should make clear, then, we're already *on the same page*—even in your extended outreach. There is certainly no attempt, I scarcely need repeat, at any rigorous delimitation in my shifting focus. In this book's threefold division regarding the investigated ways of the word, these procedures—in concentration on page, stage, and inner screen—are hardly advanced as *the* three ways, but intuited simply as discerned medial proving grounds. Mindful of Pound's metaphor for the responsive mind's "dance . . . among words"—among and with them—one might also approach the coming chapters as a wide-ranging choreographic notation: tracing out the lifts and spins, the thrusts and leaps, but also the held postures and dramatized musculature, of words underway—and quite selectively under study—in their dance of enunciation. In short: curtain up on the kinetic word.

Part I

Paged

Wording in Place

1

Lexical Timelines, Phrasal Timings

Literary words in their native place on the page; artful prose at home in prose fiction among other genres: that's the main remit of part I, the broad ambit of its attention. Wording in place—but only when understood as a mobile placing of words by syntax in action. On exactly this wide-open terrain, to recur again to an introductory way of putting it: "Words work overtime in literary prose." *Overtime*—the inference doubles in the very word: duration over a split second of lexical time; the surplus of overtime labor. As with many a verbal move to come in the traffic patterns of phrasal process—including unsignaled turns and precipitous brakings in the variable ways of the word—lexical congestion and convergence, let alone collision, impend at the speed of reading. All of which may, at any time, seem very much *in the way of the word* in both senses: a routing and a retardation at once, literary writing slowed by its own unpredictable momentum, its inward and continuous revision, as syntax presses forward.

So it is that the activity of wording—a fact as obvious as it is vital and multifaceted—operates in time as well as in place. Obvious, vital, and ripe for an always fresh investigation: each sentence yielding itself to analysis in terms as unique as its own run of words. At the macro level, this book's three parts, in closely linked partition, consider the ways of the word in aspects first linguistic, here in these first paired chapters, then, via stage and screen analogies, recitational and cross-medial by turns—with wording ultimately conceived as syntactic, dramatic, and kinetic all at once. All such "conceiving" involves various kinds of time: not just grammatically performative and more broadly narrational but genealogical as well—and the last whether etymological or literary historical (with each variable line of genealogy often borne by allusion). Part I tracks these temporalities of literary reading in poetry as well as fiction: the syntactic time such reading takes; the deep time its lexicon takes stock of, often by irony or wordplay; and the temporal framing at stake, concentrated by example in chapter 2, in the organizing force of grammatical tense. If one were to identify these first paired chapters as this book's defining "takes" on wording's structural function, any sharp demarcations would clearly be artificial. Call these aspects of attention more like "angles," slants: complementary perspectives aimed at syntax's moving targets in the wording moment.

Before embarking on these episodes of attention, one might pause over an allegory of such close notice, turned to undue heed, in Edgar Allan Poe's ghoulish story "Berenice" (1835). In the lexical sonority for which Poe's wordage is renowned, he begins with this wrinkle of writing: "Misery is manifold," with a metaphor for such multiform strands of anguish coming next: "Overreaching the wide horizon as the rainbow, its hues are as various as the hues of that arch." The reference of *arch* to bent chromatic bands is verbally prefigured in the near anagram—and spanned alphabetic array—of the double-*r*'ed *Overreaching*. Such are the ways of Poe's febrile wording. His narrator would be among the first to notice the likes of this latent alphabetic scramble in "over(re)a(r)ching," for symptomatic reasons about which we soon learn. In describing the cataleptic atrophy of his beloved cousin Berenice, he adds that in "the mean time" his own fate worsened, parsing the very idiom of "meantime" in clocking an interval of diagnosed monomania. This he does in noting that his malady is found to be "hourly and momently gaining vigor" (*momently* conspicuously archaic)—until, by an encroachment of wordiness itself, it "at length" succeeded in "obtaining over me the most incomprehensible ascendancy" (ten syllables all told in those last two words of comprehensive dominance).

The gargoyle irony of what follows, in the mode of audience acknowledgment, has to do with the difficulty of communicating the nature of this disease—as if by way of its own symptomatic perceptual temperature—to readers who, not themselves given to fixation, are likely to skim such passages for the building melodrama of plot rather than phrase. It is just this readerly orientation that remains implicit, but unmistakable, in the insinuated etymology—as well as allegory—of fevered attention unfolding so grudgingly in front of us. "This monomania, if I must so term it, consisted in a morbid irritability of those properties of the mind in metaphysical science termed the *attentive*." Here is the suspected readerly incomprehension in a sudden (and symptomatically overwritten) present tense:

> It is more than probable that I am not understood; but I fear, indeed, that it is in no manner possible to convey to the mind of the merely general reader, an adequate idea of that nervous intensity of interest with which, in my case, the powers of meditation (not to speak technically) busied and buried themselves, in the contemplation of even the most ordinary objects of the universe.

It is just such a "general reader" who is not likely to pick up on that last alliterative twist in "busied and buried" either—even following the *intensity* spelled into "*interest*" and then spun out further into two "internalizing" prepositional *in*'s ("in my case . . . in the contemplation") that are also heard by dint (or muted "din") of echo in "ordinary." With the narrator having successfully overcome any temptation to "speak technically," we have been offered instead in that antithetical rhyme ("busied"/"buried")—drawn straight from the reservoir of Poe's quintessential phonic technique and gothic predilections alike—not just a bland verb for activity but a metaphor of energies devoted to their own entombment. Language verges on, veers into, the empirical reality of an eventual graveyard tale—but only, so far, for the fatally obsessed, where the exponential "vigor" of his dis-ease is the rigor (mortis) of his fixation.

So it is time for Poe to tighten the noose of readerly investment. Not accidentally, as the first in a litany of evidence, the narrator offers as example a distraction from within the throes of reading itself: that parodied cliché of being "buried" (his previous term for something like 'immersed') in a book. The narrator's condition inclines him to "muse for long unwearied hours, with my attention riveted to some frivolous device on the margin, or in the typography of a book." Some peripheral filigree is likely, that is, to seize his eye and mind. Or he might, perhaps more to the point, grow momentarily preoccupied with something in the imprint (if not quite content) of that typeset volume—rather as we, one level in toward meaning, are no doubt presently caught up, or meant to be, by that mild phonetic idée fixe, however fleeting, in the studied fricative nexus "*riveted* to some *frivo*lous *dev*ice"—as well by the phonetic adjacency of "marg*in* or *in*." It is, in short, hard not to suspect that this exacerbated page-based overinvestment on the narrator's part is being put forward emblematically, in the looniest of circumlocutions, as more than *just one among* "a few of the most common and least pernicious vagaries induced by a condition of the mental faculties, not, indeed, altogether unparalleled, but certainly bidding defiance to anything like analysis or explanation." Bidding defiance to—or, that is, forbidding—any analysis but one modeled on that verbal attention luxuriously induced here by the lexical and syllabic monomania of prose's own bedeviling episodes.

But no cautionary tale in this, at the metatextual level. More like an inferred homeopathic cure. From any such inflamed, derailing fascination with graphic patterns on the bound page—drawn to "devices" and mere "typography," rather than to the proximate imprinted language—one way back to an actual reading of the words is through auditing their secret passage-ways. No one knew better than Poe the sounds words make in silence as they choreograph their weird ballets of psychosis in his narrative art. It soon happens again, this crossing at once of word borders and the limits of sanity, when Poe's narrator dwells, transfixed, on Berenice's "excessively white" teeth: "*They—they* alone were present to the mental eye, and they, in their sole individuality, became the essence of my mental life." Gasped out with that repeated pronoun, then personified, "they" gnaw at the speaker's own "individuality" in reducing, by phonic liaison, his entire overfocused "menta*l life*" to the "mental *eye*" (and feverish first-person *I*) of this dental fixation. In Poe's prose poetics, the way of the word is to bite off only what it can further chew on.

Lexical Backstories

So where were we, before the specter of monomania set in? Let's pick up again at first assumptions—about writing as a time-based medium, paced by the syntactic manifestations of grammar, with their own aftertones. We've noted that such paged and emplaced words have time on their side as well. In prose fiction, for instance, they come bearing histories of their own (or the shroud of archaism itself) in telling whatever new story they are sentenced to. These histories are a matter of etymology and allusion, of provenance and other precedents. Whether kept tacit or brought to exaggeration, such lexical histories are braided into succession at the time scale of the sentence: the build of sequence at the grammatical plane. This plane is something other than the duration represented in the story world, of course, whether tumultuous or evenly prolonged. The stumbles, arrests, and redirections in play at this verbal level, the periods of hesitation and suspense, are those of grammar's manifestation at its own syntactic clip, as much *paced* in verbal format as paged in the form of plot moves.

"Form is vertical. Style is horizontal": this is how Jeff Dolven arrays the interaction.[1] Such a distinction can well apply, at the scale of a single sentence, to the basic choices of diction launched upon a given run of grammar. From the vertical paradigm of word selection: a chosen lexeme—weighed against its close options—operates in structuring the axis of combination.[2] In this sense, words are the pivotal features through which the differential rudiments of form become the variable increments of style: where choices fetched from the stack of functional possibility—including its alternate genealogies—help contour the arc of any phrasal trajectory. Words, once chosen, are made to count, add up.

Genealogies, yes, structuring histories: ingrown plots and backstories of the word's own, but with stray mysteries to boot, odd syllabic byways and false philological cul-de-sacs. Against the history of morphemic roots and their derivations, for instance, what happy "literary" accident makes *languish* something like the functional opposite of *anguish*? Let alone embedding the letters of *style* in the *proselytizing* of many an aesthetic agenda? To put either of these odd word-couples near to each other in a given sentence isn't to answer the question of their accidental echoes, merely to raise it: to lift phonemes and graphemes (the audiovisual coordinates of minimal semantic function) into unusual awareness—exposing those linguistic enigmas slipped into wording on the underside of meaning. Etymology has no genuine foothold in such cases, even in the first pair. *Anguish* comes to us from *angustus*—Latin for "narrow, tight, straitened"—via Old French. By a fluke of antinomy, *languish* arrives via the Latin *laxus* for "slackened." To pitch the one against the other in any imagined syntax would be to override linguistic association with the license of style. Yet in matters of etymology more broadly—including the intuitive feel one may have for the so-called hard word descended in its formality from Latin or Greek, the homely and quotidian from the Anglo-Saxon tradition (back through frequent Germanic origins)—the tendency to track down such intuitions is very much to this book's purpose. Along with the lineage of idioms, such derivational backstories speak directly to the word's ways of arriving into the lexicon in the first place, en route to whatever literary manifestation they achieve.

Novelistic prose may sometimes pause over its own language, its own idiomatic cast, even with regard to straightforward grammatical usage. In the demotic London setting of Zadie Smith's *NW*, simple description can veer into free indirect discourse over the very grammar of word choice in participial common parlance: "Number 17 Ridley Avenue is being squat. Squatted?"[3] Language is never relaxed in Smith's hands. Beyond grammatical punctiliousness, conversation's layered immigrant patois in *NW* keeps many an idiom on edge, and can even turn a likely mispronunciation into a telling Freudian slip. In a case of elided syllabification and diverted etymology alike, an asocial addict named Annie is apologized for by her estranged lover ("she's got this agrophobia"), only to have narrative omniscience immediately intercede, with the thought that "his portmanteau version expressed a deeper truth: she wasn't really afraid of open spaces, she was afraid of what might happen between her and the other people in them" (145). With this slip evoking "approach" or "attack" in the Latin etymology of *aggre*ss, rather than the more spacious trisyllable derived from "open field" in the root *agora*, it is as if the protective distance the character fears collapsing between her and the world were intuitively performed by the closing in and down of an extra phonetic breathing space. The wrong word goes right to the heart of an epitomizing character sketch. Bad form is redeemed by stylistic extrapolation in a poetics of solecism.

This is the covert literary capital of phonetic anagrams by which descriptors seem to coagulate in the most sonorous of prose, as, for instance, in Smith's own "aqua*marine* of the *minar*et" (77). More thickly entwined yet, in Ralph Ellison's *Invisible Man,* is the erotic vision of a "fair b*ird-girl girdled* in veils"[4]—as if the very word *girdle,* enwrapped by the assonant alliteration of *fai/vei,* were always related to *girl* in the substrate of language, inclosing her tightly. A syllabic constriction is thus teased into the open in this compressed move from lexical form to style—rather than being heard in a tacit descent (as *girdle* actually is) from *girth* and *gird.* To rule out such virtualities in philological terms is not to defuse their lurking literary charge. Nor is it to mute our regret when prose has squandered all freshness or surprise, strangled by the pre-cut yardage of sheer verbiage—a condition closely excoriated by the pen of George Orwell in a famous essay and novel alike. Taking his wry diatribes under advisement is a way of highlighting not only the time-release work of diction in a given sentence, including its frequently disclosed etymological burdens, but of anticipating a further temporal dimension of prose style (explored in chapter 2): a grammar of tense crucially manipulated in the orientation of story time. Leagued with Orwell's famous "politics" of "language"—suspect in both the flaccid and the artificially fabricated inventories of its dissemination—are thus the many linguistic particulars to be brought out in a literary poetics of prose.

Prose Style Proselytized

Orwell is the author of two merciless dissections of impoverished writing in its rhetorical and hence moral—and thus ultimately political—decline. In separate lines of attack, first essayistic, then fictional, he skewers a discourse rendered in two different senses rankly utilitarian, either by the carelessness of sheer verbal filler or by a totalitarian constraint on expressive energy. Orwell's charge against the normal morass of contemporary writing, in "Politics and the English Language" (1946), diagnoses the bland malaise to which writing has succumbed in the piling on of words. *Malaise:* a word he'd never use, too French (hence ultimately Latinate) a borrowing. Say, rather, a pervasive virus of blather. What he finds everywhere in published prose (examples coming) is a crisis of lazy phrasing whose wordiness is a misjudged convenience, a depleting facility. More notoriously yet, three years later, there is his novelized version of totalitarian language reform in the near-futurist *1984*: the nightmare of Newspeak, with that buzzword's own self-exemplified compaction of verbal act ("to speak") into stunted noun—together with its propagandist absorption of all "news," plural, into the truncated utterances of its innovative but grotesque protocols. A sloth of phrasing is the earlier diatribe's target, whereas a studied reduction—and corruption—of linguistic scope centers the novel's later satire.

In "Politics," it is the otherwise healthy word—especially the Anglo-Saxon word not crowded out by the Latin and Greek pretension Orwell detests ("ameliorate," "clandestine," "subaqueous," etc., 161), the word in its native vigor—that falls victim to unexamined phrasal annexations, swaddling itself in twaddle, bulked up by flimsy window-dressing. In the coming dystopian novel, *1984*, the crisis goes deeper. It's the word itself that has been shrunken, gutted, or grafted with noxious adjuncts, robbing it of any force beyond that which polices it. Exposed in these paired works is a routinized degradation of the word as communicative unit: the one habit a rampant complacency of civic speech, the other a barbarism actively enforced by regimes of terror. The perverse lexical revisionism of *1984* is deliberately meant to shrink the thought quotient of words, shriveling all invention. In "Politics," by contrast, it is the word before capture by robotic phrase—in its potentially invigorating precision—that is spoiled by association with others automatically brought along in unthinking tow, weatherworn phrases hauled past in tatters ("ride roughshod over," "fishing in troubled waters," etc., 159). At stake, then, is the enforced rot of the lexicon versus the single word's unguarded sloppiness in combination.

Verbal decorum appears to Orwell everywhere disheveled in midcentury prose, a mode of writing unkempt, slapdash, even when ponderous. Orwell's term, twice said, is "slovenliness,"[5] four lumbering syllables, in low-country derivation, set against the mandarin bombast he satirizes. Even when citing another's lament over certain colloquial formulas, Orwell is unforgiving, deriding the critic's limp metaphors as much as his inflated phrasing. The culprit expression: "Above all, we cannot play ducks and drakes with a native battery of idioms" whose tendency "prescribes egregious collocations of vocables" (157)—this last three-word echoic thicket, even if parodic, being a wasteful phrasing of the term "phrases." Wasteful, yet lethally tempting. To Orwell, such "lumps of verbal refuse" (164) come not just easily, but with a facile music that is one lure of wordiness: "If you use ready-made phrases, you not only don't have to hunt about for the words; you also don't have to bother with the rhythms of your sentences since these phrases are generally so arranged as to be more or less *euphonious*" (164; emphasis added), with that final honorific epithet all but sticking in the craw of his contempt.

Orwell is certainly little smitten with the phony euphonies of alliteration and assonance, having no sympathy (regarding an essay satirizing the effete standards of BBC English) with even a tongue-in-cheek chime in spoofing the verbal "languors of Langham place" (158). Near the end of "Politics," an important disclaimer (in just this implicit respect): "I have not here been considering the literary use of language, but merely language as an instrument for expressing and not for concealing or preventing thought" (170). When one turns from muddied exposition to literary invention, however, even in the most facile of satiric alliteration, it is clear that prose rhythm, including the word choices that channel it, can be ironic in both its meaning and its massaged idioms. Take, for instance, the dead metaphor of traverse in the standard-issue phrase "to arrive at a conclusion"—rather than "to conclude." And here take Zadie Smith again, when the parting lovers in *NW*, in finishing one last hasty coupling reported in the arch solemnity of the Queen's English, "came swiftly to reliably pleasurable, reliably separate conclusions" (156). It is only the premature reader who has been teased into assuming the adverb *swiftly* to have completed a verb phrase from the vulgate.

Despite Orwell's mockery of the dead metaphor "native battery of idioms" in pallid mix-up with those "ducks and drakes," this sense of entrenched phrasing offers a clear baseline of "native" ground from which to throw the arsenal of style into oddity and prominence. In light of the "idiometrics" broached in the introduction, one may say that all language operates on the flat plane of the vernacular until it is inflected by invention—that is, by style. Style is a deliberate veer from the idiomatic paths and ruts of utterance, warping any prefabricated norm. In this way, swamping the probable form of a word by the distended stylization of phrase can have a power operating against the drift of those "swindles and perversions" (163) that Orwell sees in everyday published "claptrap," his wry rhyme parodying the "gumming" together of words as a matter of sheer "humbug" (163). In *1984*, the gum becomes a corrosive glue, squeezing the life out of conflated word forms to choke off any premeditated dissent. Anticipating the redrafted dictionaries of the Minitrue (Ministry of Truth), "Politics" finds constraint of thought already contagious in the malfeasance of hackneyed prose. Implicitly, hope lies only in extricating the word from the phrases to which it is sentenced: making it count again as a *unit of thought*, rather than just accumulate in some received phrasing. The novel *1984* crushes that hope altogether.

From the lucid disgust of Orwell's essay and novel, two indirect lines of fictional succession serve to point up an ongoing stylistic crux for the fate of the word: one descended from the grotesque lexical compressions of *1984* transposed to contemporary marketing, one from the broader ethical critique of "Politics." The twin legacy is legible in two novels over half a century after Orwell, themselves a decade apart: the first from an African American novelist satirizing the loss of racial empathy amid the buzzwords of the marketplace; the other, in the mode of linguistic sci-fi, from a lionized American ironist and "euphonious" wordsmith turning to futurist speculation in imagining, for the subjects of cryogenic resuscitation, a posthuman language. This is a reborn phonetic and somatic tongue, far more alien than Newspeak, whose prevision only serves to remotivate the power of present literary wording, and its incessant self-reflection, in monologues recoiling from its pending implementation. Between these two oblique derivations from Orwell: the difference between the word abjected by commercial propaganda and the word ruminated for renewal.

Stylized Desire: What Sin a Name?

A decade before his Pulitzer-Prized historical novel, *The Underground Railroad*, Colson Whitehead seeded its liberation struggle in a satire of corporate jingoism, *Apex Hides the Hurt* (2006): a matrix that may seem far afield, if only at first, from the historical trauma riding on the hidden railroad.[6] A member of the "pre-eminent identity firm in the country" (105), as he puts it, the (ironically) *anonymous* black protagonist (a yuppie Manhattanite Everyman in denial) is a vaunted "nomenclature consultant" (22) who would be quite at home in the lexigraphic department of

Orwell's Minitrue. "He came up with the names," and "like any good parent he knocked them around to teach them life lessons" (3). Such brand words, having no true patrilineage, no natural etymology, are the genetically modified spawn of an originality that disappears into them as pure corporate medium. Yet such progeny must be made "ready"—wait for it, the merchandizing pun on the warehouse of ideas—"for what the world has in store for them" (4), must be readied not just for their reading, but for filing away in their so-called recognition value ever after. Abused into submission, the names are "bent to see if they'd break, dragged by metal chains, exposed to high temperatures" (3). In this monetized phonetics, "sometimes consonants broke off and left angry vowels on the laboratory tables" (3). Yet in the novel's free indirect discourse, vowels can be otherwise recruited in the recall of failed lexical bondings, as, for instance, with the assonant match (the dull soft "u") in conjuring the neologism's frequent fate: "Clunker names fell with a thud on the ground" (3). Or when the merely routine name turns out to click, we have the harmonized verbal assurance that "success shushes" all "accusations" (51).

As the plot opens, our consultant "neologist" has been retained by the midwestern town of Winthrop to rebrand itself with more pizzazz. Earlier rechristened for the town's richest businessman, the waspy name "Winthrop" made more business sense than "Freedom," the settlement's original designation by the southern blacks who founded it when "they dropped their bags here" (76): a name that the consultant deems a mere utility of 'packaging' (his implied market term) in which "they forgot to pack the subtlety" (76). It is "so defiantly unimaginative" as to be a "moral" as well as a mercantile "weakness" (83)—indirectly parodying Orwell's claim for the political as well as stylistic deficits of sodden prose. This African American agent of the salesworthy is conspicuously indifferent to the racial legacy of the founders. Yet it radiates, as if metagrammatically, from the page. They had escaped the Georgia of plantation shackles, and, when they stopped running, in relief they "called it Freedom" (192), *it* being the very condition of arrival.

Whitehead's novel repeatedly skirts issues dear in this way to language philosophy as well as to racial history and its erasures. The recent translation of Giorgio Agamben's essay "On the Sayable and the Idea" comes to mind.[7] That titular conjunction is what produces language. In the present case, again, when giving a name to their escape and arrival at once, "they called it Freedom." That fit of the thinkable and the sayable is, in variant terms, a mantra of Madison Avenue. With the goal in *Apex* always that "the name" should become synonymous with "the thing," this "Holy Grail" (87) is not some metaphysical "it is that it is"—not logocentric but only logo-minded: the sought usurping of all competitors, as in the case of Kleenex or Band-Aids. Is there not a better idea and a better brand than *Freedom?* In pursuit of this question, marketing research constitutes the novel's plot. Previously, the protagonist's career-making coup is to have remarked Dr. Chickie's Adhesive Strips (78) with the catchier, indeed stickier, name Apex, together with a tag line that became a nationwide pop-cultural meme, where the highest recommendation for any saleable pleasure is that it "hides the hurt": eponymous slogan of the novel itself. At one point the marketer dwells in self-bedazzlement over his inspiration: "Apex"—with "that great grand plosive second syllable. Quite the motherfucker, that" (99)—worthy, he fancifully thinks, of a "fascistic crescendo" (100) in the mouths of the public (rather like the plosive "B B" chant at the hate rallies in *1984*: the abbreviated Big Brother as the foreclosure of all individual being).

The wordwork of branding is typically sublexical, phonemic, in just this way. "He dealt in lies and promises, distilled them into syllables" (153), a sleek finesse on exhibit by secondary association in that very phrasing, as the long *li* of "lies" is palmed off as the muted belling *ill* of the appositive phrase ("distilled . . . syll—"). A similar logic of advertising seems, in reverse, to have been flexed by the austerity regime in *1984*, not to induce desire, of course, but to wither the very idea of it. Amid the many iterations of terms cycled through the social text, think "Miniplenty," a governmental office whose oxymoron exposes the starvation protocols of the Ministry of Plenty. Or the bureaucratic subsection called "pornosec," which—given the truncation of real sex in the celibacy strictures of the Party—operates to disseminate addictive smut only to the underclass as "prolefeed": what a later period's portmanteau would compress as "sexploitation." Or the portmanteau "telescreen" inscribing the tele-scopic access of a surveillance state in the remote detection of "thoughtcrime." To say nothing of the dictaphone apparatus at the hero's work desk, called "speakwrite," whose alternate hearing as term, under the corrective arm-twist of "speak right," drains writing not only of all truth but of all subvocal music. The regime of "doublethink" (a jamming of 'doubled/think,' like New-speak of 'News speak') means only falsification in context, not the felicity of second thoughts—where, in the tensile play of literary language, doubles speak.

In any descent from Orwell to Whitehead, there's more than just the linguistic link between mangling and jingoism as two sides of the deceptive coinage, the entrapping versus the catchy. In the marketer's mounting disaffection with his verbal finesse, Orwell's *1984* looms as an all but explicit intertext for a fever dream induced by the infected, Apex-bandaged toe of this antihero, who keeps stubbing it against dumb names as well as curbs. Recalling the nightmare of Room 101 in Orwell, his dream is beset by pests "making little rat noises" (52). "They were everywhere, and he knows that even though they wore the skin of rats, they were in fact phonemes, bits of words with sharp teeth"—bitten off by forced conjunction—"and tails" (confected suffixes?). The anxiety continues: "Latin roots, syllables to be added or subtracted to achieve an effect, kickers in their excellent variety, odd fricatives, and they chased him down" (53). Even awake, on automatic pilot, with no product in view, still he "crunched the names, fed them into the input slot of his particular talent," where, for instance, a sound cluster like "Dark the Field" is compacted to the elided "FieldDark" for how you feel there (196).

Earlier, too, in a more explicit literary allusion, our promotional agent is hounded by "Frankenstein names, lumbering creatures stitched together from glottal stops and sibilants, angry unspellable misfits suitable only for the monstrous" (21). In their common portmanteau collapse, these words are ripe for what the latest slang—popular since Whitehead wrote—calls the Frankenword. His narrator is keenly alert to the awkward seams between syllables, whether forced by the "glottal" swallow or the hissing slur. I tried imagining an instance of the glottal device (mentioned at first without example)—and, jotting in the margin "Angrip" for an anti-aggression drug, I later forgot that the term wasn't his and vainly searched for it in the book's pages. But the text itself rewards patience with subsequent hints of the glottal hinge (unflagged as such) when "TelKing" (tel[e]king) was saved from bankruptcy by rebranding as "UnyCon" (169), with the lurch toward "unique" caught in the very throat of that compound (and a fantastical *unicorn* evoked only to be averted). Or, in allusion to Lego in the combinatory playground of the "plastic" syllable as well as product (118), there's the "snap sound" (117) of its fantasized alternative Ekho: a "hook," in every sense, "for a good stretch of childhood" (117). The novel's guru of nomenclature is proudest of what we might call his Frankenfolds when they brandish, by openly enfolding, their own branded etymology, as with "Loquacia" (138) as a drug for shyness. But he remains his own strictest censor. For bad breath, "Halitotion" (44), he realizes, won't work. Elsewhere he hits on "weathertique" (as both noun and verb), as in the familiar "antiqued" effect—"Apply Weathertique for that lived-in look that will turn your house into a home" (43)—but decides it has too many syllables. For receding chins, an idea finally "came to him: Chinplant. Not his best work" (8). Call it the result of an ungainly verbal implant.

The tinny chink of such marketing coinage is diction gone formally awry in the slippery poetics of deception, words both hung, and wrung, out to dry. With the vertical axis imploded into the horizontal, these lexical distortions represent a collapse of form with no opening to style. Epitomizing the fantasies pandered to in this way, our wordsmith even harbors such terms on hold, names without material signifieds—allegorizing the artificial middle ground between desire and act, anticipation and fulfilment: "Tantalasia" (135) is held in tantalizing abeyance for a miracle product not yet emerged—or "Redempta" (36), one of his early coups for a product not in fact described for us. Name and thing float free of each other in the ether of the sayable. Much of the signifying work is formulaic, but the urge toward originality on the heels of the preformulated inflects the discourse of his own narrative, as when, in a rut, he "suffers through a month of suffixes" (4)—rather than a proverbial month of Sundays—during which he and his team "hung the staple kickers on a word: they—*ex*'ed it, they—*it*'ed it." In ironic derivation from their shared Latin prefix instead—*sub*, for bearing up under versus affixing from beneath—such is the unmarketable play between *suffer* and *suffix*. Or "they stuck," in a further internal echo, "good ole—*ol* on it." (One imagines a name like Levitol for a Viagra competitor.) In the terminological fray, there is always the chance of "incipient revival" for some word fragment of faded glory, a syllabic rebound: "*Pro-* and *anti-* would stumble back to the top, bruised and lacerated but still standing, this month's trendy morphemes and phonemes lying at their feet in piles" (51).

Among the marketer's favorite conflations, there is the vocalic elision of "Aquaway" (8) for a water-repellent leather spray—itself syllabically liquefied. Shades there, or phonemic shadows, of Morrison's "saliva away" from the introduction, marketable in that case only if some condition opposite to "dry mouth" were to need medication. Indirectly aligned with such border trans/fusions, an odd refrain in the novel puts the established term "shuttle bus" (with its unmentioned assonance and alliteration) into iterative celebration. "Say it five times fast, he maintained—shuttle bus shuttle bus sounded like leaves whispering to each other in your textbook primordial glen" (101). Speed is always part of the neologist's calculations, of course, not just fancifully here, but in timing the rear-end syllabic collisions of his combines. And beyond the inferred sibilant circularity of the *bu/ss/huttle* loop, these named vehicles of transfer are "perfect containers of that moment between anticipation and event," so that they "cannot be blamed" if it is to be discovered that "the destination disappoints, if desire is counterfeited" (101). I think here of my own campus's punning portmanteau "Cambus." Recall Tantalasia, with its four interwoven *a*'s as a scrim of invitation in the wholesale absence of product, of referent itself. Such phonemic blur may recall the other Whitehead, Alfred North, when celebrating algebra's precision as reversing the priority of sound to script in the vagueness of "ordinary language," which his dismissal went so far as to travesty—in his own assonance—when calling speech, in contrast to writing, "merely a se*ries* of sq*uea*ks."[8]

In *Apex Hides the Hurt*, the marketing of strategically manipulated noise eventually disheartens the hot-shot brander, who recognizes how the "textbook primordial glen" he fantasizes has become a despoiled Eden. Until then, with the whole panoply of "organics" in mind, he had considered "nature" as the ultimate "strong brand," a ruse to package all effective n(omencl)ature. But with another part of his mind, he realizes that branding is a counter-nature, an overtended glen, a hothouse internalized. Early on, vistas of facility generate a *locus amoenus*, a "magnificent and secret landscape" where "beautiful hidden things scrolled to the horizon" (35). It is a wordscape whose strange flora, lushly summoned, and evoking the proverbial "flowers of rhetoric" under market pressure, include "saplings that curtsied eccentrically" (34)—waiting, no doubt, to be pruned and cross-bred, as well as "low shrubs that extruded bizarre fronds," perhaps in the form of mutant suffixes. Yet, in his mounting disillusion, the nomenclaturist yearns ultimately for a prelapsarian world, even pre-Adamic, before the imposition of names: "Isn't it great when you're a kid and the whole world is full of anonymous things?"—ablaze with presence before the "light goes out" of them—until suddenly "All those fly*ing* glid*ing* th*ings* are just birds" (182). The seeming lexical inherence of the mobile *ing*—floated in the two participles and then enfolded by the volatile "th*ings*" on the wing—is finally grounded by category, say pigeonholed. And enfolded twice over, at that: first, more freely, by the fleet elision at "flying gliding"—yet smuggling in, at the same time, a lexical model, corrupting even his nostalgia, for the "hooks" of marketing craft (and their alphabetic grafts) achieved by mastering the ratlike nibbling of phonemes that bites into his sleep. Alerted by this counter-memory of linguistic innocence, we may wonder if the withholding of the character's own name is part of some Edenic remission from the blitz of nouns.

Long committed to the premise that "wording and phrasing," when anchored in the branded bonding of syllables, articulate "the essential grammar of modern business" (96), our antihero finally breaks away into a more familiar grammar of human agency, where phrasing releases itself from terminology. Until this turning point, his proposal was to rename Winthrop "Prospera," boasting a formulaic, aspirational "romance language armature" that would give it, according to his abiding philological instinct, "a glamorous Old World aura draped over the bony shoulder of prosaic *prosperity*" (52). In this target of Whitehead's satiric prose, the prosaic per se is what must be avoided, torqued, even mangled and refashioned—prose and the individual words at its base. But in the protagonist's quest for the trendy original, he ends up with second thoughts—those, in fact, of another. It turns out that one of the town's two Black founders had wanted the city elders, in a proposal dismissed as "cockeyed," to see how a better name than "Freedom" would be "Struggle." The contemporary rebrander actually likes this one. When taken up by an existential syntax, the name "Struggle" spells an "anti-Apex," all climb, no peak, where there is no effort to hide the hurt, to "camouflage" the "wound" (210), let alone wholly heal it. Since his contract obliges the township to retain the name for a trial year, he thinks they might grow "comfortable with it," living within its resonance "as if it were their very skin" (211). Letting slip away his perverse linguistic vigilance, he falls asleep hearing the random conversations: "They will say: I was born in Struggle. I live in Struggle and come from Struggle. I work in Struggle," and so on (211): historicizing the site, and the longer plight, of endurance per se. And in nothing less than a triumph of idiometrics. Where Orwell saw the potential vigor of English diction enervated by rote phrasing, this marketer's confected word forms, so often isolated, fetishized, and debased as trade names, are returned to vitality by phrase: say by prose itself, rather than nomenclature, in the lateral plane of stylistic rescue and lived speech.

Just before this closural replacement of Prospera by Struggle, the novel's wordplay so closely anticipates the climax of Toni Morrison's *A Mercy*, two years later, that Whitehead's verbal move shimmers as intertext. Morrison's seventeenth-century historical fiction about the Portuguese trafficking in human labor for the New World, before the American institutionalization of so-called slavery, never deploys that abstract noun for such bondage—except in its final defiance by cross-word phonetic irony. In the heroine's climactic speech, she is trying to break free with her own abrupt end-stops: "Slave. Free. I'll last."[9] In Whitehead's millennial novel, set long since official emancipation, the portmanteau collapse—quite apart from any of his character's marketable ingenuities—runs (together) like this: "Before coloured, slave. Before sla*ve, free*" (192), with wording's inescapable sounding of the *slavery* to come. Even for narrative discourse itself, it would seem hard to recover a memory free from the shadow (phonetic, ethical) of that curse, any "before" kept clear of its encroachment. Remember the neo-Orwellian rat dream in the gnawing revenge of its neologisms, an assault by "kickers in their excellent variety, odd fricatives"—fricatives like *v/f* in this worded return of the historically repressed. It is no doubt a final irony, in the metalinguistic satire of Whitehead's novel, that even this kind of subliminal, even subversive, prose poetry may find its demeaned obverse in the smoke-screen facility of the marketer's Frankenfolds. Nonetheless, in the dialectic of word versus phrase spurred here by Orwell's critique, for a tensed moment the phrase, the chronological sequence *slave, free*, is heard struggling, in Whitehead even before Morrison, to liberate itself from the manacling syllables of a single convergent noun.

Prime Words vs. Cryophonemics

After *Apex*, Don DeLillo's very different version of "Politics and the English Language" comes a decade later in *Zero K*, in a bizarre sci-fi plot about a Wall Street billionaire entering into a contract for cryogenesis (the title, *Zero K*, referring to Kelvin's discovery of "absolute zero").[10] His skeptical unnamed son is the narrator, permitted top-secret access to the underground laboratories of "Convergence" (the trademarked intersection of life and death, as well as the unmapped junction of the three former Soviet-y/istans of Central Asia), where the frozen bodies are wired and stockpiled. Among the most chilling prospects of such a thawed-out immortality is, for this narrator, the melting away of human language itself, which has been his lifelong fascination. He grew up chasing words in the dictionary, wading through one new synonym after another—from, say, the overheard paternal accusation of "fishwife" through "shrewmouse" to "insectivorous" (25)—and he now pauses repeatedly to comment on linguistic curiosities or to reach self-consciously for his own best nugget of expression. "There was," for instance, "a word I wanted, not crypt or grotto," he comments when his mental thesaurus is under strain in the dungeon of the banked dead: "bodies on both sides of me, and the sight was overwhelming, and the place itself, the word itself—the word was *catacomb*" (133). Only such a knotted polysyllable could summon the honeycombed necropolis through which he stumbles.

For all his repulsion, the narrator revels with perverse fascination in the argot of this rejuvenation enterprise, with words like "vitrification" and "cryopreservation" (141) being, in his view, linguistic prods to further notches of molecular discovery—goads to his own lexical investigations in a resistant vein: "Cherish the language, I thought. Let the language reflect the search for ever more obscure methods, down into sub-atomic levels" (141)—as in the nuclear combustion of the anagrammed *chersh/serch* dyad. He is continually probing his own discourse for the inner linings of association. Distracting lexical fragments are dwelt on in a way that might "draw other words out to lo*cate* the *core*" (166)—with the vocalic core there chiastically targeted. A mannequin is seen as "reddish brown, maybe russet or rust" (24). Sounds redouble, embed, retone, and bracket each other. A favored Catholic ritual entails a phonetically smudged "splotch of ash" (15). With words understood as "dense realities" (201), the one that comes to mind in responding to his father's diminished spirit, after delaying his euthanasia, seems suited to their conversation on the banquette of a posh New York restaurant: "desuetude" (201) feeling just right for the fancy ambience, whether upholstered in velvet or actual suede.

Elsewhere, the wording of a "purer aura" (47) seems to rarefy itself by syllabic iteration as we listen, *ur* purified via *er* to an open-vowelled *aur*. In recalling the notion of "prime numbers," he "needed to find the precise and perpetual and more or less mandatory wording that would constitute the definition of a prime" (151). A search, in short, for a prime wording.

Orwell had his hero Winston Smith reach for the right word, too, while dodging the monstrosities of Newspeak. In a spurt of free indirect discourse made plain to us only after the fact, and thus placing a further rhetorical accent on invaded privacy, Winston's unpoliced thought takes shape in just the right four-syllabled metaphor—producing exactly the kind of compelling "image" Orwell's "Politics" essay finds blurred in the murk of contemporary prose. "Winston was gelatinous with fatigue."[11] No sooner said than glossed—and in a reflex pitched this time halfway between narrator and character: "Gelatinous was the right word. It had come into his mind spontaneously"—that very adverb indicating a minor triumph under the crush of Newspeak. "His body seemed to have not only the weakness of jelly, but its translucency," all the more penetrable in turn by telescreen surveillance, with that etymologized soft *g* of "gelatinous" having operated to sap even the glottal closure effected by the very noun "fatigue."

More often yet, DeLillo's protagonist in *Zero K* is caught listening in on his own wordings—as hooked on syllabic latches and aural "cores" as any marketer's playbook from *Apex Hides the Hurt*, yet in a mode curious and investigative rather than instrumental. This is the DeLillo who, in a famous *Paris Review* interview, explains that being a writer means, for him, writing sentences acutely attuned to the syllables of words. "I'm completely willing to let language press meaning upon me," so that "I might want *rapture* matched with *danger*—I like to match word endings":[12] poetry by another name. Exemplified in this very sentence is less the particular seesaw of rapture and danger than the slant rhyme of the match. This match can take hold at the beginning of words as well: in *Zero K*, a backseat taxicab video submitting him to the "*dead*ly *sed*ative *ten*or of picture and sound" (176). Or there is the underground postmortal epiphany of a spectral monk present "on this *ben*ch" in "the context of an im*men*se *emp*tiness" (126), with the minor plosive echo, *b/p*, deflated by the surround of emphatic flattenings. Blind spots of criminal negligence about one's own motives are called "little *fel*onies of *self*-perception"

(108). Although he imagines a frozen body trying to picture her own verbal memories not by seeing "the letters in the words but the words themselves" (162), in the throes of his own self-expression he often sees letters in their separate insistence, his own version of "subatomic" recognition—as with the pivot-like (and erotically feminine) *v* of the mesmerizing word "lover" for his girlfriend: "The idea alone consoled me, the word itself, lover, the beautiful musical note, the hovering letter v" (158). So gratifying is the word that, beyond the alphabetic (and inevitably sexed) *v*, the whole fetishized disyllable nearly returns, as if by erotic addiction, in "ho*ver*/ing." Or, back in the cryogenics lab, there is the lexical "savor of that word" tasted on the tongue of the internally chimed—and then reverberant—polysyllable "Fore*ver*more. He*r word*" (258): just the kind of wording that will have no place in the newspeech of artificial rebirth.

Instead, for the posthuman agenda to which he's been made privy, the "occult language" (245) of the futurists, shaped by commissioned "philologists" in the revamping of "roots" and "inflections," traps speech within an "opaque bubble" (244) of phonemes and gestures that communicate nothing to the living. This is a condition parallel to a speech-disabled student of the protagonist's girlfriend in Manhattan, who, in his apraxia, is stumped by "the specific motor movements" that permit speech. In his case, regarding so-called natural language: "Nothing is natural" (191). This sentence reads two ways at once: a positive *is* for the natural lapse into nonspeech; a negation of all normal articulation in the boy's case. Saying nothing is the easy default—here where a litany of rare and "unnatural" disablement hangs in the air without a sentence grammar of its own, just a word list of inefficacies in regard to what doesn't come naturally: "Phonemes, syllables, muscle tone, action of tongue, lips, jaw, palate" (191). Similarly, in the subterranean labyrinth of Convergence, the "congested syllables of 'regularly' " (17) are heard by the narrator at one point to trouble a dying tongue. Back in New York, when the hero's own embarrassed stammers in a job interview find him "murmuring microdecibles of assent" (166), we may think by contrast—in the same sibilant groove—of those subatomic rumbles of *dissent* regarding Convergence that he is working to choke off in this scene. When this same narrator is heard asking rhetorically near the story's end, "Isn't that why I was here"—in this novel as well as the underground lab—"to subvert the *dance* of tran*sc*endence with my tricks and games?" (242; emphasis added), we can hear an instance of just such prestidigitation in the smoked out "trance" of artificial animation—syncopated against the already choreographed two-step of d*ance/dence*. Where better to instance Pound's "dance of the intellect among words" than in this kind of telltale spin as a fugitive pirouette? And the "tricks" can be more constrictive yet. In his colorless cell in the lab, he spews a quartet of monosyllables that shift from nouns as rudimentary descriptors—"Wall, floor, door, bed"—to a "monosyllabic image" (271) of his claustrophobic room. Even this side of the future's posthuman newspeech, the narrative's own "natural" language may in this way, under duress, appear cramped—or is it purified?—in confrontation with the perverse horizons of a cybernetic beyond. In their own sense of linguistic genealogy, the quartet of Anglo-Saxon nouns ("Wall, floor, door, bed") works to encase scene per se as a "monosyllabic" space, even in narration's distressed guesses about a timeless postmortem enunciation where all linguistic "roots"—including their verbal progeny over etymological time—will be remade by the new futurist philologists.

Precisely because language is always at risk of expressive default, the narrative voice must stay alert to a semiotics of aurality beyond its own lexical register. As much as Whitehead's novel dreams of embodied natural flight in a time before the word "bird" names such agency, so does DeLillo find cleansing words of his own for the pre- (rather than post-) linguistic affect of living energy. In the novel's contrapuntal structure, a final return from Convergence to the open-ended seethe of metropolitan humanity achieves a moment of contingent secular grace in the last paragraphs, when, on a bus route, a radiant New York sunset happens to align its glowing orb with the cavernous city streets—and when a child's squeal of delight, seeing the burning shape framed so symmetrically by cement walls, serves to voice, without exactly uttering, a burst of affirmation. Celebrated by the narrator as eloquently "pre-linguistic," the child's delight is also solemnized by DeLillo's typifying syllabic craft: no flat monosyllabism of *red* occupies the epiphany of a "great round *rud*dy mass" amid the assonant "urban *hud*dle" (273) of stone. Beyond the modest personification of the phrase lies perhaps the displaced intertext of America's "huddled masses." Not all *prime wording* is definitional, but rather imagistic as well, evocative, allusive, revisionist in its own play of vocables.

In Orwell's "Politics and the English Language," the bane, beyond formulaic phrasing, is "staleness of imagery" (158)—whether in the mixed or the dead metaphor. This remains Orwell's charge against modern prose, the colorless writer as "a cuttlefish squirting out ink" (165), though the phrase itself has an acid bite. The inveterate phonetic grain of DeLillo's syllabic prose doesn't rest easy, above, with its image of the sun, but finds in the echo (*rud/hud*) an animated and momentarily centered metropolis. Such imaging (figurative beyond pictorial) is the glory of the crisp fictional archive out of which Orwell's own writing emerges—and to which we can return for a concentrated, if extreme, Victorian example. George Meredith puts into the mouth of his novelist-heroine in *Diana of the Crossways* (1885) a flamboyant instance of the imaging word at its own syntactic crossings, track-switching from one register to another in a running pun on the locomotive grammar of gender. Under such figurative extrapolation, even an unworded term can inflect an entire passage. Marriage is the heroine's literal topic, the resources of language her metaphor (with my italics) in this extended conceit: "We women are the *verbs passive* of the alliance, we have to learn, and if we take to activity, with the best intentions, we *conjugate* a frightful disturbance." The bravura energy of this whole lament may well seem extruded (by exclusion) from the unsaid word *conjugal*. Then, too, any phrasal impetus in "we have to learn"—any quest for knowledge we might expect—is nipped in the bud by the antecedent drag on this phrase as a matter not of open inquiry but of belated recognition.

On it goes, with these verbal *crossway*s facilitated by the abrupt shunt to an unexpected shifting rail. In the straitening custom regretted in the heroine's next clause—"We are to *run on lines,* like the steam-trains"—it is as if an enjambment by run-on in the literary line itself were being commandeered for prosaic routine, followed by an insistence on the abiding railway-figured threat: "or we come to no *station*"—not just no resting *place* but no social *standing*. In the double logic at just this switch point of impasse, where the risk of independence is that we "come to no station, dash to *fragments*," one may hear in the parallel predicate "dash to" the finality of "dash(ed) to." In the vocabulary educed from DeLillo, and related in fact to Whitehead's (and Morrison's) "slave/free," we may say that prime terms serially chosen from the formal paradigm can become primed terms for their cross-word manipulation by the ligatures of horizontal syntax.

At the figurative intersection of Meredith's *Crossways,* the grammar of predication returns explicitly to clinch the point: "I have the misfortune to know I was born an active"—the seemingly impending next word, "verb" (in chiastic symmetry with "verbs passive" at the start), going unsaid. The genetic trope "born an active" keeps possibilities open—even while only a firm grammatical sense holds them together. "I take my chance"—a submission to contingency already well illustrated at the level of lexical drive across the rails of syntax. If form is vertical, style horizontal, what has been anomalously fashioned in the space of these three sentences—by the resolute double valence of formal selection from the stack of verbal alternatives—is staged to guarantee that each word has a philological as well as a psychological traction. And a momentum all its own. En route, formal tension restyles the contemporaneous railroad image of Victorian progress into a double-tracked irony of syntactic and social mobility alike. In the spirit of Orwell, here is the *gender* "politics of the English language"—as, before in our examples from Whitehead and DeLillo, the racial and the ontological—at work overtime yet again, word by forked word, in the transforms of figurative diction over the energized time of reading.

Time-Release Phrasing

Underlying the extravagance—and vagrant metaphoric shifts—in the multi-tracking of Meredith's conceit lurks a blunter bifurcation (though hardly unliterary or unprecedented): like train engines, we women either *stay on track or put*, in the latter case stuck forever without chance or change. Idiometrically calibrated, these are the split wordings of an ongoing present tense necessary to support such splayed effects from within the same, so to say, grammatical frame of reference. So back once more to Zadie, rather than Winston, Smith for a moment. Recall the slow reading, the rereading, induced by the opposite descriptor "swiftly" in, not the foreplay, but the byplay, of idiom in those previously cited nonmutual orgasms of the estranged couple in *NW* who *together*, if only so to speak, "came swift*ly* to relia*bly* pl*e*asura*ble*, relia*bly* se*p*arate conclusions" (156). Yes, timing is everything, with syntax here building—even in its vernacular irony—across the syllabic build of *ly/bly/pl/ble/bly/p*. If, however, one were to render the split—then splintered—idiom in a different context, in a vein of long-standing wordplay (traditionally called zeugma, or alternately syllepsis) from Austen through Dickens to the Marx Brothers, the forking template would be all the clearer: 'She no sooner came than also to a final conclusion about the relationship—and went at once.' No such strain in the novel's actual wit. But Smith's delight in the whole diasporic range of London patois makes her also edgily alert, one might say, to migratory possibilities in the most mainstream of idioms.

So timing is everything—but only if this includes the syncopations by which, in their staged delays, the ways of the word can reroute syntax in the texturing of time-release sense. This is to say (idiometrics again) that one of the places where words, like women in Meredith, don't always keep to their station—and in this fashion take syntactic time into their own hands—is in resistance to vernacular formulas. Idioms can be made, when even slightly dislodged from the norm they crystallize, to give tactical pause on the page. What these distortions often give voice to are *spaced-out* displacements from codified phrasal routine, exposing in the process, to locally heightened attention, certain new regimes and reigns of estrangement. Puns allowed. The loosened reins of idiomatic control can install (or at least instill) fresh rules—adjusted orderings—of recognition from within the grooves of worded pattern. High formalism once enshrined deviation and its consequent estrangement as the mark of literature's inflected language—not just the local mark but the sign of literary writing all told. Sometimes that aura of alienation is managed notably by writers for whom English is a "secondary" tongue, superimposed on an earlier language template—and thus ready to usurp the artificial norms of idiom for a wry repurposing. The hybrid London sociolects so often reported upon in native speaker Zadie Smith's fiction tend to work this way. Imagine, then, the dictionary, the English word book, in the hands of a prose genius for whom English as a Second Language is not an entry-level course but an aesthetic mode. It's easy to do. In the manner of lexical slapstick, famously, Russian emigré novelist Vladimir Nabokov seems always to be "hearing things" in English of the sort that few other novelists since Joyce have—and none so memorably before Dickens, whom Nabokov taught among other British novelists during a post at Cornell University. Under this quirky audition of English idiom in the turn of a given word, even before phrase—idiom in its wild prepositional variety, for instance—wording, as we'll see, often comes apart at its syntactic seams even while sounding out unexpectedly from within its separate lexical textures.

This is wordsplay in its time-release grammar, and sometimes phonetic aftertones. Dickens, in his last completed novel, *Our Mutual Friend*, epitomizing a career-long fondness for splayed grammar, has one character succeed in tossing another into a dung-cart, a feat "a*chie*ved with great dexterity and a prodi*giou*s spla*sh*." After the swift syllabic chiasm of "*great* dex*ter*ity," the two senses of "with" (cause and effect)—latched aslant by *and*—set us up perfectly for the thick squash of Latinate upon Anglo-Saxon diction in the last phrase. As often, too, internal alliteration (as marked, from the first *ch* phoneme) bridges what wording, even syntactic compounding, divides.[13] It is all skewed for comedy around a not quite logical "and," a kind of forced parallelism verging on redundancy. Nabokov is the true heir of this interplay between echoing sounds and a forked English grammar. In *Lolita*, with his car stuck in the thick mush of damp clay, the narrator moans out that "my rear wheels only whined with slo*sh* and angui*sh*."[14] The turbid alliteration is in both cases the verbal bonus of the grammatical joke. *Slosh and anguish*: one can just hear Nabokov hearing not just English, but the English word *language*, stirring in this mimetic mire.

Dickens's most famous example of *and*-compounds unraveled by two different senses of their predication entails the play on another idiomatically disposed preposition, *in* rather than *with*. This happens in the off-kilter form of verbal event, a phrasal as well as a human departure, when an irate character in *Pickwick Papers* (textbook example of syllepsis) "went home in a flood of tears and a sedan-chair." The interplay between material and spiritual condition, concrete and abstract, is beyond "character": it is what characterizes this syntactic device in its underlying structure. Such hyperkinetic forkings of syntax can often seem, in Dickens not least, an ebullient master key to the word's parting of its own ways. A tenth-generation derivative of this effect sponsors the Mexican beer ad "Drop everything and a lime." With the Dickens example, it is worth lingering over the effects of such time-release wordage for their comparable estrangement of a norm. Undermining any implied parallelism of compound grammar, the jolting syncopation—dropping everything in midstride until the jokey mismatch drops by surprise—is timed to reanimate the most neutral monosyllables of the English vernacular: in a flood of tears, in a chair. The syntax is briefly pitched to a no-lose comic battle between wording and grammar, part of speech and its divisive phrasal participation, native expectation and exotic disruption.

Reigns of Estrangement: The Foreign Near

Typically, Dickens holds such time-release effects—whether in the non-metrical beat, or sometimes even the quasi-iambic feet, of his broken cadences—to the dropped shoe of an immediate afterthought in a blunt twofold format. Slightly separate senses collide divisively in an even-handed reciprocal estrangement, so near and yet so far. In contrast, the foreign ear of Nabokov, reveling in the shifting paradigmatic resources of his adopted language, goes so far, in *The Real Life of Sebastian Knight*, as to produce such a highly "literary" version as the triplicate "having missed trains, allusions, and opportunities"[15]—as if working through the OED under shadings of "v. to miss." This is the same Nabokov who has his narrator describe the crisis of that stalled getaway car in *Lolita* as an impasse, a quagmire, at once physical and emotional: "All was dark and muggy, and hopeless" (281)—and making for an enforced delay over diction, as well as extrication, by the sheer spin of words rather than tires, "tortuous and tortoise-slow" (even in its lightning-fast assimilation of the French *tortue* for such an amphibian analogue). Whether it is a copula like "was" caught blooming in two mildly different registers, atmospheric and mental, or a transitive verb like "missing" loosening its grip on three objects at once, the strain of the strangeness exerts its own new hold on attention.

Slavic speaker Joseph Conrad, the anchoring language in his case Polish rather than Russian, was just as alert to inadvertent verbal kinships in English. We've overheard his own ear for the metaplay of contingent syllabification in the introduction's mordant "Hazard has such accuracies." When he turns in *Lord Jim* (1899–90) to full clausal disjunctures, his fanning out of options tends, unlike Nabokov's, to be more metaphysical than whimsical, as when (with three different senses of "in," inflecting the interlaced three of the verb "fills") the hero has a sudden repulsed revelation "of everything vile and base that lurks *in* the world we love: *in* our own hearts we trust for our salvation, *in* the men that surround us"—in the very mystery, that is, of inner and outer lives. Across such an anaphora of revulsion, the "ion" of "salvation" seems to have sprung the leak of its own hidden "in"-flection—a phrasal contagion at the same time felt "as well as in the sights that *fill* our eyes, in the sounds that *fill* our ears, and in the air that *fills* our lungs." As if such a disclosure is mobilized with a dictionary in hand, there are almost as many ways to "fill" us with despair as there are to be "in" evidence. An overt and more openly metaphoric wordplay like 'my heart was as full of fear as my ears of rumor and my eyes of tears' would only make explicit the kind of shifting vernacular registers against which Conrad is playing off his picture of a blanketing—and more to the point, a penetrating—anxiety in *Lord Jim*.

The so-called ear for idiom that doesn't feel quite right in this novel, and whose effect is a refused normalization of its multiple existential crisis, is recruited, in the same year that *Lord Jim* began its serialization, to estrange audition in *Heart of Darkness* with a more claustrophobic patterning. I refer to the penultimate paired clauses, in its closing occluded panorama, that compound both themselves and the famously brooding gloom: "The offing was barred by a black bank of clouds"—via alliteration and assonance, in a mimetic pileup of phonic as well as foggy murk that casts its own auditory shadow over the tailing-off of the sentence: "and the tranquil waterway leading to the uttermost ends of the earth flowed sombre under an overcast sky." The *ank* of "bank" serves to unsettle and begloom the very chance of complacency in the torpor of "tra*n*quil"—before this syllabic matter further dead-ends in the head-spinning rhythmic foreclosure of "somb*re* und*er* an ov*er* . . .," securing the viselike shutdown of all ocular prospect. This despite the fact that a grammatically indeterminate dash is then used to append—and in this way suspend, morally upend, any hope of finality—an odd free-floating simile: predicating the way in which the river, by grammatical addendum, "seemed to lead into the heart of an immense darkness." Which is, of course, the by-now metaphorically inescapable fact of its colonial outreach. What transpires in this whole last channeling—and moral drain—of phrase is the syllabically braced equivalent of an ethically emblematic grammar like 'Under the shadow of the overwhelming, the river flowed past, out, and nowhere, beyond all acknowledgment, in its routes of exploitation.'

Even reined-in this side of any overt wordplay, but skewing the passage's inert neutrality of tone by phonetic contamination, such wavering ways of the word become figures of uncertainty and blockage in their own right, of burden and arrested progress. If Conrad isn't quite writing a transparent English here, it is in part because the novella, in its critique, refuses to speak British. In terms of narrative wording in the often frictional mode of prose fiction, the very least we can say about the residuum of "bank" in "tranquil," for instance, the aural atmospherics of such roughened lamination, is that it evokes the prose equivalent of those fog-banked lap dissolves mobilized in departure from Kurtz's compound by Francis Ford Coppola—along with the acousmatic echoes of Brando's "horror"—in the filmic update of Conrad's story for *Apocalypse Now* (1979). Conrad's auditory kinematograph got there first, of course, just as the exhibit from *Heart of Darkness* (only by happenstance from the same half decade that saw the London debut of motion picture technology) anticipates a fuller account of exactly those tempting equivalents between phonemically cued syntax and screen montage to which we turn in part III. For now, we can hear how the shared sounds operating in Conrad under cover of alphabetic difference, or retained residually by just such difference (*bank/tranquil, sombre/under/over*), find a counterpart in the frequent silent letters of English orthography—a ubiquitous challenge to the new learner. In *Lolita*, a muted letter within a word, as in the self-exemplifying term "dip*h*thong," seems, for instance, an inextricable part of the metatextual seduction for Nabokov's aesthete narrator in that more than alliterative shapeliness—and extra graphic rather than phonetic cross-stitching—involved in the silent (but not entirely repressed) lip-smacking *b* of the "ny*m*phet's li*mb*s" (257) in spectral echo with the differently pronounced p. Phonically, a quasi-erotic caress of wording lets loose not those silenced plosive puckers (*p/b*) but the titillating hint—amid the rhyming nimbus of English orthographic quirks—concerning the half-said *slimness* of that *nim's/lim(b)s* stroke.

With Conrad and Nabokov, certainly, there is a connection often noted between these preeminent master(er)s of English as their adopted narrative tongue. In turn, the great postwar heir of the latter, in the irresistible lure of wordplay, is the Nobel Laureate Joseph Brodsky when turning from Russian verse to the phrasal poetics of English prose. It's not easy to pun on "was," but Brodsky opens his self-elegy for years spent intermittently in Venice, *Watermark*, with a deliberately atmospheric dead metaphor and a lighthearted grammatical forking: "Many moons ago the dollar was 870 lire and I was twenty-two."[16] Explaining his earliest encounter with Venice, the poet in him also hears an adventitious slant rhyme between two alliterating monosyllables, springing a further double alliteration: "This is the *way*, and in my case the *why*, I first set *eye*s on this city" (43). The phonetic echoes only serve to flag the more interesting symmetry in the bifurcated grammar. His principle of narration, such as it is in this pastiche of reflections, is in fact a principle of prose sequence at large, since "what makes a narrative good is not the story itself but what follows what" (37–38). Which is true even with barely any story involved, as in the prose of the present meditation, where another forking grammar arrives in almost as dampened a form as the foggy season itself, "a time for reading, for burning electricity all day long," and, in sync with the spirit of such reading, "for going easy"—like the (invisible) alliteration here, again in train to a dominant syntactic doubleness—"on self-deprecating th*ough*ts or c*off*ee." Behind this phrasing lies, no doubt, the more common idiom "going easy on yourself." Brodsky's English often catches us just fractionally off guard in this resuscitating way. The cliché "awe-inspiring," itself verging on a pleonasm for "inspiring" alone, when implied to the waking dream of a city like Venice, is countered at the level of diction by the reminder that the amateur interpretation of dreams can be so tedious, so "yawn-inspiring" (121), as to send you right back to sleep.

Other and odder English anomalies captivate Brodsky's foreign ear, including a discrepant homograph like "flounder"—in its noun/verb rift, meaning (so to speak) both "a fish" and "to foul up"—that would seem responsible for generating an extended conceit strung out in the description of canals like "eels" leading the hapless Venetian visitor to some unintended "flounder of a campo" (45). Brodsky's prose is not shy of exaggerating such effects—indeed, with Nabokovian comic echoes toppling over into blunt puns—as when, in this same vein of piscatory geography, the flapping hands of Venetians, when giving futile directions, "don't so much help you as kelp you" (46). On the model of "what follows what," Brodsky's idiomatic splayings at the syntactic level can be even more intricate than Conrad's or Nabokov's. Enjoy sorting this out, for instance: "For all the time, blood, ink, money, and the rest that I shed or shelled out here, I never could convincingly claim . . . that I'd become, in however minuscule a manner, a Venetian" (122). It goes down smoothly enough, until you try bringing its logic to light. Pushing beyond the triplicate festivity of Nabokov in the taxonomy of idiomatic predication, Brodsky mounts his nominative quartet on the sly avoidance of two separate idiomatic paradigms, "to spill" and "to spend," encapsulated instead by the telescoping of "shed or she[lle]d out." Blood shed in the vernacular sense, unlike ink spilt, is usually another's, and the way time and money are comparably "shed" depends on a separate subsidiary forking of sense that presses beneath the written, as in a phrase like 'spending more money than time on that skimpy meal.' In retrospect, we recognize in the thick of Brodsky's slipknot wording—perhaps more clearly than in any of the previous examples from Dickens, Conrad, or Nabokov—the stylistic leverage of syllepsis: where word and sentence, wording and sentencing, are not just inextricable but disruptively cross-wired and self-revising. Like the slippage of syllables within and between words, the splay of diction across a canny fanned-out grammar becomes a figure for reading in action.

This mix of soundsplay and sense-play is typical of Brodsky's majestically sustained estrangement in prose from his acquired poetic tongue, where syllables themselves may obtrude as resident aliens within English lexemes. This most extreme prose-poetic tendency is nowhere more haunting than in his extended conceit, near the end of *Watermark*—the title itself linking page texture to lagoon and canal surface: "this Penelop*e* of a cit*y*, w*e*aving her patterns by day and undoing them by n*i*ght, with no Ulys*s*es in s*i*ght. Only the *sea*" (114). The long *e/y/ea* alliteration gives way to the echo and contrast of "night" with "sight," the latter word turning to an irrelevant homophonic half pun ('no sees' ["ysses"]) before its flip to singular noun form in *sea*. Recurrent phonetic patterning—mainstay of the "poetic function" in its theorization, for prose as well, by Slavic linguist Jakobson—has found, in Slavic poet Brodsky's ear for English syllabic accidents, a new and thrilling subtlety. In reversing Jakobson's formula, once you strip the surplus equivalence from the axis of combination, you get just what Brodsky's music has transcended, something as banal as 'with no Ulysses in prospect, only the horizon.' Prose has made sure we hear it otherwise—through open rhyme ("by night"/"in sight") as well as by sublexical resonance in the audited rather than seen *seas* of *sses*. In the play of word forms as a formative energy, the graphic can also dictate implications. Joyce's *Ulysses* might almost be heard, thanks to Brodksy's variant of such play, to approach some insinuated version of its own title scene in the last line's run of reiterated "yes" words when releasing their own erotic "sigh" ("yes *I* will yes *I* will") in the breathed desire ('yes, sigh') of

Molly's Penelope—and so returning the *y(e)sses* of heroic affirmation to the very name *Ulysses*.

For Brodsky: no sign or sight of Ulysses, only the impersonal "sea." This lexical play, sheering off a lone monosyllable from within the name Ulysses, is clearly related to the broader spans of split wording in Brodsky's syntactic wit: semantic vestiges and leftovers folded back into a divisively tracked grammar and its disjoint compounds. Often the very structure of the word, and of any word's way forward to the next, can be understood as a faster wafting of aftertones than the subsonic ear can detect. This is by no means the special province of bilingualism, of polyglot authorship. It is inherent in the linguistic function itself, founded on the native alienation of each signifying unit from its necessitated differential other. Aligned with the pitched battle between cliché and invention, here is the main way in which Orwell's writing about the "politics" of English, on the one hand, and major international stylists, on the other, coming fresh but belatedly to its poetics, speak to each other across this chapter. Noting the primal force of differentiation is a way of snapping phrases free of their formulaic links in the forging of new associations. Contemporary narrative writing has its own way of inhabiting such abstractions about linguistic pattern and its generative differentials in a knowing theoretical vein—as we've seen with DeLillo and Whitehead and will again with Richard Powers, among others—and in between, soon ahead, with the ironies of discursive framing and temporal structure in Paul Auster. The timelines of lexical etymology—surfaced by inference within the timing of a given syntax—articulate phrasal routes that are often charged first of all, and then further, by the variable wording of tense, that cardinal node of difference in narrative orientation.

2

The Tensed Word

In verbal response, to muse upon is to take the measure of. To ruminate on the ways of words is to *weigh* those words—as well as to take their pulse: alert to the syntactic time they take in the rhythms of their distributed substance and forward force. Among the frequent measures of lexical mass and gravity, and hence of momentum, is how the grammar of tense weighs in at the baseline of a sentence, its burden sometimes subtly shifted as we edge from one load-bearing clause to the next: tense manifested now as the ballast of a sentence, now its fulcrum, now its ironic dead end. Yet tense is, of course, only one aspect of wording's temporality as meaning is rolled out. Inherent to the relation of diction and syntax, lexicon and grammar, is the pervasive sense that words situated in time are also words clocked in process.

To say that the horizontal pacing involved might be compared to a tracking shot, or even a rapid swish pan, in cinema—revealing and revising a space as it goes, requisitioning the off-frame from one moment to the encroaching next—is one way to apprehend the mobile wording of sequence and flow in prose. Time is everywhere taken by syntax—even if not taken up as narrative topic. But sometimes both—and the latter even, on occasion, by one literary work in the weighing of a predecessor—by citation and contextual inference. Inset within the last page of Richard Powers's *The Echo Maker* (2006), with its pointedly open-ended closure (its cognitive neurologist hero returning to New York for airport pickup— or *not*—by his estranged wife), is to be found an earlier piece of closural rhetoric from the American canon.[1] The protagonist has been reading the increasingly "wide and wildly" marked-up copy, flagged by "the swathes of shakey highlighter" (451), of Willa Cather's *My Ántonia* given to him for the trip by a patient.

As his descending plane follows the vector of a privately uncharted future, the narrator's attention has been almost literally *drawn* to the heavily overscored end of Cather's novel, in uncertain match—or mismatch—with the probabilities of his own life story. "This," sums up Cather's narrator, as if referring to her own plot as well as its figurative route, "had been the road of Destiny; had taken us to those early accidents of fortune which predetermined for us all that we can ever be" (451). The sentence looks forward and back, not just in perspective, but in its own syntax—and twice over. Such is the way of the world paced in the circuit of words—and further cued, first, by that grammatical hiccup (and swallowed transition) at the semicolon, with a tacit parallelism split down the middle of "had"—marking two different modes ("been"/"taken") of the past perfect: attribution followed by summarized action or direction. And not just that elliptical split, marked by the missing second demonstrative "this." In regard to such temporal impaction and latent overlap, there follows the momentary phrasal resting point at "predetermined for us all," as if 'for everyone.' Such, if only for a microsecond, is likely to be the first adverbial gist of the appended subordinate clause—as if in the universalizing plural of collective wisdom.

But from that false plateau, we realize instead that wording, in syntactic fact, immediately plunges forward toward its clear and momentarily unfolded thematic intent instead—via a swift prose enjambment: "predetermined for us all // that we can ever be." The noun phrase as subordinated verbal object that kicks in at "all" ["all that . . ."] has thus finally caught hold in its miniscule loop ('for us all all that') across the very time of reading—as had grammar previously looped back on itself at the semicolon. I realize that this double sense of serial blur and recursive hesitation may be for some readers (of mine, of Cather's) hard to see, hard to hear. So (with part III on the cinematic sentence in prospect) try *picturing* those sentences instead. This is what the metaphor of "loop" is doing just above: tracing a profile of their time-release progress other than syllabic. Those two recursive grammatical effects—as far from cinematic in their context of metaphysical abstraction as possible, and quite smoothly assimilated to the author's classic prose cadences—have nonetheless a filmic quality, a certain dissolving overlap, in the melt of one sense into the next.

And *The Echo Maker* has yet more to share with us, in its citation of Cather, by way of a muted grammatical hermeneutic, as exacting as it is tacit. Picking up again, in immediate continuity, the balance of that exit passage in the nested Cather text, we encounter an understated rolling force dilated, quite unassumingly, over a less impacted grammatical span, one clause each for its mounting recognition. From "had been" through "had taken" and on, now, retracing exactly the same grammatical shift, to a return of the so-called verb of being in newly aimed usage. What plot's *via negativa* was once, and had since permitted, was yet to be fulfilled: "Now I understood that the same road *was to bring* us together again" (451; emphasis added)—where, by the odd idiometrics of the English helping verb and its infinitive completion, the word "was" (as simple copula in the past tense) has migrated across some missing middle stage from "had been" (in past participial form) to full verbal force in a colloquially predictive tense: its auxiliary use being part of an assured future subjunctive.

And there is more convergence yet around the adverbial "together again" for Cather's coming last sentence: "Whatever we had missed, we possessed together the precious, the incommunicable past" (451). What at first seems like a paradoxical inversion of receding past tenses in a shared roster of loss ('We possessed together the deprivations of whatever we had missed') is not so much corrected as transfigured by the amplified noun form "past," lifted as luminous word above the *ed* sequence of grammatical distancings. We've at least had our story, tallied losses and all. Steered to a shared vanishing point, not just in this passage but in its contemporary host novel, are convergent lines of narrative foreclosure: first Cather in citation, then Powers's hero in his highlighter-flagged access to this embedded novel-within-the-novel. At such moments parallel lines do sometimes, uncannily, converge. To speak of the "host" novel is also to speak of the emotional mediator—through whose inset lens one reads, as if magnified by reframing alone, the undulant subtleties of what we might think of, in such a prose regress, as tense structure squared. And this, too, is borne out by another complication in the plot so far, apart from the hero's uncertain marital closure.

Telling "Ourselves" Backward and Forward

The symmetries of life in *The Echo Maker*—as "echoed" in advance by Cather and yearned for in the neurologist's return to his wife—are part of the typical master plot of those "case studies" that have made Powers's lead character famous in professional circles. One in particular: the delusional psychosis of "an otherwise healthy man who thought that stories turned real" (414). This is only true, of course, for something like the virtual reality of a novel—and especially one, unlike *The Echo Maker*, as overtly pivoted as is *David Copperfield* (as noticed in the introduction) on the subsuming of biology to biography in a so-called life (or life story). Powers's gloss on the narrative reality credited by his unhinged patient: "Journey, complication, crisis, and redemption: just say the words and they took shape" (414). A clinical delusion, to be sure, but also part of the scientist's own analytic procedure. The aberrant patient stands forth here as a metanarrative prototype for re*storative* practice: "That one delusion—*stories* came true—seemed like the germ of healing" (414; emphasis added). The oxymoron passes almost unnoticed, since the "germ" of delusion, the toxin of unreality, is instantaneously transferred, in the other dictionary sense, to the seed of restitution, as germinal as it is infectious.

Far more salient in its alienation of idiom, the syntax to follow catches exactly the fulcrum of this narrative transaction: "We told ourselves backward into diagnosis and forward into treatment" (414). Transitive grammar has rarely indulged a more pointed departure from the norm. The accusative case becomes reflexive. The wording "told ourselves" is deployed not as the transitive verb and indirect object of some therapeutic procedure like 'told ourselves the tales that would bring repair,' but instead as the autonomous predication of ourselves in the objective case. In the full logical strain exerted linguistically at this turn, it's not a matter of what we tell ourselves, but of who we tell ourselves we are. If mere invention can translate life to reality, then subjectivity can be redefined as sheer narrative construct. This convalescent brain science of narrative rehab is next internalized as textual performance through the displacement of a cross-word chiastic slant rhyme: "St*ory* was th*e sto*rm at the c*ortex*'*s core*" (414). Such is an assonant mash-up in response to which we may be forgiven for hearing an "or" matrix centering the sentence's whole phonetic bracket, operating there in a telescoped or portmanteau expansion of an etymological tipped hand: "Sto . . . ore." In tracking the electric discharges of such syllabic weather, the ways of the word are the backdrafts of story in its fired synaptic mappings. In mental therapy as in narrative catharsis, everything hangs in the balance between memory and prospect, turmoil and alleviation, regress and progress. Everything is in this way caught up in a grammar of tense. The general rule stands, even when, as enhanced by Cather's wording, the way forward ("together again") is understood—and figured—as the way back round ("we possessed together") within a circuit of the irretrievable.

If to read the Cather extract in these terms, under pressure of its embedding by Powers, could rightly be felt as a recalibrated weighing of even our most normal words, and in their most fundamental assignments as discursive activators, then we have the pleasure—a uniquely aesthetic pleasure—of recognizing a set of almost imperceptible gradations on a sliding scale of temporal orientations ranging from elegiac to anticipatory. These complex orientations are grammatical at base. Again, the deceptive lyric simplicity, and twin micro-reboots, of "This had been the road of Destiny; had taken us to those early accidents of fortune which predetermined for us all that we can ever be." Even the seemingly ineluctable "road of Destiny" forks between classic ambivalences in genitive (possessive) grammar: figure for fate's given route ('Destiny's road'), inherent to time's plan, or the serial repositioning ('the path amounting to a Destiny') that alone maps such fatefulness in process, and does so, again, as a mere metaphor for any sense of life's predestined vector—and in either case where the etymological bond with *destin/ation* surfaces as effect to revealed (if amorphous) cause.

To borrow in summation Cather's terraced, split-level predicate in the hairsbreadth shift from "been" to done ("had been"/"had taken"): this scale of differentiation has been our emphasis, has brought us back to the weight of wording from the stream of meaning. I have dwelt so long on so brief a span of transformational wording—as I imagine Powers did, and wanted us to do—because of the way it taps the indwelling mystery of idiom itself, even in the most seemingly neutral increments of predication. The locally dramatized, however much underplayed, modulation from being to doing at the narrative plane—a shift paper-thin and feather-light—can be analogized to that between the fact of print and the act of its decipherment, the given and its unfolding. Narrative reading enforces the temporality of sentence pace under the overarching sense of story, with first moves, turning points, the reach for closure, all endemic to sequential expectations. The sentence is, in this respect, the microcosmic form of narrative—and words make up its internal episodes. Episodic in both senses: unitary and fluid, self-contained and rhythmically determined, inching forward from syllabic cluster to cinching phrase within an adjusted temporal frame. In Cather's finale, and all the more so when foregrounded by mental "highlighter" from within Powers's very different prose, what the meditated path of destiny does to differentiate what life *was* from its past actions, the *had been* from the *had done*, is perfectly vernacular and ingeniously nuanced at once.

Imagine a version of this distinction far from underplayed, but forced to preternatural limits, by the gap between a lifeline in process and its storyline already known, already foretold: right down to the wire, because already transcribed in a tortured script of premonitory death. Such a text exists, involving a total implosion of that organic and biographical "life" we saw held in balance at the launch of *David Copperfield*. This travesty text is George Eliot's *The Lifted Veil* (1859), its plot seeming a deliberate perversion of Dickens's wordplay, where in this case clairvoyant biography elides biology, the written "life" sucking the very life out of its subject (in the tacit formulation 'This, I see already, will have been my life'). In the hands of a master logician of grammar like the Victorian realist Eliot—even in this, for her, rare excursion into the supernatural gothic—the overheated manipulation of verb tense can seem like a test kitchen for its appreciated role as narrative ingredient at large. We'll return in detail to Eliot's finesse of tense after some recent and extreme treatments of story time far more aggressive than the subtleties entailed in Cather's incorporation by Powers. These more assertive turns take their lead from certain bold moves of inverted grammar—and even from its cognate metaphysical forms of fantastic narrative temporality.

Speaking Backwords, Writing On

Reverse action: on screen, a matter of image progress and spatial regress at once, each phase of temporal advance made to look like an impossible backpedaling on action. Inverted grammar is a different thing, a matter of rhetorical emphasis, in imitation at times of sequence, but hardly ever exactly backwards. No typical inverted grammar—as, for instance, "In from the imploded window burst, the broken glass with it, the flung debris from the tornado"—operates such an impossibility as we find in the black-magic realism of a novel like Martin Amis's *Time's Arrow*, its story told via normal grammar but in reverse-action sequence. Narration is no talking cure in this novel, certainly not for an escaped war criminal, a Nazi doctor, dragged back into an inescapable past. Retrospection is involuntary and gradually effacing. Nothing like Powers's sense that, in narrative, "we told ourselves back into diagnosis and forward into treatment." In Amis's tour de force of one-way return, the narrating protagonist stands idly by at his own dying away in reverse, back toward his birth. In this regress, he must acclimate himself to the way acts like rising from bed are rendered as a falling back upon it, gulping food is registered as (re)gurgitation, and so forth. "Why am I walking *backward* into the house?"[2] So he quizzes himself in the first phase of backtrack after his heart attack and death. Not: 'Backward into the house walking am I, why?' His discourse is clear and forward tending in its bafflement; the events, not their verbalization, go in reverse.

But in the realm of words, dialogue is an event as well, and to set the novel's template early on—in this case its besetting problematic—we do get actual spoken words run in phonetic reverse. This bafflement accompanies, for the narrator, the backward sounds of birdsong on a shopping trip that involves the unwrapping of a purchase and the handing of money back from the clerk to the patron. Here is what is heard; but in order to *read* it, you need to move from bottom to top, right to left, in this rearward way of the word:

"Dug. Dug,"says the lady in the pharmacy.
"Dug." I join in. "Oo y'rrah?
Aid u too y'rrah?" (7)

As the faintest counterpart to these brain-boggling reversals in actual enunciation is the first line's normative inversion in the predicate "says the lady." As lexical luck would have it, there is also the surprise chiasm by which "u too" spells out its place in "you to/day" in each direction (*u too/oot u*). But that's a minor accident within the broader temporal irony. A more intriguing turn (almost a full about-face), as part and parcel of the bizarre disorientation in which the *youthing*—rather than ageing— protagonist is caught up, lurks in a wording more phonetically entrenched yet. This occurs when the middle line's answer to the tongue-twisted slurring of a formulaic "How are you today" (*harr'y oot u dai*) carries—at its unsuppressible first (graphemic) glance—the existential overtone, and undermine, of an internally inverted 'who you are?' (*Oo y'rrah?*) in this no-man's-land of temporal subtraction rather than accumulation. Be that syllabic contortion as it may, it's hard not to see this whole moment of reverse-action enunciation as finding its deepest models not just in the chiasm (*abba*) but in that form of anagrammar known as the palindrome (*bab*). Time rotated into reverse—at levels narrative and lexical alike.

Although characters are talking backwards in this one matrix scene, springing devilish cryptograms of compromised identity in their own alphabetic characters, in the rest of Amis's novel it is up to normal sentencing to backtrack through fateful eventualities to first things. When the dwindling adulthood of the narrator, participant witness to his own eroded timeline, comes finally to anticipate his birth from the throes of infancy on the last page—not as a prenatal vision but as a literal return to the womb—normal syntax, for the most part, is still needed to activate such temporal collapse. When from these earliest days he anticipates his pending vanishing point in the unborn, he realizes that "relations" with his mother, "already very intimate," will soon be "more intimate *still*" (164, emphasis added)—and beyond that, having actually entered rather than exited her body, he will have succumbed, or plummeted, to the yet more liminal stillness of a life unborn.

Nearing this point of no return, his caressing of her naked breasts "will be allowed. He can't stop it" (164). The jealous father goes without naming in this "he." And the Oedipal defiance intensifies when parturition is inverted to penetration, as if in a lampoon of self-conception. For "eventually our corporeal bond will be tied, with Solingen scissors" (164).

In parody of a connubial knot: the umbilical re-stitch—accomplished here, not via grammatical inversion, but by a non-Caesarean cut at the disjunction induced by the breached vagina. At just this crux of reincorporation, the mother's cries offer a preternatural mockery of convulsive orgasm, with the infant's designated fate handled by a kind of mortal euphemism: "When I enter her how she will weep and scream." Drastic syntactic caesura next, punctuating the reverse rupture: ". . . weep and scream. That I am gone" (164). His whole retracted identity is captured by a grammatical fragment of severed subordination, in all the moment's introverted final dependency. Culminating this book-long reverse-action shot, back to larval promise only—to speak with apt inversion—must barge the neonate, crawl the fetus, burrow the embryo, thus burying the character.

It is as if Ian McEwan's later novel *Nutshell*, about an unborn hero eavesdropping in the womb upon the villainous plans hatched by Trudy and Claude to murder his natural father—and named for the line from *Hamlet* about a life bounded in the cramped space of a nutshell (with the fetus's own variety of imprisoning "bad dreams" in utero)—is self-consciously designed to reverse any such natal (subtr)action yet again. It does so, more in the mode of the embryonic meditations of *Tristram Shandy*, in order to tickle itself at the start with the kind of erotic punning lurking as an idiomatic seed for closure's reverse parturition in Amis's book: "So here I am, upside down in a woman. . . . waiting, waiting and wondering who I'm in, what I'm in for."[3] There, grammatical tension in that tensile "play" of the contracted double "I'm," released from the opening "I am," is precisely the shift from spatial to temporal parameters—with the vernacular "in for" as future-aimed variant of 'what is in store for me.' Then, too, when the hero's birth in *Nutshell* finally aborts, as it were, the escape plans of the homicidal couple on the novel's last page, the imagined prison cell the narrator is to share with his mother lends an extra ex post facto reverb, in the sense of criminal sentencing, to "what I'm in for." In the distended interim before this, the coterminous patterning of the murderous suspense plot along with the hero's dilated gestation—as the convergence point of an ominously postponed closure—has made inescapable the "to be or not to be" antithesis from the source text, unspoken prompt of the whole narrative arc. In contrast, the unbecoming paradigm of *Time's Arrow* buries all either/or logic in radical paradox: *to be and then not yet to have been.*

Less parodic narrative timelines—if no less macabre—than those in a black comedy of prenatal surveillance, or in that historical epic of reverse maturation, may put special pressure, in the mode of the fantastic, on the grammar of being in the full conjugation of its tense structure. So we return now, more fully, to the bitter prolepsis of Eliot's *The Lifted Veil*. In turning back across the centuries to that novella's rarefied laboratory of tense in narrative enactment, it's worth framing such a Victorian prototype through the rearview mirror of the film medium's own intermediate arrival into cultural consciousness as its own kind of time machine—as anticipated obliquely by Eliot in allusion to cinema's lantern-view predecessors. Yet the mechanics of narration I want to italicize have less to do with hallucinatory optical thematics, in Eliot's case, than with the technology of grammar. The eerie force of prophecy in her tale depends on the inner gearing of syntax by the marked deployment of certain monosyllabic helping verbs—"tensed" in every sense to propel the time-based medium along its remorseless and preordained narrative path. Given that its turning point episodes, in this regard, take place after the hero is sent to Switzerland for schooling—and not just to Mary Shelley's gothic Geneva but to Calvin's as well, perhaps—one senses the theological mysteries of fore-ordination being backed up into the traumas of living premonition. In this enacted curse of clairvoyance, any analogies with the machinations of cinema can be more narrowly specified, as we'll see, than just a case of flash-forward.

With part III in view, such cinematic parallels certainly benefit from being made clear early on. In regard to its timed effects over the long century of its dominance, celluloid film harbored an open secret on its every surface—surfaces transparent and reflective in turn, on strip and then screen. This was the abiding duplicity of the so-called frame: an illusionist picture window in projection, opening to a continuous view, as well as (and because of) a serial segmentation on the plastic strip, operating there more like a mechanized photographic flip-book. It is precisely the functional blur of those small-scale millimetric frames, as they are beamed through the aperture of projection, that gets magnified by the focalizing lens into plausible motion within the rectangular frame (big F) of the screen view. The race of successive imprints in mechanized displacement gives way to an envisioned place—and its imaged action. By alphabetic approximation, then, one can call this tightly geared engineering, tabling its literary equivalents, the off-Fframe cause of the motion effect: gauged at different scales, micro and macro, small *f* and its supervening capital. At the basis of the process, in its sheer (both senses) procession, an off-frame dynamic (what we see, impelled forward by what we don't quite yet) is installed at the level of the cellular unit (spooling photograms on the track, like aggregate phonemes in writing), only then, at rare turns of disclosure, to be projected at screen scale—at least by cognitive association—in certain unique modes of visual technique like jump cuts or freeze-frames. It is there that the strictly sequential is sensed in the visual. The open secret of scalar relations amounts in this way to a defining synecdoche, with the disappearing act of each incremental transparency on the strip assumed in (and as), in fact resumed by, the motoring force of the whole. As a necessary point of departure, then, all celluloid motion pictures are sprung from the moving of still pictures. Photo trace becomes film only when its delimited cellular frame is shoved forward by another almost identical, arrived from beyond its own speeding (and border-marking) frame line. Resembling some of the lexical blendings sampled so far, rapidly elided difference sparks perceptual shift.

Which "reads," on screen, as gesture or action: an event in time. From instant to instant, that is, the previously excluded unit renews the mutation and sustains the viewed "movie." And this off-frame impetus on the spinning track, this inbuilt displacement, or say this continuous lifting of the veil, notch by notch, is, I repeat, homologous on screen to movement within the larger Frame, as well as to displacements of (rather than within) that Frame (via the moving camera itself). Those last include the gradual shift of the image field, laterally or vertically, in a panning or tracking shot, for instance, traversing the recorded space in its chosen direction. At macro as well as micro level, then, image depends on what it surrenders to, at one margin, and annexes from, at the other: again, the always impinging latency of the off-frame. The question for us: What analogies exist between, taken together, those two correlated levels in the function of actual cinema (Fframe as visible image plane and plastic aggregate at once) and the semantics of the read sentence in its comparable roll-out?

The suggestion so far is that there certainly are such points of comparison. And the self-revised syntactic tracking we've recently examined should make this apparent enough. But it should also be made clear that the preceding two paragraphs are not broached as some concerted interdisciplinary inroad to the third part of this study, where homologies between media will be rigorously secured. Rather, the invocation of cinematography as a lexical or syntactic equivalent in these pages is never mechanically exact, just instinctual, responding to the material flux of phonemes in the reeling past of a given wording—and to phases of semantics in the pace of syntax—by a popular analogy ready to hand. Along the unwinding spool of verbal continuity, enunciating the macro through the churn of the micro, we've seen wavering temporal predication in Cather; chiastic mayhem in the reversible dialogue of Amis, not to mention a caesura (or jump cut) of reverse parturition; self-differentiated puns of futurity ("in for") in McEwan—as well as all the various means in chapter 1, from Orwell through DeLillo, by which what might be called the buried time-signatures of deep etymology can inflect either a Latinate or a Saxon word choice, way beyond matters of tone, with a subplot all its own, emerged as if by a fleeting sematic superimposition from within a given word.

Across all these variants and more, in whatever we might single out as a cinematic sentence—often equivalent to a moving shot (a nondiscursive "statement" like *this happens next* or *they do this*)—a structuring synecdoche of sorts also prevails, in writing as well as screen projection. That is what attention to the double structure of Fframe-advance has wanted to get clear. In literature as well as film, parts are as serially determined as the whole. In making our way along the cognitive chain of meaning, phonetic lettering flashes past into gathering word forms even as these so-called parts of speech, one after another, cede syntactic space to a sometimes unexpected next-in line across the resting spots or run-ons of adjusted sense. This is the *drama* of writing—and its kinetic art: the never stabilized ways of the word whose temporality cannot therefore be dissociated from the flicker effects of screen motion. The fact that the emergent screen image, the photogram-impacted gesture, can never be returned (in unaided ocular experience) to the file of cellular frames that induces it, whereas in prose a suspected lexical echo in segue, a hovering grammatical ambiguity, an ironic slippage between script and phonetic enunciation—whatever reading is intrigued by—can always be double-checked before spooling forward: this fact does not disable the transmedial comparison; rather, it can only help sharpen our sense of prose resources in whatever cinematographic ambition they may at times evince—or whatever tacit parallels they might reveal. What prose sequence horizontally unveils from phoneme to phoneme, what cinema lifts vertically to view in incremental image cells: such are the moving targets of activated syntactic recognition in each narrative medium. Whereas such cinematic correlates to prose motion are offered here as a brief trailer to the perverse temporal compressions of Eliot's narrative, as well as to the alternate euphoria of elided time in Whitman, it will take the final two chapters of this book to unfold fully the inferences of this comparison for the time-based medium of literary wording.

Tense, Tension, Tensility

And now to the prolonged ordeal of Eliot's *The Lifted Veil*, where a normally curtained human future is made cruelly visible—and by just such nuanced (here excruciating) temporalities of verbal (here verb) forms as we've considered above under the category of micronarrative succession, its paradoxes and existential reversals. The fact that part of this bedeviling clairvoyance in Eliot's plot anticipates a frequent brand of flash-forward editing through allusion to the "dissolving views" of a magic lantern show—its slide shifts a precursor of cinema—does more than round out the apparatus of prevision in Eliot's metaphorics. It also foregrounds the scale at which words do part of their work through the slide-effects of syntax itself. "The time of my end approaches" is an arresting first sentence, locating and postponing at once. The protagonist Latimer could have said 'My end approaches,' but the syntactic prelude of "the time of" adds a broad existential redundancy to the witheringly specific. Such is the nature of time, spatially figured, that any and every end is always and already approaching us, as we it. Latimer envisages and describes the moment itself, in its fully lived—and died—texture, in its disclosure to him from behind time's normal veil. Even as the verbal distension holds off such a doom, Latimer rehearses the medical diagnosis that "I may fairly hope that my life will not be protracted many months." Verbal protraction and hopeful contraction at once in this lugubrious declaration—for a downbeat elegiac rhythm capped by the lament-heavy internal rhyme of the next sentence: "I shall not much longer groan under the wearisome b*urth*en of this *earth*ly existence."

In between now and then, between life and its punctual end, pure prose—a textual deferral: "Before that time, I wish to use my last hours of ease and strength in telling the strange story of my experience"—with s*trength* in loose phonic sympathy with its decidedly *strange* narrative object. That's the set-up, but this last sentence opens the fourth paragraph, already preceded by two given over to extensive, dense, and complexly tensed premonition before being admitted as a self-conscious act of documentary writing. The strange story, in other words, is already underway before a commitment to it, at least as a written record, is spelled out: a narrative already dependent on the traumas of syntactic temporality under proleptic compression. "For I foresee when I *shall* die, and everything that *will* happen in my last moments." Punctilious here, the mere future "shall" for first person, the fatalized "will" for third. Where the comma might lead us to expect a compound sentence in which "everything that will happen" is a subject on the way to a waiting predicate ('and everything that will happen afterwards will be blank to me'), instead the whole clause is the compound object of *foresee*. The way of the word, so often slipping out from under supposed clausal containment, is here boxed in by syntax. It is only as the plot has begun building momentum toward this terminus ad quem that subsidiary previsions are introduced both to validate and to equivocate Latimer's prescience, including a bout of clairvoyance inducing a notably labored alternate simile of mechanical translucence (magic lantern and its "dissolving" slides) or natural illumination (dissipated mist) as it enfolds a rephrasing of the story's very title: "But I could not believe that I had been asleep, for I remembered distinctly the gradual breaking-in of the vision upon me, like the new images in a dissolving view, or the growing distinctness of the landscape as the sun lifts up the veil of the morning mist." Optically, the scene alludes to precinematic attractions. Grammatically, by its preternatural flash-forwards, it seems in its gerund force to anticipate, beyond its own plot, the eventual common wisdom about screen images being always in the present tense of becoming. Reflexively, as the "new images" overlap the old, the precinematic "dissolving view" (again the implied laterna magica prototype) of a lifted morning mist—as a vertically elevated "veil"—points back to the story's own eponymous metaphor for prophetic time travel.

Before picking up the proleptic ironies of this story again at its early node of premonition in the opening paragraphs, a broader sense of tense-based narrative expectations is of use. In her famous and very short story "Happy Endings," Margaret Atwood mocks this titular convention by giving alternate marital plots for a couple, and then declaring, with redundant flair, the unhappy end for all such storylines: "The only authentic ending is the one provided here: *John and Mary die. John and Mary die. John and Mary die.*"[4] But it isn't just that Eliot's novella thematizes death as narrative closure; her plot preternaturalizes it—in a story of clairvoyance where the character knows as much about his end, in advance, as any narrator could. The historical present tense that Atwood casually deploys in "John and Mary die" is a slyly perverse instance of a narrative norm, since "die," rather than "are dying," entails its own finality. Human presence passes away altogether into an unnerving present tense. With a closural model only deceptively more open-ended, as we'll see, compare for now, in the matter of Eliot's present-tense grammar, the first rather than final moves of Paul Auster's *Ghosts*, where grammar is its own kind of time travel, dividing representation from what it reports upon: "First of all there is Blue. Later there is White, and then there is Black."[5] What we may take to be a logical priority converts to chronological sequencing: "Brown taught him the ropes, and when Brown grew old, Blue took over. That is how it begins" (161). Convention wants "began"—or even "was begun," anchoring the backstory where it belongs. Instead, we topple into a different narrative tense altogether, a metanarrative present: "The place is New York, the time is the present, and neither one will ever change" (161). Because this, not any other than this, is the story.

The perpetual present is the secret time of all written story. Any narrator plugging directly into that authorial tense, as does the executor of *Ghosts* (or Eliot's narrator), will find that plotting is at one with prolepsis, accident with prophecy, contingency with imminence. All is foretold, all laid out on the same plane of invention. It is according to such a premise that the end of Auster's doppelganger plot of psychic and narrative distinctions implodes, with a final reveal. The detective hero ends up reading a confiscated text of the story that has just transpired around him, in the hand of the man he's been surveilling: a text whose closing tense is more clearly that of a manuscript than of an immersive narrative, operating not in real but in scriptive time. "But the story is not yet over. There is still the final moment, and that will not come until Blue leaves the room. Such is the way of the world: not one moment more, not one moment less"

The Tensed Word 73

(232). The way of the "world"—and of its wording. "When Blue stands up from his chair, puts on his hat, and walks through the door, that will be the end of it." Not the idiomatic "end of it" (say no more) but of the story itself. We're free to imagine Blue "booking passage" to China, if we like, but no passage in this book will confirm for sure. Have it your way: "Let it be China, then, and we'll leave it at that" (232), ambiguously fiat or concession—and where the elided *will* or *shall* in that contraction also embraces both determination and relinquishing. The "then" is not temporal (narrative by now bled of all duration), just logical. Or less: a sop to plot. "For now," as already predicted, "is the moment that Blue stands up from his chair, puts on his hat, and walks through the door. And from this moment on, we know nothing" (192), the adverbs of duration (*now* and *on*) chiastically flipped under graphic cover to the double phonic negation of "k*now* *no*thing." The curtain that curtails all future in the normal narrative finis is turned back, in Auster, to the immitigable present at the launch of story in a timeless enclave of fictive event. Auster's temporal contortions (textbook postmodernism) foreground the radically foregone conclusion of this narrative as a mere writing act. It differs from the fevered narration of Eliot's Latimer only by its flagrant ironizing of narrative convention.

So much for narrative "suspense" in these forecast finishings. All fictionality, in whatever plot form, knows this clairvoyant double vision of the now and the coming. In *The Lifted Veil* such double vision torques— all but warps—the narration right from the start. No opening page so radically premature could do more to rehearse, at the level of linguistic function alone, the temporal ricochets of the plot to come—with its broad fabric of prevision and whiplash return played out here, from the first, at the scale of internal echo and syntactic disjuncture. As described in the second paragraph, the ominous last scene is set as follows (with emphasis added on the remorseless "helping" verbs): "I *shall be* sitting" there (future participle of the ongoing moment, yet soon truncated). The next sentence burrows down—and tunnels forward—to an inhabited present tense. "Just as I *am* watching a tongue of blue flame rising in the fire," and so forth, the future intrudes again from its own *anticipated* temporal plateau—for it is then that "the horrible contraction *will* begin at my chest." Is this simply to say that the heart attack will begin—or that, beginning at his chest, it will spread to shrink his life to extinction, as might seem the figurative overtone of this anatomical "contraction" over against the temporal "protraction" previously negated in relief? "I *shall* only have time to reach the bell," pulling it violently for help. But the future tense of futility—"No one *will* answer my bell"—shifts again into a yet more immediate "historical present" (or say, instead, future present) of recognition: "I know why." He knows now, in often reiterated forecast, and will then, by the bitterness of confirmed expectation, when a then of premonition has come round to the now of event. The only effect of his double "bell"-ing, in echo against *shall* and *will*, is narrative's answered knell.

That blunt trisyllabic sentence, "I know why," is pivotal. Its switch point between what might sound like the work of deduction versus the slam of precognition is parsed, by way of immediate explanation, across a compressed and belated subplot of upstairs/downstairs intrigue, in which an inset romantic melodrama is squeezed tight into a further allegory of narrative tense itself: "My two servants *are* lovers" (presently, in this time of my end), and "*will* have quarreled" (just before the onset of my attack). Yet again, as in each channeled veer of tense across the entire passage, it is the rigorous *logic* of the grammar, not any slipperiness it licenses— a logic upheld within the fantastic premise of the narrative itself—that renders the temporal focus so unnerving: so much a reflex of sheer verbal event, pressing the normal resources of human speech to their alienating limit. The name-fated, belated Latimer, his life robbed of sense as well as suspense, is tortured on the rack of foreknowledge for which, in his own script, these exactions of tense are the tightened screws. Wordwork at its lower limit: the helping verb "will," in a curse of the auxiliary itself, executing the temporal baseline of these premonitory sentences—under sentence of death.

While Latimer—across this infranarrative servant subplot, fully dispatched in that second proleptic paragraph—is continuing to script his own undeflectable death, we return with him to the (future) present of the servant Perry's absence, all within the overtale (supervening and overt) of the narrator's unattended lethal fate: "Perry *is* alarmed at last, and *is* gone out after her." In this muted melodrama of grammatical time frames, that last formal (dated) use of the present as perfect tense (rather than "has gone")—call it word choice degree zero—keeps the immanent desertion of the narrator front and center in the compacted time zone of his unanswered need. Finally, putting a last ambiguous nail in the grammatical coffin, the closing phase of lethal inattention hovers in a phantasmal space between the iterative tense (of continuous obliviousness) and the panic of a onetime fatality: "The little scullery-maid *is* asleep on a bench; she never answers the bell; it does not wake her." Never, from day to day, whenever it rings during one of her furtive naps—or never at the fraught moment of this one mortal impasse? In the flash-forward of this prose scenario, spectral and self-foreclosed, it hardly matters. She is dismissed by plot alone. It is only we who are put on notice as we read.

After this frustration of all material succor, the one-sentence third paragraph of the story's opening prolepsis then tracks the narrator toward a final ellipsis. This progress is transacted across a present participial tense—disappearing into the past as soon as inscribed, and this across a shift in idiom from euphemism ("passing on") to obscure spatial metaphor—when "I am *passing on* and on through the darkness." Accompanying this marked *phrasal* passage, and closing off the last of the narrator's premonitory reflections, the microdynamic of grammar's building tension has collapsed upon an indeterminate closure: one sentence fragment trailing off into another rippled with homely slant rhymes that seem meant to remove its enduring music, and predominantly native diction, from the pending nullity: "Agony of pain and suffocation—and all the while the earth, the fields, the pebbly *brook* at the bottom of the *rookery*, the fresh scent after the rain, the light of the morning through my chamber-window, the warm*th* of the hear*th* after the frosty air"—what, 'all this persisting without me'? Or expected words to that effect? Where does this grammar, long in tow to the adverbial *all the while*, find its point of rest? Nowhere, finally. Instead: only a truncated litany of the receding world broken off, by a last breathless dash, from a present-tense syntax in the throes of subjective shutdown: "—will darkness close over them for ever?" Again, wording's two temporal parameters in collusion, etymological and synchronic. First, there is all that homely Anglo-Saxon normalcy choked off by the Latinate agon of "pain and suffocation"—with its further clench of a sundering, then yoking hendiadys (instead of "painful suffocation" or "suffocating pain") distending the fatal ordeal by coordination rather than subordination. And, second, all this within the swollen moment of "the time of my end" and the tense structure that paces it.

It's not just a negligible digital accident, then, but a potent one, when Project Gutenberg mis-scans, near the end of the first paragraph, "the miseries of true prevision" as "provision"—not bad for a phonetically charged contrast with the preceding clause about the "age most men desire and *provide* for." This blip is its own kind of alphabetic epiphany, alerting us to the likely selection of *prevision* over a plausible *provision*. The prefixes intersect one another at cross-purposes: the natural course of forethought—finding its eerie antithesis and parody in clairvoyance—recovers the genealogical time of "pro-vide" as a forgotten etymological composite of "fore-sight." It is as if Eliot's coming fantasy plot were being prepared by a manic tutorial in the estrangement of normal language by the "lifted veil" of genealogy as well as its structuring syntactic energy. Primed in this way, we are ready to hear how expressive speech can at any moment turn, under intensified concentration, elusive and uncanny in its own right.

Almost a decade before Eliot's novella, Melville brings *Moby-Dick* to a close with an opposite and even more insinuating twist of tense. The ship has gone down, but the vortex still exercises its unforgiving suction. More for sound than for sense, or say for a sound dialed up by the near redundancy of sense, we are suspended in the present adverbial framework ("Now") of a fateful aftermath: "N*ow* small f*ow*ls flew scr*ea*ming over the yet y*aw*ning gulf...." The screams grate across the prose tempo with their own mourning keen: "Ow, aw, ow, ee, aw." And the gulf, beyond description, is immanent there, as well, in the widening of "ye-" to "yawn" (origin Germanic, not as strictly "imitative" as it sounds). Now, next, finally, after a semicolon in this one-sentence last paragraph, "a sullen white surf *beat* against its s*teep* sides; then all collapsed, and the great shroud of the sea rolled on...." The only sides are those, not of the ship, but of the gulf, not elevated but submarine in measure, so that even with the *ea/ee* assonance building again toward a sounding of the previous *ow/ee* matrix—a wake narrative and phonetic at once—the dentalized sibilance built up across "against its steep" releases the oceanic truth of "deep" from this demonic crater of hellish elevation.

The sea, yes, "rolled on as it rolled," with the momentary natural rhythm of unexpected pleonasm—felt as the nondifferentiation, and cosmic indifference, of eternal return—until we realize, from the emerging backwash of sense, that an invariant past tense has flattened the grammar in lieu of a more normative conjugation in the perfect or pluperfect. Not an oceanic pall that rolled as it *has done* for millennia, or *had rolled*, but as it always and ongoingly does, uninflected in its own immemorial time frame by the human grammar of bounded temporalities: ". . . rolled as it rolled five thousand years ag*o*"—a starkly arbitrary numerical figure, rather than the less conservative 'five million,' for instance—that undulates, beyond any human harmony, in the pitiless echo (after the sentence's opening "N*ow* small f*ow*ls . . .") of "th*ou*sand" with "*sh*r*ou*d." Even in its flat incantatory dirge, prose like this lifts off the page into a veritable performance of the inexorable, syllable by cresting syllable. And where Eliot mobilizes the tense of the future perfect, in the 'I will have been dead by then' format, Melville lends to the leveling and uninflected past tense the indifferent burden of obliterated life. For an embodied enunciation of such lexical and syntactic cadences, we'll be turning in the next chapter to an experiment with aural activation—*Gatz,* the fully personified theater of words in a "staging" of *The Great Gatsby*—that also subsides into something like the nautical nihilism of Melville's closing sentence, figurative rather than literal, equally drenched in the American tragedy of disillusioned quest.

Charting the ways of the word, we may say that etymology is the pedigree of diction; syntax its path; the grammar of tense its plane of orientation in discursive time. The deep time of the word connects in its sequencing with the temporal frame of discourse, whether narrative or otherwise. This ongoing poetics of the paged word courses through poetry, too, especially when tense connects with the genealogical time of wording, not just in origin but in transmission. Where Cather's sense of destiny is defined by that which "predetermined for us all that we can ever be," poetry itself accomplishes this for Whitman, paradoxically inscribing all futurity in onward-echoing words. If one telos of Cather's futurity finds itself in an embedded citation by Richard Powers, the pace of Whitman's wording leaps over time to stage its own impact to come. A single famous pun sums this up at the start of *Leaves of Grass*, where what "I assume," asserts Whitman about the axioms of his vision (present tense), "you" the reader "shall assume": in the alternate sense of inherit (in the immediate reading future) as the very mantle of attention.[6] And what a single play on words can achieve when bifurcated across its implicit subentries in the lexicon—in the very conflation of achieved writing with its future reading—is accomplished elsewhere in *Leaves* across a more uneven and

78   Chapter 2

elusive cascade of structured variations in the tense of attention and its worded channels.

Paging All Readers: Whitman's Time Machine

Within wildly various frameworks, from the etymological manipulations of the marketing department in Whitehead to the syllabic flips of reverse-time garble in Amis, we've traced a disparate but representative spectrum of the word's time-emplacing work on the page. But sometimes language's extraliterary assignment is precisely not to stay put there. Words are rarely called upon so immediately, beyond their own print medium, to outplay—without of course outlasting—themselves, their own condition, as they are in the temporal extrapolations of Whitman's "Crossing Brooklyn Ferry," in verses first appearing under that title in the 1860 *Leaves of Grass*. Words rise to the occasion there, in microcalibrated links with—and within—syntax, to escape any quotidian frame with an uncanny quotient of defied authorial finitude. Moreover, beyond the obvious thematics of affective time travel in this poem, the fact of it as poem, in our momentary sidestep from prose fiction, has to do with—and much to illustrate about—the tense structure of lyric apostrophe in contrast with the unfurled durations of narrative time, even when the latter are bizarrely overlapped as in Eliot.

Whitman figures this transtemporal bardic power even while implying an impersonal and transtextual diffusion of his own will. It's not just his text that would find citation in the future but, in an unprecedented end run around mortality, almost his very self—virtually reborn in the cognitive bodies (not just readers) of those he has motivated. This happens when wording, conceived as no longer page-bound, prompts a futurity not properly its own—except in the endurance of reading. In "Crossing Brooklyn Ferry," the poetic "appeal" (its attraction, but also its call) is transmitted—via continuous broadcast in Whitman's public address system—through the heady circuit of ingrained readerly (p)recognitions in the throes, hopes, and snares of a temporal rhetoric. It begins right from the jarringly inverted title of what ought logically to have been "Brooklyn Ferry Crossing." But one catches the almost literal drift, over the river of time, soon enough. "Crossing" as a present participle implies an open-ended temporal action; as a noun form, or gerund, it would more typically mark a space for this transit, limited at both ends of the itinerary. And well beyond the title's nonfinite suspension as written, the recurrent force of Whitman's syntax is to produce this logic at almost subsensory levels.

"It avails not, time nor place—distance avails not," opens the famous third stanza, as Whitman lays claim to a destined presence in the lives of "ever so many generations hence," future readers all. Vaulting across potential centuries, his is so vaunting a confidence that it can seem to encroach on a medium not yet his to imagine—though his addiction to photography may seem to anticipate the "perpetual present" of the cinematic image. It is this mode of temporality, within the schematic transfers familiar later from film's montage logic, that allows the kind of flashback structure with which each of Whitman's famous analogic lines is experimenting—given here with emphasis on the predicate transitions, and recombinations, across intransive, linking, and passive forms:

> Just as you feel when you look on the river and sky, so *I felt*,
> Just as any of you is one of a living crowd, *I was one* of a crowd,
> Just as you are refresh'd by the gladness of the river and the bright flow, *I was refresh'd*,
> Just as you stand and lean on the rail, yet hurry with the swift current, *I stood yet was hurried*,
> Just as you look on the numberless masts of ships and the thick-stemm'd pipes of steamboats, *I look'd*.

Punctuated by the iterative *Just as you,* these five end-stopped lines of recurrent analogy, with a not quite parallel grammar, produce a heady overlay of conception on reception. The spectacle is in fact one of sheer projection, a past record in re-presentation, the free verse lines "crossing" the gap between storage and retrieval characteristic of any medium. Hence the quite specifically textual sense in which "distance avails not," where that inverted negative highlights the Latinate derivation of this hyperformal diction (*valere*: to be strong, to be valued). With these a priori categories vitiated in part by the aura of dated formality, what is valorized is the demotic, homely diction (Germanic, Anglo-Saxon) that ensues in framing the whole sequence: *I felt, I look'd*. Stretching right in space and backwards in time, the verse format waxes nearly emblematic in its own right—as we, in reading, are made part of not just a recursive line but of an imputed spiritual lineage.

For starters, the "so" of "so I felt" that anchors analogy disappears after its first saying, the template clearly set. Further adjustments sneak up on us—even from within an overarching and unmistakable pattern. In this litany of inhabited futurity, the visionary point is clear enough from the insistent tense structure. A poet from the past, *once* (*back then* and *ever since*) intensely immersed in his lived space, can be present to all future readers in the same resident setting: the lively enduring g/host of all embodied response. This effect is won not just by verbal tense (*Just as* I do now so will you; *just as* you do now, so I did then), nor by the present effect of the incantatory parallelism, but by a reverse engineering of the future as a vision from the past. And this reverse is the least of the versework. As the flash-forward/flashback structure accumulates, there is a narrowing trajectory (the lure of temporal convergence) as well as an expansive, iterative scope. It goes something like this on rereading, after that agenda setting "so I felt" is retired: 'since I felt it, so thanks to my poetry will you.' *Since*: in consequence, logically and temporally. The recursive anaphora—from "Just as any of you is" and "Just as you are" ('thus once was I') through the intransitive "Just as you stand" ('so stood I')—leads to a shared point of view in reading and imaginative seeing: "Just as you look on" (its sense of 'upon' so different from the "lean on" in the line before). This latest phrasing involves a quaver between a verb of appearance and a transitive of perception (*look/on*): 'Just as you look when [on the occasion of] looking on.' More importantly, it's not just a comparative *as,* but in that ghost-way, a temporal marker again, the poet's present look and feeling simultaneous, across time, with the reader's. Here, unmistakably, amid the grammatical armatures of projection, lies the pivotal work of wording: *since, as,* and not least the inaugural *Just,* all mobilized in two-way transit in the crossings of a *passage* as much verbal as waterborne: not just a levitation but a hydroplaning of wording's grammatical reach.

By now—in some preternatural telescoping of time, which is of course the indisputable point of the passage—the frame of crossing feels twice filled in, crowded with occupant senses for *Just as:* including *even while*; *at the moment that*; *in the very manner that*. Syncopation builds to temporal implosion. This capping sentence doesn't go so far, beyond its opening equivocation, as to argue a radical telepathic simultaneity; but it does tantalize us with just such a notion through the hovering invitations of phrasal slippage. It is as if grammar were complicit with theme under the wavering sway of the word. The cognitive, rather than pictorial, effect traced along our decoding of the line resembles the kind of calculated cinematic pan that rapidly corrects a perceptual schema as it goes, accrues new data in swiftly graded advance, backfills recognition through some unforeseen explanatory slant, eschews the same false expectations it has elicited, and completes the picture in its own serial sweep. But a verbal medium, not governed by the master gaze of a camera, lets us reread, reexperience, crossing the lines again.

Given the asymptotic horizon of Whitmanesque prophecy, where diction is at one with prediction in the tense of projected readerly epiphany, the passage certainly invites a reading never over till it's over. This is a text where—for all the seemingly genial ceding of perception and affect from writer to reader in a transcendentally generous passing of vitality's baton—we are actually being called to by an omnivorous grammatical imagination. We are, in effect, being (fore)told what to think in those crisscrossing ways of the word that appear almost surreal, hallucinatory. Or say pre-scripted, since it isn't hard to imagine certain moves in an experimental film made of this passage, including its longest, most layered and "poetic" (phonetically inflected) last line: "Just as you look on the numberless masts of ships and the thick-stemm'd pipes of steamboats, I look'd." To capture the unnerving ocular introversion of this line: how better than with dovetailed POVs of past and present—to be filmed with contrastive, lap-dissolved shots of a contemporary corporate skyline and a (perhaps digitally reconstructed) former urban seaport vista? 'Just as you see, my eyes have looked—as of course their transcribed impressions here and now confirm, the sine qua non of the only vistas in play.' A potential reverse shot, then, in that lyric film: the camera-operator's own anonymous visage in overlay with Whitman's iconic one. Such is the double exposure (or ghost effect) of screen rhetoric that might answer to Whitman's protocinematic sentencing—including, at the level of diction and syntax, its inscribed future verdict on its moving phrasal pictures, a verdict delivered in none other than the medium of verbal delivery. No accident that one metaphor for such prevision seems to lurk unsaid in these lines: namely, that in the case of you my readers in future generations, *it is written.* Nothing considered so far, even in the prose reversals of Amis's *Time's Arrow*, can seem more perverse in its inverted timelines—in Whitman's case, more like a perceptual boomerang returning continuously to its source. Whitman's whole futurist liturgy is a case of divination in reverse, celebrating the fiat of literary words at the vanishing point of their own conjurations—and striving to naturalize the telepathic rhapsody. 'Just as you will one day take your place onboard this ferry *passage*, so do I in writing it out.' It is we who live the poet's words, keeping them alive in their crossing of the page.

In all this, I can't be the only buttonholed reader to have sensed a temporal confession coming at the final turn of that fifth line, however dashed that expectation in what actually follows. The momentary oscillation between "look" as *to appear* and its immediately corrected understanding as *to view* only masks the more suggestive slack in in the adverbial "Just as" (coincident rather than just comparable). Until this point in the parallel syntactic series, tense has operated by negotiating a kind of diachronic counterpoint of association—an alternating montage, so to say. In this way, we agents of future cognition (incarnate readers realized in advance) are systematically shunted back into touch—via rhetoric's own kind of graphic match cut—with our past analogue and avatar in that poet of the summoning voice. On the fluid boundaries between present and past, we seem to have encountered the momentary spectral skid of the synchronic. And so another cinematographic function comes to mind's eye. At exactly the ambivalent temporal switch point of "Just as you look," the alternations of the ongoing montage rhythm have fused instead into a kind of ocular—and, by further association, grammatical—*superimposition*. It is in this sense that, even though ultimately disappointed, I wanted to hear the comparative adverb ("too") skewing syntax into present revelation; wanted to hear the always implicit *also* in 'Just as you look . . . I look'd [too]': present lifted from past ("look[ed]t—") in an anticipated and strictly lexical blur: a phonemic palimpsest. To my ear, that is, Whitman's mobilized poetic thrust just misses—just barely and stirringly misses—its chance to round itself *up* with the extra syllabic (and temporal) ambiguity of 'Just as you look on . . . I look('d) too,' where the poet's copresence with his readers would have been captured precisely in his enacted emergence from past into lettered present with that implied unwritten inheritor ('too') of the passage's original "so."

The adverb of analogy was so readied by the poem's logic that I heard it coming, lexically inexorable even though technically absent, when the lines were read aloud at a 2019 bicentennial celebration by my colleague Ed Folsom. It would have been no less sublime than subliminal in its temporal slippage. 'Just as you reader now look at these words, so in the moment of their writing I looked too, look too, then and now both'—with past disappearing into present as the verbal flashpoint of the poem's whole transhistorical destiny. The conventional metric syncope of "look'd" would thus have abetted the further dental compression (elision answering to contraction) of 'look'*d t*oo' in a moment of voicing freed from writing, persona from inscription. Again: the poem's whole point. Hardly lost, of course, in the flat emphatic version that calls rhythm up short with insistence itself: "Just as you look on the numberless masts of ships and the thick-stemm'd pipes of steamboats, I look'd." But the phantom final "too" is hardly a phonetic ghost laid to rest as we move immediately forward into the poem's next line—to which the eye may well drift in anticipation, and with a pressure as impingingly phonic as it is semantic. For inscribed there is the very adverb in question, the privileged match of 'likewise,' as if in iteration of the unsaid—and this time front-loaded in a nonsubordinate clause of immediate phonetic byplay, outpaced by grammar but not entirely erased: "*I too* many and many a time cross'd the river of old." Hardly *eyed* too often, the waters of this symbolic transit of space as time: the "of old" of geology and biography alike. Such is the whole point, again, of that parallel "too" in its correlation between textual persona and future reader(ly) experience, but of course with one decisive proviso—since "too" isn't ultimately, has never been, the real issue. Whitman hasn't *also* looked, let alone looked "too many" times; his inscribed, iterative view is the one and only.

When a living poet hears a comparable cross-lexical effect to the tacit past/present of the anticipated 'look'*d t*oo'—and later in this same poem (as my epilogue will submit this writer-critic's particular audition to a further attentive playback)—its whispered aftertones will take their place alongside the unactivated undertone (and addendum) of the present phrasing, "I look'd (too)." Yet we needn't wait for this extra testimony to the eddies and drifts of Whitman's wording. Very much in the spirit of these opening chapters is any tendency to find enigmatic ligatures in the ways of the word—to find them, that is, no less exemplary when they merely tempt expectation than when they reward it by actually hitting the page. Language, if not writing, is equally at work on the inner ear in each modality of verbal event, each enticement—in other words (decidedly other), in each incitement even to a glancing sense of the unwritten, the uncitable. In this sense one may take even the idea of negative evidence here as something like the aural correlate of "Ffilm" processing as screen event, where the speeding photogram or imprint cell (again the microframe) is the unseen propellant of the optic Frame on screen. What isn't visible there in the single (af)fixed image is the molding of what is—is projected, that is—as motion picture: the difference that fashions, in its activating of contrast even before racing interchange, the pictorial base of depicted flux. This is to suggest that even negativity can have its own imprint, syllabic as well as optic. As we listen in to the "lyric" moment (text as "sung" utterance) in either poetry or prose, contributory peripheral inferences are just as likely to be *periphonal* as semantic. In the present case, one may think of them in scalar terms as Whitman's V/voicing. Or put it that noise in either the metric or the grammatical channels of wording can induce a vacillating static as well as trace a scripted lexical glitch. With our reading never quite taking a stabilized oral dictation from the page, even at writing's most vocalic, we are always *in line* for hearing things, stray tracings, shadowed forecasts overwritten by the given. Such are the word's ways even in abeyance or displacement.

This is hardly to deny, however, that Whitman's whole visionary gambit is one that remains, aside from the odd spectral expectation of the present tense 'I look too,' only and resolutely *legible*. And if the future of "Crossing" is a writing-effect, its signature as such is at its most marked in the slight figurative inflections of the riverscape that comes between the two *looks* of this fifth line: again "the numberless masts of ships and the thick-stemm'd pipes of steamboats." The uncountable in the phrasing "numberless masts" is affixed alphabetically—*mb-ss/m-sts*—to "*steamboats*" (*st-mb-ts*) in a figurative slant rhyme with "thick-*stem*med pipes" (the only whiff of metaphor in any of these anaphoric lines: exhaust tubes as pipestems). The literary effect, however modest, signs itself into notice as part of the *writer*'s claim on future efficacy. As its own generative origin, the "crossing" in progress is the *transport* of poetry itself. "Look on" all you need to.

Reading lyric poetry: a way of experiencing the world *otherwise*, through a borrowed and internalized vision. But any such cliché is alchemized in Whitman's channeling of response by the paradoxical vectors of prophetic temporality. With each new human subject (not just reader) whom the Bard pages and inspires down through the generations—such is the rhetorical fantasy—it is as if he, not we, could imagine himself *seeing the world through new eyes*. In its taut balance of tense, "Crossing" advertises itself as something like the transcendental obverse of Eliot's gothic: in Whitman's case, the lifted veil on the reader's future as the poet's own. The ways of the word are transversal, in this case a crossing of time as well as lateral (syntactic) space. As the word *pages us* in Whitmanesque appeal, it also calls on the flip side of part I's subtitle: words in their place on the page, yes, but more like running in place, wording their own kinetic way forward.

Beyond his inversion—or extroversion—of Eliot's nightmare of premonition into a state of willful, wistful projection, Whitman's place, as poet, alongside prose's own lexical and phrasal byways, should be clear. The shared maneuvers have been crystallized in the present example around the operation, again, of time Fframes in their scalar relations: organized, negotiated, and hedged on a broad grammatical template of predication across the least creases of syllabic superimposition, the ordinarily unassuming service of helping verbs, the elisions of grammatical sequence, the collisions of logic, the whole hinged wording of duration casting forward and back at once—including those time-release syntactic forkings of idiometric irony, as well as their phonemic miniatures, that we've seen favored, among other writers before and since, by Conrad, Nabokov, and Brodsky. Time Fframes—and their sometimes ironic frame-ups: circular and self-fulfilling (Cather), violated by reversal (Amis), radically premature (McEwan), proleptic (Eliot), collapsed by metatextual irony (Auster), millennially leveled (Melville), and extrapolated to eternal present (Whitman). Such verbal transactions do repeatedly operate at the conjoint scales indicated by that emblematic *Ff* typography, where the ingredient minim of the operating framework, from phoneme to lexeme, often pushes the agenda—as the flashpoint of a retooled impetus.

In Whitman, that anticipated, wholly spectral *too*—seemingly provoked by analogic momentum in the transtemporal fusion that unsettles the so-also of "I look'd" with the backflow of 'I look d(too)'—would surely count, if actually incurred by the line, as a subperceptual Fframe-advance. Within the broader ambit of diction, idiom, and syntax canvassed in these first two chapters, the suppressed afterbeat of such expectation alone—off-page, but encroaching—marks a typifying intersection, tensile and self-adjusting, of wording's syntactic sequence with an underlying grammar of tense. It's as if the wording of memory as present inscription ("I looked") has been marginally breached as a sign of the broached continuum between an inked then and the apostrophic now. In contemplating the shadow play of that repressed conjunction "too," there is as well, beyond a general sense of poetic latency, another reason we don't have to wait until this book's epilogue for confirming evidence of such aftertones in Whitman's rhythms. For this is the same Whitman, it bears noting, whose "Song of Myself" later in *Leaves of Grass* celebrates the continuous balance of Thanatos and Eros, with no more living or dying now than ever in the world, "never any more inception," nor "end." The poetic measure in itself insists on this vitalist momentum, at one with death, when throbbing in phonemic bursts across the enjambed apposition "Urge and urge and urge, / Always the procreant urge of the world." With its own hopscotch of internal and overlapping phonetic enjambments ("Urge an*d urge* an*d urge*"), this wording keeps no metaphysical distance, nor even monosyllabic, from something like the world's *urgin' urgent dirge*—and then only to reiterate this one more time, in a further slippage between lexical Fframes, at the fused juncture of its assonant summation (and angled-off rhyme) in "procrean*t urge* of the wo*r*ld." Such is the surge and swirl of words to which we now return with further prose examples in order to continue auditing their pulse and backbeat alike—and next, as it happens, in an actual auditorium.

Part II

Staged

Text Out Loud

3

Reading-en-Scène

Literary words live a collective life of their own, always in commute (and sometimes mutation) between page and inner ear. But the *live theater* of words is something other—and further: the staging of wording per se, and not just in its world-building force. One is used to seeing actors in person, not just on screen, in performances "live" rather than recorded; why not actors playing the part—or parting the plays—of language itself in straight-ahead narrative prose? Twenty-first-century experimental theater has an answer ready. The question rephrased: How to enact the subvocal theatrics of wording's private reading in dramatic progress? One such staging (as if there were any real precedent) exhaustively plays out—the prose's occasional mordant wordplay included—the verbal as well as affective contours of a classic American novel in its complex layering of phenomenological via phonetic cues: the whole spectrum from lexical foundation to imagined narrative space. The recessional manifestations of a famous frame story are themselves reframed in this way before our ears, then eyes—as if a whispering prompter from the pit were lifted to featured status as engine of event. I'm raising the curtain here (though in the event there wasn't one) on the conceptual extravaganza of *Gatz*, premiered off-Broadway in 2010 by the award-winning Elevator Repair Service—and caught by me in a traveling revival at Princeton's McCarter theater in 2019, where I was steeped in its vocal inflections for hours on end the day before teaching on the other side of campus, as a visiting Humanities Council professor, a course in narrative prose as *medium* rather than just text. My commitment may have been overdetermined, true enough, but my attention was wholly earned by the riveting show (and its lengthy tell).

The eponymous monosyllable *Gatz* is the only thing truncated about *The Great Gatsby* in this (re)production, a novel whose every printed word—word by (and for) word—is unfurled hour by hour, six of them to be exact, almost to the minute. Each linked phrase of F. Scott Fitzgerald's novel is delivered up to varying densities of dramatic manifestation within that wording's ongoing generative orality. The novel's black-comedy-of-manners becomes a multi-act play of ensemble phrasing, at times a melodrama of the mellifluous—and of the cacophonous—within a Roaring Twenties thematic of indulgent ease, careless flux, inevitable stagnation, frenetic outburst, and contingent drift (climactically "accidental," a word that occurs in a final and spectral verbal repetition). Sometimes the sporadically dramatized Roar threatens to deafen the oralized text in its continuous delivery. Yet hours in, after two breaks and a dinner interval, the audience is still on the edge of their seats, their surrogate reading-chairs, catching the internal "accidents" of phrase (in approach to the final murder scene) as well as the verbal insinuations of pending doom. The star turns of literary language remain the featured action throughout. What might have been a celebration of theater's advance over fiction, in its vivid disposition of lived bodies, is just the opposite: a transformation of words themselves into a cast of thousands in the collective labor of invention.

Everything one might ever want to say about the "performance" of literary phrasing, prompted from the wings if not the pit—stage left and stage right alike—by syntax's choreographic directives in the "dance of the intellect among words"; or, in the same vein, everything one might want to imagine about the manifest convergence of Pound's melopoesis (music) with logopoesis (the linguistics of wording) in the live enunciation of a sonorous prose: all can be at least intermittently glimpsed, which is to say heard, in this tangible *production* of a novel in embodied space, yet without the associated reduction to which the "performance" trope is sometimes prone. We do not entertain borrowed feelings directly, oversee the gestures of others in the enactment of text; linguistic texture does not disappear into the customs, or costumes, of projective identification. This is not a novel "acted out"—but prose out in action. On the stage of *Gatz,* even as in the reading of *The Great Gatsby*, words retain their strictly verbal tenor and tension even as they enact affects well beyond, but including, their own triggered vocal sensations. Here words are the protagonists in the dramaturgy of their own sentences, subordinating human agency to readerly absorption and uptake, staged before us in exact simultaneity with our own reaction time, word by word.

Now, it's not uncommon to hear in dramatic poetry, when "read" in performance, certain effects lost or forgotten when closeted with a play text, as when Ralph Fiennes, in a recent National Theater production of *Antony and Cleopatra* (2018–19), delivers what amounts to Shakespeare's own sublexical reprise of his deathless lethal echo, "Put out the light, and then put out the light," from the earlier tragedy *Othello*. This time it is the heroine who has extinguished herself, so Antony has been misled into thinking. The staggered lines of his agonized speech, by no means fresh in my mind there in London, were in fact momentarily misheard by me in the balcony. My ear couldn't catch a grammatical enjambment at the following swivel into paired, self-goading imperatives (surfacing from his call to Eros for the sword of assisted suicide). It goes as follows in the text, Antony's compound injunction closing down upon a nullifying verb form ("mars") whose effect was, in contrast to the enjambment, very much audible in its grammatical surprise—standing forth as a touted proper name bent into a predicate in its deconsecration of the hero in his previous association with the war god Mars:

> So it must be, for now
> All length is torture: *since the torch is out,*
> Lie down, and stray no farther: now all labour
> *Mars* what it does (IV.xiv.46–49; emphasis added)

The shift from the heroics of Mars to a marring labor is one thing. But lineation rubs it in. On the page at least, there is the bitter false lead, in this suicidal avowal, at "for now"—as if there were any future left in which change might be imagined. But the word "for," as wording, shifts at once from preposition to conjunction. And the bracketing grammatical ambiguity that follows actually spells out its own lexical shift, via internal variant, in the mode of a homophone rather than a homonym like "M/mars"—as the diphthonged *tu* of "torture" grates against "tor*ch*"—even while the adjective in "all length" soon returns via alliteration to rob action as well as time ("all labor") of its meaning. Just before that, however, rather than the text as intended, and precisely because of its silent colon, I heard in the theater—impelled by this *tulch* skid—the syntactic sense of the second line lengthened to complete a freestanding grammar all its decisive own, unpunctuated even if chokingly delivered.

It is, in fact, hard to imagine the actor who could prevent, or would even wish to, such a mishearing in the thrust of desperate expression. The pause that would regroup, re-gear, for the onset of a wholly detached subordinate clause at this bare lurch into a new thought ('And moreover, since the torch is out . . .')—still with its precondition of misery—simply hangs in the air at first as a grievous caesura. Caught there is a silent ga(s)p before seeming explanation: morbid effect to be confronted by figurative cause. The waver amounts to a kind of explanatory implosion. And the longer it takes to explain here, in wordy secondary commentary, the more powerful its compressed wording may seem. The meaning of this bereft status of meaninglessness for the hero toggles, that is, between the temporal latch of "since" as "ever since" (her death) and the resulting afterthought of restated despair sprung from its alternate sense as a newly predicated *because* ("[S]*ince* the the torch is out . . ."). But this split grammatical (and of course lexical) hinge is as fleeting as the smothered flame, especially when the line's whole iambic span is bonded by the internal slant rhyme that wafts the trace of loss across the syntax-defying arc of causality—or, in other words, that so bitingly lodges, in its own miniscule drama of phonic longing, the snuffed "torch" in its resulting elongated "torture." With my collected Shakespeare an ocean away, I couldn't wait to get back to my laptop in the London hotel to reboot this brilliance, only then discovering its phonetic syncopation as the result of a solicited but mistaken "line-reading" (mine, not Fiennes's), erasing as my racing ear did a phrasal flange that only further collapses the language of futility, however momentarily vectored, upon its own punishing dead end. Yet it is important to note, regarding the theater of words in these overwrought lines, that the famous double grammar detected and celebrated by William Empson in Shakespeare, operating here in full flower, is also caught up at the same time with the more narrowly gauged syllabic byplay of wording's phonic drag on syntax.

Live Words: *Gatsby* via *Gatz* in the Transmedial Theater of Text

That's one high watermark in a dramaturgy of the word: Shakespearian dialogue, verging on soliloquy, expertly drawn out, even while folded over itself, by professional inflection. It's another thing (though not quite) to have the words of a novelistic text brought to bear on the ear—in their full syllabic as well as narrative impetus—by delegated recitation on a theatrical stage: words read out, called out as such, intoned even as internalized, what have you. What you get, in the audience of *Gatz*, is the stray surprise as well as the gradual pervasive involvement, the sponsoring words never verging on full transparency even when enacted. And sometimes warped by obtrusive ambiguity. Without the novel closely in mind beforehand, one may well be taken aback, for instance, when rain-bound characters at Gatsby's mansion, staring out at the storm, are heard to be (that is, said to be, read out to be) "looking at the corrugated surface of the sound." There the unheard capital *S*—in a phrase clearly short, of course, for Long Island Sound—may cause the word itself to perturb the ear as much as the pictured liquid surface is disturbed, this with a weird synesthesia more like late Woolf or Joyce than Fitzgerald.

Such is the phonic anomaly that proves the rule of a more lucid reading aloud in this monodrama of literature's subvocal drive. Discounting the likes elsewhere of any such overt and perverse sound puns as that on the word "Sound," still at any turn we may audit—through the conduit of recitation—what the silently reading eye might be more likely to pass over with Fitzgerald's text simply open before us, lexically tracked, rather than activated by the deciphering voice of our peripatetic onstage mediator. This audial surplus is certainly in evidence in a late retrospective passage concerned with the first fetishistic attachment of penniless Jay Gatz to the glamour of Daisy Buchanan's upper-class social scene. In narrative flashback, we hear (of) him smitten with an "artificial world" that "was redolent of orchids and pleasant, cheerful snobbery and orchestras which set the rhythm of the year"—where the last word of this triad ("redolent" faded away to metaphor by now) has harmonized the sentence's own rhythm by the moral discord of internal echo. The luxuriant aromatic lending of syllabic stems from "orchids" to "orchestras" (in all their false etymological league, the former from the Greek "testicle," the latter from "choric" space) makes the haze of moneyed leisure all the more artificially perfumed and diffusely continuous. A kind of moral synesthesia in this case: words cutting both ways on the knife edge of figuration and free association. As may often happen on an open page as well as on stage, words can steal the show.

Same with the laugh-getting turn of phrase earlier (though easier to register when heard in the theater than merely read) about Daisy's wayward life after marriage, the Buchanan couple flitting about from one prestige location to another wherever people "played polo and were rich together"—with the second phrase offering a satiric vagueness punctuated by that leapfrogging last adverb. It is a tempered case of the same forking grammar, naturalized here one might say, that the opening chapter found maximized in the acquired English of Conrad, Nabokov, and Brodsky. So it is that this send-up syntax for an idle social set splits down the middle (all but sylleptically) in a variant of 'played together both at polo and at being rich,' where wealth emerges—even in the given phrasing—as an empty signifier, a blasé role-playing. Jokes and minor echoes aside in the novel (except when the aural drama of the play spotlights them), the exponential power of *Gatz* on stage—with its remediation of *Gatsby* in the theatrical auditorium of uneven elocution, by a reader only slowly getting the hang of the text, its tone and rhythm—is precisely to foreground the medium of prose in its cognitive, imaginative, and ultimately projective function: from syllabic substrate to phenomenological vantage point, from lexical manifestation to ethical stance. In the normal choreography of a theatrical drama, bodily positions are typically blocked out on stage, by chalk or tape; in this case, language is almost tangibly traced out, one aired sentence at a time. Wording doesn't just center the poses and gestures fitfully mobilized by it; it upstages them front and center.

Set back in the unspecified technological space of the 1980s business world, let's say just over half a century on from Fitzgerald's 1927 flapper landmark, the media of writing and wired communication in *Gatz* are updated from a former epoch of typewriters and teletype only by portable (not yet cell) phones and a primitive console computer in a low-rent bonds office. In the breakdown of the latter tool, and in retreat from the commercial urgencies of the former, the "lead" character (ushering us into Fitzgerald's textual space) absents himself from his disabled office instrument and picks up a novel about, and narrated by, another bond salesman, who transmits his tale of decadent pre-Depression New York into the thick—and mostly thin—of the reader's colorless present. On this historical cusp of emergent e-text culture, the seizing up of a computerized medium throws the atavist back on a residual manner of "word processing." Our enunciating protagonist begins to while away the time, and his cares, with one Nick Carraway, inheritor from Conrad's Marlow of the canonical caretaker role in the frame-tale preservation of a dead man's memory.

And other medial intertexts converge on this textual, this literary, election by default. With nothing to read or write electronically, even when the protagonist slams both spread hands at once on his dormant computer keyboard, the whole time—behind him, on the set's back wall—there stretches an unusually wide rectangular window, shaped like an elongated movie screen, behind which in turn, when its own slatted curtain is open, certain moments of narrated action, and mostly stunned reaction in profile, are intermittently played out. This happens when they are "projected" there from the scene of reading onto this delimited and reframed sector of its impersonated narrative scenario. In allusion, perhaps, to the many movie versions of this beloved novel, this optic aperture throws into relief, by contrast, the audial interface through which, far more often, an action more faithful to the text than any moving-picture event is here scanned into visibility by the drama of recitation alone.

Moreover, in adjacent medial terms, the inevitable risk of this play's underdramatized tour de force may be mitigated, if only slightly, by its being conceived and mounted during the growing popularity of the audiobook, rapidly evolved past tape and disk to MP3 file. The production's demanding conceit of word-by-word "adaptation" has to this extent a certain potential audience waiting: readers used to having books "narrated" (orated) for them, often by moonlighting professional actors, and—even more to the point here—with ambient sound effects to round out the diegetic world. *Gatz*, however, does more than produce, it performs, this circumambience. It does so while at the same time enacting the (never entire) takeover of signifier by signified. Indeed, the staged text—rather than stage story—dispatches in histrionic fashion the very way words keep their hold on us by reaching back, for renewed lexical traction, from depiction to lexical process. In the throes of this two-way traffic in verbal extrapolation, certainly no already-familiarized terrain of the audiobook can detract from the gamble or extravagance of the play's conception. It is the Elevator Repair Service's great and winning wager, its reparative literary move in an era of competing media, that reading *out* a text could be made to sustain attention as a figure for reading one's way *into* its world: in other words, that the dynamics of volume and intonation alone, textured by what we might call its referential interference from conjured bodies and their subsidiary voices, could virtualize Fitzgerald's own narrative *volume* in its inhabited verbal parameters.

At least four salient and building features of *Gatz*'s incremental stagecraft serve to pace the escalating metadrama of imaginative literary access—even while, in the process, no fewer than another four explicit articulations of transferred desire from the unaltered novel arrive, in sequence, as if to gloss the motives for this whole theatrical transposition: the rehearsed triggers of its inspiration. In that first quartet of marked formal ingenuities in stagecraft, the launching arc of theatrical transposition—routing us from decoded rectangular page to an encompassing mental stage—involves, in order and in cumulative force, matters of discourse, mise-en-scène, tacit phenomenology (in the presencing of the narrative world), and an ultimately embodied participation in the language that generates it. Such is the conceptual path by which this famous frame narrative of Fitzgerald's is progressively reframed by the auditory's proscenium arch.

In the first phase of our anonymous actor's retreat to reading, the surround of everyday office language seems muted by the very force of his surfaced oral fascination—illogically filling the room with the vocal upload of story. As the actor/reader makes his tentative, halting way, with slips of enunciation and sometimes stumbling emphasis, through the smoothly lucid cadence of Fitzgerald's prose as devolved upon the Carraway narrator, and may seem all the more to be broadcasting (illogically enough) the inner rhythms of a skimming silence, the office workers around him go all but mute, either barely whispering—or miming their words in total silence. The effect comes across as a wholesale metaphor: part of an ecology—and a dialectic—of private and public audition in which it is implied, by a bold trope of subjectivity, that a subvocalized narrative, compelling enough, can drown out the world.

In a second formal departure from the dramaturgy of realism, *Gatz* works a fascinating variation on anything like the omniscience of free indirect discourse (a narrator siphoning off the worded thoughts of a character). When the variable population of the reader's (now narrator's) lived office space begins to figure the depicted bodily (and erotic) agents of his enunciated storyline, suddenly one or another of these converted office personnel (translated to narrative personae) breaks in vocally to speak lines identified, often after the fact, as spoken—identified, that is, by the seated or standing reader: "They'll keep out of my way," for instance, completed across the stage by the narratorial "she insisted." One ventures to call this a transmedial case of freed direct discourse. At such pivot points, we are catapulted into a diegetic space not that of these mercantile functionaries; instead, the novel as event, if only by a coercive identification radiating out from its generative voice, is struggling to "come alive" from its referential gestation on the page. Even while still tethered to it until very near the end.

As a third facet of this parturition from wording to narrated world, we gradually realize that the male figure long buried in obscurity stage left—first presumed (at least by me) to be an office coworker, a nearly faceless prop of commerce—is more like a noncharacter fixed at attention before an anachronistic open laptop more high-tech than the jammed console of our stage-center reader. For this amorphous noncharacter has a supervening role to play, it turns out, rather than just a few minor ones later, in this metaplay. Repeated fussbudget attempts at IT intervention (concerning the reader's frozen computer)—performed by the actor who will later play the low-tech garage mechanic Wilson, cuckolded murderer of Gatsby—can easily distract us from this other peripheral body and his own latent computer agency. But only until it dawns on us that the extradiegetic figure to the left is all along operating from his laptop the electronic instrument panel that activates the lighting and sound cues for the entire production: installing a tech metalepsis (production manifest within product) that seals the thematics of mediation at the play's core. The point can only sneak up on us, receiving no onstage emphasis. The diegetic space of Gatsby's story is hereby being programmed from within the same mise-en-scène as its reading, each feature of materialization operating on a participatory, invested, and ultimately uncanny continuum: a leveled playing field between page and stage.

A fourth and curiously related jog to the logic of present theatricalized event, also to be noticed by audience members in their own good time, is at least as intriguing. We eventually recognize that the sudden disruptions captured in Fitzgerald's plot in the course of its dialogue-heavy progress—the abrupt gestures, the harsh stares, the sudden arresting noises, the flashes of a car headlight, the minor distractions of almost any sort—are for the most part enacted in *Gatz* (sometimes comically, always disarmingly) to precede just slightly, rather than proceed from, their vocalized textual indicators: say their novelistic stage directions. They are recurrently marked by the orator's (let's call him vocator's) double takes in real space—followed by his return to the textual page, often with a wry smile, to catch up there with the text's belated cue. Gradually, tapering away from mere words into dramatic embodiment, we have entered a world we are asked to imagine unfolding on its own—merely recorded and confirmed by text—rather than one in fact entirely produced, in hallucinatory fashion, by said text, said aloud or not.

All the while, as the "play" of language builds in our auditorium—hour by hour, in its early afternoon slide into late evening, with fewer breaks for refreshment, liquid or otherwise, than the novel's characters themselves take—the attentive listener may, as suggested, also register a widely spaced quartet of passages in the novel that add up to an organizing subtraction: the removal of its pivotal character from action to mere oversight. These passages may seem in this fashion to provide a linked psychodynamic matrix for *Gatz*'s whole theatrical incarnation as a twice-mediated framing of report and rapport alike, of narrative identification per se, where Nick's transmit of Gatsby's meretricious dream (supposedly "incorruptible") is clouded by his own passive romanticism and vicariousness, his instinct for a care-away purge of urgency. In light of Nick's double vision, these fourfold touchstones stand out in part because of their emphatic delivery by our onstage vocator, mantled at these moments in narration's borrowed, self-searching words.

First, after the drunken and ultimately violent Manhattan party thrown by Tom Buchanan and his mistress, with Nick the narrator eager to break away from the joyless chaos, he yearns to be out on the street, escaped from the madness. Yet it is from this desired but now deputized vantage that he can only imagine a split-screen refocalizing of his own experience: For "high over the city our line of yellow windows must have contributed their share of human secrecy to the casual watcher in the darkening streets, and I was him too, looking up and wondering. I was within and without, simultaneously enchanted and repelled by the inexhaustible variety of life." Indeed though twice "within" on *Gatsby*'s fictional terms here (as partygoer and spectator), he is, by the telescoped perspective of *Gatz*, consigned in several stages to the "without"—as actor playing a reader playing a narrating as well as a narrated character.

Next, in this roster of metanarrative prompts, the Carraway figure is repeatedly enlisted within the story as a participant witness to the ethnography of idle wealth. At a later ill-fated party at the Plaza: "At this point Jordan and I tried to go but Tom and Gatsby insisted with competitive firmness that we remain—as though neither of them had anything to conceal and it would be a privilege to partake vicariously of their emotions." What else does fiction do but license such vicarious partaking, here by the further theatrical taking of parts? To enjoy this "privilege" at the distance of viewer or reader—here viewereader—is to inhabit its testimony secondhand, to bear witness at a sustained remove.

As a third nexus in this chain of exposed surrogate engagement, there is Nick's alternating role, as character rather than narrator, when veering between cicerone and chaperone for the adulterous liaison of his frivolous married cousin and his filthy-rich neighbor. As go-between, Nick feels increasingly de trop in the crossfire of their rekindled romance. Within the plot, this mediator figure is rightly uneasy—structurally as well as emotionally—with a diegetic role that may seem to undermine his "outside" narrative stance. As Daisy waxes increasingly romantic in one embarrassing episode with Gatsby, "I tried to go then, but they wouldn't hear of it; perhaps my presence made them feel more satisfactorily alone." The guess is as much structural, finally, as psychological. Nick doesn't just finesse and oversee their liaison, but in his textual role as recording secretary of this overwrought passion, his take on their romance—for transmission to us— is a definitive part of his "privilege" to "partake vicariously" of "emotions" not his (nor our) own, let alone—except by transferred vicariousness— those of the onstage reader in our stead. Textual eavesdropping, if we may call it that—when figuratively projected out loud, and reverbed in turn among stand-ins and avatars for plot agency—has become a theater of voyeuristic displacements. It is still up to Nick to accept this fully, cured of any prurience but willing to superintend events from within his world, to *commit* rather than merely report, obligated by bonds beyond the sheer binding of the pages he has inscribed in retrospect. *Gatz* is yet more powerfully emphatic on this point, as we'll see, than *Gatsby*.

While we sit listening to another read, we are aware, with this dramatized text, of a narrator (and his POV) self-consciously both inside and outside at once; next, enjoined in the latter aspect to vicarious interest as a surrogate insider; then recruited as functional outside to another couple's enhanced solitude and privacy. That's the threefold sequence so far, waiting only a final acquiescence in the ultimate postmortem legacy of delegated "interest." For fourth and finally, after Gatsby's death, when dutifully trying to assemble at least a few mourners for the funeral—like Marlow, again, as emissary of Kurtz's memory—Nick is at first surprised by his role (operable all along, of course) as narrative conduit, where every "surmise" about Gatsby's fate, let alone every question of fact, is "referred to me." But realization finally arrives. In attendance on Gatsby's corpse in the mausoleum his mansion has become, "hour upon hour it grew upon me"—across the shifted pressure of that preposition, from succession to oppression, and in unusually crisp and knowing delivery from the stage at this point, each accretion in the clarified phrasing pointedly hovered over—"that I was responsible, because no one else was interested—interested, I mean, with that intense personal interest to which every one has some vague right at the end."

Off Page/On Stage

The play breaks open here—even as the book, the well-thumbed novel, is unexpectedly closed tight. For it is just this lone apogee of "intense" attachment, with the screw turned further by the narrator's gloss on it—just this divestiture of self in "personal" as well readerly investment—that is distilled from here out in a sustained soliloquy rather than in page-turned decipherment. The ratcheting up of immediacy is as stunning as it is immediately obvious in its inference. Alchemizing the actor's mimesis of everyday reading until now—avid but uneven, throttled by phrasing at times even in its eager lurch forward, at best rough and ready—his textual access is here transfigured by full-bodied impersonation. Wholly and unreservedly, the nameless bond dealer *becomes* his narratorial counterpart in (and as) the novelistic perspective at large: the individuated medial function not just "simultaneously enchanted and repelled," as is the character, but—more important, in terms of a structural bonding or osmosis from character to narrator—operating yet again "both within and without." It is by way of just this double play, as in the overall medial reframing of *Gatsby* by *Gatz*, that Nick and his onstage double enact, at a new pitch of conviction, both character and reader at once, actor and reciter, unnamed person and the always-other of persona.

And it is this latter role now, once "personal interest" has taken hold in its deserved "intensity," even its internalized intention, that allows our vocator—though still clutching the closed book, clinging to it—nevertheless to suspend the material fact of text for the open horizon of story. Over the course of the next bravura half hour or more, in touch with the bound novel only as if he were swearing to its authority as on a courtroom Bible, our fully inhabited Nick (the gifted Scott Shepherd in a show-stopping turn, preparing for his several standing ovations) gives the story over entirely to a mesmerizing metanarrative soliloquy, delivering the rest of the novel in a full-bore channeling of memory and exacting enunciation, with all the melancholy verve of a prose that has previously seemed to elude him around the edges of its artful cadencing. If this is the way Nick writes, and in reading I feel it from within, then these are my words now, wholly owned. As vouched for in the register of unforced dramatic inflection alone, he has become what he reads. And through the conduit of his newly mastered (because internalized) dramatic enunciation, we make our headlong, stirring way back to the reopened text itself for the famous writerly last sentences, implausible in any extemporaneous monologue, anchoring this prolonged burst of empathic transfer in its recovered status as a reading effect. With *Gatz* coming to this head of immersive identification, Georges Poulet's signal claim about the phenomenology of reading could be the epigraph, motto, or mantra for the whole production: namely, and by whatever name assigned to the source of text as reporting agent, in the heat of reading I have the thoughts of the other as if they were my own. It is just this bodiless transference that has found its rare stage enactment.

Characters in drama are always delivering the speech of the other as if it were their own. Here that discourse has dropped all existential pretense in its centrality as text.

Certainly none of the play's climactic innovation was lost on the chorus of positive reviewers. When the show reached London, *The Guardian* critic Michael Billington, though having "spent much of my life attacking adaptations," finds the "glory" of *Gatz* that it offers instead a "complete rendering" of its literary source.[1] Complete—and complete with an unexpected internal momentum, which a play on words in an earlier Chicago review by John Beer (in *The Point* magazine) flags as its true metatheatrical coup.[2] Whereas, in ordinary theater parlance, getting beyond a play script to its memorized rehearsal is called "going off-book," here, in Beer's turn of phrase, with the book being actually a bound fiction, "Shepherd, playing Gatsby's narrator, Nick Carraway, literally goes off book and recites the last sections of the novel from memory." It is in this sense that the actor is indeed "playing *Gatsby*'s narrator" every bit as much as he is impersonating the character who channels Fitzgeralds's text: having, one might add, *taken to heart*, moment by moment, what has been learned by heart—committing to it, in a sense, more than just it to memory. The effect of this is what Ben Brantley, in the *New York Times* review, is singling out (with avoided spoiler) when he writes: "The blurring of Nick the reader into Nick the narrator is, I promise you, unlike anything you've ever seen in the theater."[3] Not a reviewer's implied superlative there, with the added boost of hyperbole, but a tacit measure of the extratheatrical charge of this literary enactment.

If that speech about "intense personal interest" offers the fourth and most definitive of the structural tipped hands regarding the novel's logic of vicarious displacement—and thereby provides the dramaturgical tipping point from recitation to theatrical monologue across the denouement of the novel's final chapter—we may have sensed the building pressure toward this explicitly inhabited commitment in the immediately preceding prose. For elicited there, by the remediation of *Gatz*, is the novel's ultimate narrative peripety, though deliberately floated in a wash of anticlimactic detail. It is a passage, as prose, whose bleak mortuary flux—movingly read by Shepherd with the book still open—elegizes Gatsby's swimming pool murder, where the scapegoated body (only after the offstage shooting) is found floating in slow circles, going again nowhere.

The almost numbed precision of Fitzgerald's prose at this point, in dwelling over (and within) the all-but-inert wake of a life, has never seemed sharper, more searing, than in this theatrical materialization of its phonically charged ironies. What Nick comes upon is the corpse in artificial motion on an inflatable raft, an "air mattress" as death bed. "There was a faint, barely perceptible movement of the water as the *f*resh *f*low *f*rom one end urged its way toward the drain at the other." Flux, urgency, a flash of alliteration, a false freshet of energy: all is displaced from the corpse, on its barely mobile bier, to the entrapped waters—and the faintly mimetic prose—that nudge it forward. No grand epic river-of-no-return here. "With little ripples that were hardly the shadows of waves, the laden mattress"—all but leaden in its dead weight—"moved irregularly down the pool." Down, not across, in a kind of spatialized hint of a narrative falling off. From that lapping of *a* sounds, short and long, is propelled an eddying phonetic current—and undertow—that ruffles this aquatic space as a forlorn nautical microcosm (barely "the shadows of waves"). It does so while spilling over from the five-syllabled assonant adverb in "m*o*ved irreg*u*larly" into the short and long *u*'s (as we're next to hear) that levitate and ironize the always *inflated* dream in its exposed brutal effigy—against whose book-long fatefulness the immediate iteration (with its twinning of "accidental") protests too much. All this is read from the stage, feelingly, but with a new forensic exactitude that lets through its scrupulous gloomy music: "A small gust of wind that scarcely corrugated"—that word again, from the rain-swept undulation ("corrugated surface") of the Sound, here "gust"-nudged—"that scarcely *corrugated* the s*u*rface. . . ." As a prose surface, one of narration's *superficial* effects is to redouble the *ru/ur* ripple across the stridently unemphatic repetition of "accidental." As the sentence plays out, a further gust of wording, that is, propels what I'm tempted to call phrasing's melodramatic deadpan at this turn: "was enough to dist*u*rb its *accidental* course with its *accidental* b*u*rden." All is aftermath and recoil—or, as we will come to hear such effects in the epilogue, aftertones: "The *tou*ch of a cl*us*ter of leaves revolved it slowly"— just as slowly, this material twisting of human and material debris, as its own phonetic turn is retarded by syntactic momentum in this last aimless swirl, complete with its telling trail of blood—its vestigial motion finally noted as "tracing, like the leg of a compass, a thin red circle in the water." That kind of compass, with no direction left—only the circuit of futility.

Chapter 3

All this can easily seem like the first turn of a developing travesty—this listless funerary drift, this draining away of all romantic agency in a last vicious (compass) circle of mistaken vengeance—a send-up in advance of the text's famous last sardonic nautical flourish: "So we beat on," beating with no winning to be had, just the fruitless plosive blows of windblown friction, "boats against the current, borne back ceaselessly into the past." Even while lapped by the leisure-class yachtsman argot of "beating and tacking" against the wind, the phrase breaks from its own knowing idiom of alternate, course-corrective moves with the vectored "on." This is the capping sentence—in its stressed monosyllabic downbeats, a quintessentially literary prose—for which our vocator has aptly returned, as reader, to the opened-again page. Yet, among the other effects cresting here, it is only a natural vocal retardation that can elicit the sibilant suction of that lone trisyllable: the dilated temporal adverb "ceaselessly," sliding past, into the past itself, in the faint litotes ("nondiscontinuously") of its rearward drag. With phrasing's ambivalent shift from metonym to metaphor, our deluded aspirant selves are in part the emptied vessels ("we . . . boats") of a discredited quest: an appositional sense, as against the more likely parenthetical absolute ("our boats being . . ."). "So" our unoriginal dreams go oaring forward into the lost past, always upstream, against the current, against the present itself, against the real.

And simply to put it this way is to italicize the ultimate motive for a page-based return to reading from the previous onstage soliloquizing investment. At stake at this turn, this foregrounded troping, is not just a nod to the hyperliterary, but the flagging of a strictly linguistic closure. The result is not unlike the mild uprush of muted alliteration and metaphor in the fifth and final line of that litany from Whitman that closed the last chapter: signature effect of future-projecting versification as well as vision, including, beyond a marked alliteration, that reflexive mimetic inflation of the phonetic "stem" to make way for "steam" in the phonetic thickening of those "thick-stemm'd pipes of steamboats." What we read at the end of *Gatsby*, or have read to us in *Gatz*, is even more completely literary: pure figure, pure counter-epic metaphor, pure language. No actual yachts, no present river, no Long Island Sound, no resounding romantic past in any specified lamented memory—just the sonic contours of a phrasal falling off, an abstract extranarrative cadenza in the subsiding way of the word. This is where the play's stagecraft has so perfectly "read" the literary valence of Fitzgerald's closure. After half an hour's stirring surge of personal empathy through internalized discourse, this "dramatic" break from plot into its figurative summation needs *sheer reading*—rather than the stage hero's recent claim on the ficiton by emotive declaiming—precisely because it has no conceivable staging in social space, no event base. It is the trope for all that has otherwise depletingly transpired.

Channeled by the "live wording" of *Gatz*'s sustained auditorial conceit, it is exactly such undertows of wording itself (as in "So we beat on, boats . . . borne back")—including the slippage of grammar, the spillage of syllables, incident (as well as "accidental") to the working up of image—that has ghosted many a phrasal turn of the semantic tide for six hours of now chaotic, now melancholy report. Under the proscenium arch of intermittent and fitful verbal enactment across the rippling glints and shadowy laps of Fitzgerald's prose, it is ultimately the drama of novelistic language as such, in the temporary but marked abeyance of newer electronic media, that finds its minor apotheosis in the syntactic slack of "So we beat on"—a barely discernible play between "In consequence" and a more self-exampling "Thus."

Drawn back *thusly* in forging ahead, grammar stands (out) yet again—in the Elevator Repair Service's emphatic *textual* rendering of this epitomizing last sentence—as the microcosm of a retrogressive American plot whose heard rhythms nonetheless come through unimpeded, float free, and take their final bows. After which, with the lights back up and the players dispersed, one can repair home and to the text again—not just literary critics but critical readers at large—to see if we've heard right at times amid the rush of brusque and lush phrasings alike. And in this revisiting of text, this passage again more slowly upstream, we retune our ears to the special labor of the page. *Gatsby* is *Gatz*'s true encore. For the novel's is a narrative space that in its own right, within the vocally coached theater of its enlivened silence, entails even in private—as performance medium—the activated body in muted speech production, not just borne by the current of words but bearing them into that life of their own we respond to as literary force.

Vehicular Focalization

Neither Hudson nor East River, nor any of the grander rivers of our literary classics, like Twain's Mississippi, let alone the open seas of Melville's epic, is specifically on the mind of Nick's phrasing this time. Chartless and subjective instead, the downstream current beaten against in his defeatist figure is, of course, not any less there on stage than it is in the narrative space of the novel. Both paged and staged, it is a mere metaphor for that futile human trajectory of unachievable dreams that the novel has mapped out as plot itself. The glimmering prose brilliance of *Gatsby* in its last sadness is to have found this open-ended finish for its tale—this fluvial flourish in immediate counterpoint to the bounded pool as its emblematic antithesis in the preceding death scene. The fittingly brilliant last touch of *Gatz* is to let the prose be—and do; to have taken hands off, letting a return from participatory dramatization to the strictly enunciated page serve to recognize fictional closure's novelistic triumph over all the reality that drags down its characters: a triumph embodied in this abstract and withering mastertrope for a drama otherwise so tempting to invest in. Here, at the end, is a ritual of divestment: the return of event to language in an extended allegorical turn of phrase about the defeated vehicles of our dreams (and of us too, as "boats" ourselves).

That emphatic prose quality flaunted by Fitzgerald's stylistically rich phrasing and its emblematic images, here in *Gatsby* and in his later fiction, is what always haunts the attempt at adaptation, to the stage as well as the film screen. So a further aftermath of *Gatz*, as theatrical experience, is not just that it may well send us back to *Gatsby* for selective rereading, to savor or dissect a descriptive evocation given new prominence in recitation, but that it may also call up later writing by Fitzgerald in *Gatsby*'s own illuminating light. It makes us especially alert to those moments of figuration that, being unstageable, are also at times, in the medial crystallization they foreground, all but ironically unfilmable as well—and may at times be openly, disruptively, stressed in just such an "inalienable" literary aspect. For this is where the ways of the literary word so often part company with any transparent visual report on the depicted world.

A brief moment of nautical symbolism familiar from the close of *Gatsby* occurs at a emotional turning point in his later novel *Tender Is the Night* (1935),[4] otherwise curtailed in its lyricism by the dialogue-heavy reversals of its marital plot. The exception in question occurs when the expatriate hero, Dick Diver, floating momentarily (instead of any namesake plunge) on American waters, has returned from Europe for the burial of his father. The sentence negotiating this transatlantic shift of scene seems veering off into a dangling modifier until we catch up with the sense: "For an hour, tied up with his profound reaction to his father's death, the magnificent façade of the homeland. . . ." Grammar's point is not that Diver is caught up in reverie, or tied up in knots, but that, in an impressionistic mode, the nearing destination tethered to his debarkation is itself an architectonic metaphor ("façade") for "the harbor of New York" that (to finish the sentence) "seemed all sad and glorious" (265). The transfiguration is short-lived, for "once ashore the feeling vanished, nor did he find it again in the streets or the hotels or the trains that bore him first to Buffalo, and then south to Virginia with his father's body" (265). But for a transitional moment the pathetic fallacy—and actual dangling modifier ("once ashore the feeling . . .") blending man and mood—that robes the Manhattan harbor in sympathy for the death, or for the melancholy of the survivor, has quietly served to transform the prose itself. It has done so not just in a purely figurative, but also in a partly phonetic, way (*façade/all sad*), where the syllabic cadence of fă/sahd meets its near-chiastic reversal of vowel sounds in ahll/ăd. Nothing could be less descriptive, more purely literary, letteral, phonetic: a passing resonance of affect in sound alone. And although this sympathetic vibration is made explicit, along with its abeyance, soon after landing, the mortuary path of aftermath finally returns to symbolism in the character's eyes "only as the local train shambled into the low-forested clayland of Westmoreland County" (265). It is only then that he could "feel once more identified with his surroundings"—and they, projectively with him—including not just "the moon over Chesapeake bay" but the tracked motion and channeled watercourses of other perennial, millennial energies. These wheel by in a running paratactic sequence, all on the same plane of laminated historical perspective, involving (revolving) "the rasping wheels of buckboards turning, the lovely fatuous voices, the sound of sluggish primeval rivers flowing *softly* under *soft* Indian names" (265; emphasis added). Achieved here, or audited in evocation at least, is a plateau (further leveled by that repetition) where word and thing, name and waterway, have themselves merged into a lulling transhistorical equivalence.

Unlike *Gatsby*'s rearward churning current of human aspiration, here in *Tender Is the Night* is a real harbor, then a real bay, real rivers—actual social vehiculation—but transfigured by temperamental (even verbal) echo in response to the mourning mood of the hero. Illustrated in such a passage is the typical ambient space of that novel, where setting is contoured to the course of feeling as much as the other way round. The wider *Gatsby*-like rift between description and figuration, the former realistic, the latter isolated in the metaphors of prose report alone, returns again for the first-person narration of Fitzgerald's last, unfinished novel, where a Carraway-like sentimentality is allowed to inflect the frame of apprehension for another Gatsbyesque self-made tycoon. This is Fitzgerald's deliberate fictionalization of "Boy Wonder" Irving Thalberg, head of production at MGM, as the charismatic Monroe Stahr in the novel known best without the first three-word half of its title, *The Love of the Last Tycoon*—and without the subtitle, "A Western," that already casts it in the cinematic mold of loner-hero genre.[5]

Early in that book, a metaphoric aerial "shot"—a sheer figure of speech for the producer's quasi-omniscient commercial oversight—operates in a more tangible ocular mix with plot than is the case with the anchorless nautical emblematics at the end of *Gatsby*. Closing the first chapter of this intermittently first-person narrative, the daughter of the hero's business partner at the studio celebrates the "vision" of Stahr—the aerial pun in his name put in full play—as something, implicitly, between an Olympian deity and an overreacher like Icarus. In this case, a figurative God's-eye view that provides both distance and elevation on the human lot (rather than just the backlots of Tinseltown) is then segued into an actual landing of his entourage's plane (only to anticipate Stahr's own death in an air crash later). Plot and its extrapolated optics, aeronautic trajectory and the trope of overview: as if generated in free association by the airborne narrator, the resulting interlace of vehicle and tenor, in the normal workings of metaphor, makes her motorized flight the literalized carrier for the trope of omniscience and beneficent descent in her view of the hero. The predicate of ambition is unmistakable in this context: "He had flown up very high to see," as she figures his ascendancy, "on strong wings, when he was young. And while he was up there he had looked on all the kingdoms, with the kind of eyes that can stare straight into the sun" (20). With the categorizing "kind" suggesting more like one-of-a-kind in this anomalous context, with the very strangeness of the formulation highlighted by its alphabetic link to "kingdoms," the master image-maker looks down on us all, but only in benign surveillance. And then, reminiscent of the driving force ironized at the end of *Gatsby*, comes a plosive verbal echo of that "beating on . . . against the current" here redoubled by perseverance. "Beating his wings tenaciously—finally frantically—and keeping on beating them" (20): this is Stahr's power, drawn out with the almost awkward forward thrust of the idiom *keep on*—a kind of mimetic strenuousness and verbal strain—in that twofold participial grammar "keeping on beating." By so doing, as the sentence concludes, "he had stayed up there longer than most of us, and then, remembering all he had seen from his great height of how things were, he had settled gradually to earth" (20). At which point the metaphor of nonvehicular flight and landing is reliteralized in the Glendale airport touchdown.

The producer's (the Creator's) overview of "how things were," of course, makes him the ideal manufacturer of their illusory duplication. His was an "extraordinarily illuminating flight," from whose vantage "he saw which way we were going, and how we looked doing it, and how much of it mattered" (21). We, humanity, have been submitted to the lens-eye view of commercial cinema as a mode of cultural destiny. No "accidental wind" blew him to the studios, thinks the enamored narrator, but he was drawn there—the cinematic metaphor about to become explicit—so that his "visionary" ambition could find scope for itself. He came with a mission, the narrator wants to believe: an almost transcendental advent, figured in the terms of silent cinema: "I would rather think that in a 'long shot' he saw a new way of measuring our jerky hopes and graceful roqueries and awkward sorrows"—that triadic reduction of psychological abstraction to slapstick or expressionist gesture—so that he "came here from choice to be with us to the end" (29). Perhaps "to the last," if only his own, but to the screen "finis" most of all, one completed high-profile production after another. Then, too, in the way made by words alone, there lurks here, beyond a set of repressed scare quotes on "the end," the passing phantom hint of a trajectory induced by the idiomatic (idiometric) veer from "by choice" (in an alliterative formula like 'by chance or by choice') to the more marked "from choice"—as if in a sweep "from" free creative will to inevitable finality. At which point, to keep the narrative open, allegory now comes down to earth in a hovering fragmentary simile: "Like the plane coming down in the Glendale airport, into the warm darkness" (21). From on high, that is, the plane's smooth landing traces exactly the descent, into lucrative practice, of that creative force of overview and application Stahr incarnates.

None of this could be had through dialogue, let alone through set design, neither in the 1998 LA theatrical production of the novel nor in the earlier Elia Kazan film version (1976). What can be visualized on stage or screen, here or with *Gatsby*, is not the drive of self-interested visionary proclivities—or their rank frustration—but only the look and sound of characters in interaction. Even in prose's celebration of the producer's gifted aerial ken, therefore, the evocation of any such vast overhead panorama is not a cinematic "shot" after all. But Fitzgerald is good at more plausible screen techniques as well, where prose aspires to the lens of unfettered registration, at close range as well as distant.

For an ironically highlighted and metafilmic version of that effect, we can return to *Tender Is the Night*—and to its third paragraph's introduction of a heroine we don't yet know to be a Hollywood starlet, except by association with the swish pan that lures our narratively figured "eye" from the precarious complexion of her mother to the daughter's lavishly conjured nubile bloom. Conjured, and zeroed in on—by the opposite of that "long shot" explicitly ascribed to Stahr's entrepreneurial gaze. The setting is near Cannes on the French Riviera, the lighting natural, the prose camera transfixed, once it has veered elsewhere and dollied in. At first: "The mother's face was of a fading prettiness that would soon be patted with broken veins; her expression was both tranquil and aware in a pleasant way" (4). Complexion is anticipatory, her aging alliteratively underway. "However"—an unusual and clunkily abrupt word in narrative prose, marking the rapid shift of the "camera"—"one's eye moved on quickly to her daughter, who had magic in her pink palms and her cheeks lit to a lovely flame, like the thrilling flush of children after their cold baths in the evening" (4). Whether read as object of the past-participial adjective "lit" or claiming it momentarily (and without clausal punctuation) as their own new intransitive predication, those cheeks are soon returned to in further close-up, their "color" being not just "real" but "breaking close to the surface"—unlike the mother's foretold "broken veins"—from "the strong young pump of her heart" (4). Here the capillary action of the prose itself, in what amounts to a kind of ultrasound mode, shifts in its phonetic pulse rate from the *ong/ung* buildup to the overlapping *uh/ump* sprung from "young." Phonetics aside, it is at the lexical scale where one thing is certain: that among the ways of the word, under the comparative paradigm of their cinematic energy, some moves are sideways. The passage just read has maneuvered us from objective observation to erotic valuation across the evoked focalization of film technique, its own vehicle the moving camera. Again, "one's eye moves on quickly": swish pan giving way, not to a full-body tilt, but to an epitomizing close-up. And among the charted ways of the word, such modes of giving way are often definitive, whether from one ocular detail to the next or from pictured world to its figurative inference.

We might, therefore, readily "jump cut" from here to the next chapter—except that one more stage production, a Fitzgerald treatment very different from *Gatz*'s performance piece, can helpfully intervene on this cinematic score. In the 1998 theatrical adaptation of *The Last Tycoon*, by playwright Simon Levy, the stage itself is sparked to visibility as follows, like the film within it: "In black, a light flickers—flickers again and again until the flickering turns into a silent black and white movie projected onto the upstage center screen."[6] And from the opening monologue that ensues: "People pretend to be interested in how pictures are made," but they favor illusion over fact in the long run. "Tell them pictures have a private grammar, that they're created by ordinary men and women, and watch the blank look come into their face" (9)—a blankness as if in reciprocation for the effaced mystique of cinematic presence by syntactic codes. That blankness in its own way prefigures the play's epilogue, where, with cast members gradually leaving the screening room, a documentary film about the deceased tycoon—with metaphoric overtones of the idiom "played out"—on its own terms "plays out to 'THE END.'" And then goes blank, "except for"—more mechanically iterative yet than the first time around—"the flicker, flicker, flicker of the projector light" (56), rhyming *ic/er* with *ec/or* in the spin of the very phrase. In the verbalism of this last stage direction, the spun-out way of the word seems manifest in an onomatopoeic splutter displaced from the sprocket clicks of threaded celluloid. In any case, imageless at this vanishing point, projection operates in the absence of exactly that "private grammar" of cinematographic sequencing to whose activated verbal counterparts—and yet again "corrugated" audiovisual "surface"—we turn in the next chapter.

But a clearer bridge to this material is at hand. For, not just in adapted stage directions, it is Fitzgerald's own prose, as we saw beginning with *The Great Gatsby*, that bears comparison with, rather than just invokes at times in its plotlines, the technics of projection. If the famous final sentence of that novel has drifted away from any scenic picture to sheer figure, all scene displaced by rhetoric, still what has immediately preceded works a vein of imagery that does instead call up cinematic rendering even in its language's most allegorical scope—along with subsidiary touches of what we'll be noting in the next two chapters as lexical montage. Along with the dead hero's shamblingly phrased "huge incoherent failure of a house," darkness encroaches at the end on the privileged shorelines and the rest of its mansions. "And as the moon rose higher the inessential houses" (with that loaded four-syllabled epithet playing between 'trivial' and 'evanescing'), those dimming structures, are exactly the materialist monuments that "began to melt away until gradually I became aware"—not just "melt," but "melt *away*," and in a perceived temporal direction that makes the alliterative "aware" its immediate result—"aware," that is, "of the old island here that flowered once for Dutch sailors' eyes—a fresh, green breast of the new world." Paracinematic lap dissolve ("melt away" in cross-fade) cedes to a flashback panorama of unspoiled wilderness in which the vista thus materialized seems to superimpose upon the minimal personification of "fresh, green breast" an overlay—a lexical "sound match"—of that political and spiritual "clean breast" that the New World was meant to afford its transatlantic colonizers.[7]

It was there and only then, as we read in an almost mimetic dilation of phrase, that "for a tr*an*sitory ench*an*ted mom*en*t m*an* must have held his breath in the presence of this contin*ent*"—an ephemeral revelation as if faded away again, there in the wording itself, along with its own exhaled alliteration. And whose plangent fading is there on the lips of intonation in the Elevator Repair Service's rendering of these very cadences. For what ERS has done, in its return to textual attention from memorized assimilation in this last phase of the novel-as-novel, is to repair and elevate our own attention to the heard word of even paged text. The effect continues simply by taking Fitzgerald up on his own wording. Gatsby has come far too late to these eastern shores, too late to seize his "dream," arriving from the receding eminent domain of its already violated promise. Long lost behind him, even while alive, was its elusive prospect—receding across a telescoped stretch of prepositions that induce something like the prose equivalent of a slow fade (or, anticipating digital technology, a latent cosmic zoom) and its nulled-out vanishing point. For this originary vision of possibility, receding here in adverbial dissipation, is a "dream . . .

already *behind* him, somewhere *back in* that vast obscurity *beyond* the city, where the dark fields of the republic rolled *on under* the night." Not *in* the night but (*on*) *under* it: darkness as both blanket and ban. You ultimately couldn't film this either, of course, and yet, more than those boats beating up-current, the cross-fades and fade-outs of this establishing if unrecoverable vista, its framing flashback and recursive verbal flickers, do help anticipate the emphasis in part III on a "cinematrographic" cast of wording in prose narrative.

Part III

Screened

Toward a Cinematics of the Sentence

4

THREADING THE READ

At the dawn of the film medium, the cinematograph was a device for both record and retrieval in a single mechanism. Before the lens: light, camera, action, matched behind the aperture by their intermittent trace. Later, on the reverse s/trip to the screen within the same apparatus: spool, beam, projected motion. Any imagined cinematography of the sentence is a comparable recording of segmental sequences for the purposes of their own playback. On the page: letters, lexemes, sentences. In reading: phonemes, syllabic patterning, the syntax of sense. Centuries before film, at the dawn of the codex, the mechanics of vertical scrolling gave way, page by turned page instead, to the lateral unrolling of syntax alone, with no mechanical spooling. But celluloid cinema involves—is revolved as—its own kind of coiled scroll. And even after the digital revolution, postfilmic cinema depends at base on binary triggers driven by an algorithmic rather than alphabetic code—whose oscillating differentials have their counterparts, as with the filmic photogram, in the unfurling of lexical succession. Distant counterparts in each case, granted, even beyond the very different "visualization" involved in literature and cinema. And a distance not to be forgotten—since screen image is automatic (whether mechanical or electronic) and normally irreversible, whereas prose on the page is always individually paced in reception, forward and often back. But at the many ways this difference licenses such a comparison between movies and prose motion, rather than silencing it, these next two chapters are aimed.

Their goal in moving between media is to find mobilized in verbal style the prose counterpart of cinema's twin frames, as distinguished in the second chapter: the big Frame of the moving screen picture together (always together) with the little frame of its composite photographic imprints, as those are subject to the traditional understanding of "frame-advance" in the spinning past of the celluloid reel in projection. Movies derive at base from the instantaneous replacement of these so-called photograms (and their pixel equivalents since) in generating the actual motion on which pictured movement depends. As with syllabic sequence in syntactic perception, within and across phrases and whole sentences, the two scales of "action" are in fact all but simultaneous—and functionally inseparable. Hence my heuristic typography for the momentum at play and at stake in each "time-based" medium: Fframe-advance. "One necessity of movies is that the thread of film itself must be drawn across the light," writes philosopher Stanley Cavell in *The World Viewed* about the process in its celluloid form.[1] His quiet distinction between medium and matter ("movies" versus "film itself") remains, in this sense, well within our ongoing double "Fframe" of reference.

One necessity of films is the moving of film. Cavell might have spoken, instead, about 'one necessity of viewing'—where single filmic pictures, light-seared transparencies, photo imprints, must reproduce themselves at thousands of times their plastic dimensions, and in continuous serial disappearance at that, on the reflective rather than backlit screen. Only then do the photograms on the strip, those single pieces of lowercase *film*, scale up to "the film" so called—with the masked frameline breaks on the spool giving way to the mobile screen Frame (uppercase for scalar emphasis). When one entertains it, the literary equivalent of this overall narrative field is the discursive *frame of reference* in any one textual passage, mounted of course on the internal struts and frets of the prose *framework*. In my composite coinage, such, again, is the structuring Fframe-advance in literary as well as screen fiction. In process, in procession, it is in just this sense that the projected rectangular image or shot (F) subsumes its optic increments on the strip, its photogram frames (f), the way a syntactic span (S) does the amassing syllabic units (s) of its grammar, one lexical unit advanced after another.

In verbal experience too, as much as in cinematic projection, meaning far exceeds the serial rudiments of inscription. One necessity of writing is wording. One necessity of reading is that words must be drawn past us, at first pass irreversibly, in the strands of syntax they constitute as well as in the strings of enunciated lettering that make them up. Necessary but not sufficient, this condition. Even when resultant threads of sense emerge, pulled taut or not, certain irregular fibers and kinks of phrased meaning may often invite immediate "rerun"—in a way unavailable to normal screen viewing. Yet the parallel still holds between media—at least holds out some promise of apt comparison. Subsuming the spooled band of a celluloid image track to the perceptual thread of action on screen, what could otherwise be designated as the F/film distinction—with the moving image riding on, overriding, the individual filmic cell—can be productively correlated with a similar tiered process in the act of narrative writing. And its reading. Alphabetic characters disappear into phonemes into syllables into words in the phrasing of characterization—as well, of course, as of scene or event.

Beyond this generalization, in conjuring with the idea of a *particularly* cinematic sentence, or with its possibility at least, no priority need be given to authors who have made film's "universal language" a signature feature of their style, beginning famously with the montage aesthetic of postcubist modernism in a writer like John Dos Passos, or in a different way, penetrating to the skids of word formation itself, in James Joyce or Gertrude Stein, including verbal channels of jagged seriality in everything from alphabetic flicker effects to jump-cut clauses.[2] Given the punctual linkage of word forms under sudden duress in such writing, strange surprises are pried loose from conflicted lexical junctures. These impacted syllabic segues or cross-fades flare into observation by analogy with precisely the variable tracks of that defining cinematic Fframe-advance first posited in connection with unexpected inflections of tense in a time-based medium—and next to be given a chapter of its own for a further sampling of its scalar ramifications and their prose and poetic equivalents. The densenings in question occur, by productive disturbance, in a writing whose gradations are thus seen—and heard—inching out the full reach of their descriptive scope not just syllable by syllable, but sometimes letter by abruptly unfettered letter. Process is activated by increments now routine, now subtly self-correcting, now abrupt and startling. As with cinematography, so with lexical sequence: the off-frame impends, impinges.

Associated with such calculated d/effects of inscription attendant on this quasi-filmic verbal process are the more or less comparable slippages of "tense" (sampled in Auster among others) in the alternate time-based media of text and screen narrative, including—as we're soon to screen it for analysis—the prose motoring of fast-forward synopsis in particular, where separate temporal settings, in a Nabokov passage, are strung together in accelerated resumé if not actual time-lapse. But unless the "more or less comparable" is to be *too* freely entertained—and thus of limited appreciative or analytic use—another question must precede any such analogous readings across media. How is it that the activation of a verbal code can tangibly resemble the fusion of discrete images in the piecing together of a visual system? It can't, and doesn't. Resemblance isn't the issue, but rather operational equivalence—so that, in tapping (as writer) or probing (as reader or critic) the internal mechanics of the prose medium and its material basis, in conscious comparison with the seriality of the film image, one mode of narrative may call to view, the other to mind, the workings of its sometimes recognized counterpart: always with that emphasis on the *counter*. Only in this way could literary syntax comport for analysis with that very different "private grammar" of film mentioned in the stage version of *The Last Tycoon*.

So that, in imagining the cinematic valence of narrative writing, it should be stressed again that nothing uniquely specular need be summoned. In this spirit, the next chapter's return to Pound's three types of poesis from the introduction (melo-, phano-, and logo-; aural, visual, and verbal)—though bearing on his imagist rejection of Tennysonian music—has a more encompassing import. Only when examined against the audiovisuality (the melophanic mix, if you will) of cinematic transition (cuts, fades, overlapping dialogue, etc., including the kind of aerial "long shot," and tacit swelling score, metaphorically deployed in *The Last Tycoon*) does the particular linguistic "editing" of narrative poetry or prose come into full relief—not in some medial purity, but nonetheless in the verbal integrity, the internal coherence, of its linguistic grain. Which no analogy with "motion pictures" is meant to level, but rather to set off and investigate.

Not the Same Difference

In tracking, comparatively, the reigning time-based media of modern narrative production, there is no ignoring their divergent modes of timing per se—automatized on screen, voluntary for the prose reader. For just this difference (in their differential pulse) is the reason, in a book like this, for the comparison in the first place: the better to know the powers of the latter in regard to the former, prose sensed anew in the equally discontinuous light—but mechanized and irreversible stride—of motion picturing. Cinema, screen narrative: whether spun into motion in the spooling of celluloid or shuffled across the bitmap grid in digital sequencing. By contrast either way, regarding either regime, prose operates otherwise. These last two chapters would be going nowhere fast if they weren't rooted in the *notably different* medial structures (and audience protocols) they juxtapose—and attempt, nonetheless, to correlate stylistically.

The analogy at the nub of these final paired chapters, then, in all their appreciative exertion, isn't for a moment intended to warrant a blurring, let alone a merger, of material forms, but rather a reversible *translation* between them: as in each case a mode of narrative delivery palpably inscribed—*textualized*—in and between, and behind and before, the forward march of plot. On the score of such ingrained narrative momentum, the point isn't that one reads the increments of prose the way one watches the flux of cinema, even when the latter is facilitated at the elective pace—and pause—of home video. Beyond the everyday nature of skimming and skipping in the waywardness—or tactical willfulness—of the reading eye, including its quick recuperative returns to the flow of sentence and sense, prose invites its quite distinct forms of doubling back: through echoes, second thoughts, mental addenda, disruptive undertones, what have you. It does all this in a very different way from the cognitive hiccups or segues—call them the disjunct visual tissue—sent to the screen by the motored pulsations of montage.

On this generalized model of translation (or, better, transposition) from one medium to another, any notion of functional exchange—for the experimenting student writer, for instance, as in examples to follow, testing out some movie-like moves in wording—begins in a distinct mode of analysis whose intensity *is itself transferable*. When approximating the cinematic in narrative sentencing—say the observant seriality of the tracking shot, the magnified emphases of the close-up, the iterative fixation of the freeze-frame, the variably timed cadenza of the fade-out, or the doubling overlay (and potential ambiguity) of superimposition—the point, far from exact equivalence, is that any effort at devising approximate ingenuities in prose would serve to disclose, and maximize in action, their own intrinsic medial grain. And this is vividly the case in the creative reading of prose as well as its creative writing. Ranging, under close enough attention, anywhere from the scale of a "jump cut" between paragraphs to a recursive "loop effect" of anaphoric syntax, the act of *thinking cinematically* about prose fiction becomes its own unique method of *verbal* close looking. So that, at the narrowest scope in the phasing of sequence, even a flickering surprise of phonetic juncture—whether or not elicited on the page by visible alphabetic crossover, or just summoned by silent enunciation—can, under scrutiny, or just simply underway, ring not merely reverberant but narratively true. And, in so doing, can achieve its productive cognitive skid at roughly the same relative scale—minimal, constitutive, primal—as effects deriving from the jammed or accelerated frame-advances of the optic strip.

The division of labor across this book so far has hardly been offered as evenhanded or cleanly compartmentalized. Together, the first two chapters made for a combined exposition, however spottily illustrated, on the ways of the paged word: the lexicon as variously recruited—and transmuted—by the structure of literary sentences in their exerted temporality, by turns diachronic (word history), synchronic (paced wording), and discursively positioned (tense structure). And by their subvocal enunciation in each case. The brunt of that discussion was more stylistic than narrative or phenomenological—drilling down on how words work, rather than on the emotional investments they trigger or more slowly evince, the inhabited terrain they may depict. The brief subsequent chapter turned to this latter issue in the exaggerated case of a stage performance where the embodied human designations of literary language come into, and out of, impersonation before our listening eyes. It was a chapter not preoccupied with a theatricalized fiction per se, in some familiar brand of adaptation study, so much as with the embodied epiphenomena of verbal agency and event in any theater of words. Yet that interlude in an actual auditorium did find a way forward from *Gatsby*, under orchestration by *Gatz*, to a further purchase on sentence structure in later Fitzgerald, including his own approximation—or evocation—of cinematic perspectives and focal lengths.

These final chapters on filmic writing are even further removed from adaptation study—in either direction, whether in the filming of prestige novels or the "novelization" of hit films. Both more narrowly and more broadly, discussion concerns, instead, writing itself, neither novels as genre nor theatrical or film scripts, but writing etched in the substrate of language: a prose now panoramic, now tightly framed, here rushed in its readjustments, there dialing in by dilation on a single moment, no sooner shape-shifting than iterative—a prose that may, in any case, be understood, and practiced, under the sign of the cinematic. Where the idea of editing offers one common denominator. Flow another. Overlap and disjunction as well: say superimpositions and cuts. None of this has anything to do with writing for the movies, nor (or at least not much) with imitating their narrative materials in story form, but rather with seeing filmic sequence as itself a mode of inscription that may harbor lessons for prose composition. Film is a "writing with movement," it has been famously said (by philosopher Jean-François Lyotard)—or elsewhere a mode of *camera stylo* (film theorist Alexandre Astruc): inscriptive, authorial. Conversely, but still comparatively, style in literature can be characterized as a *movement in writing*, where words are released or throttled, shoved ahead or bent back on themselves, in the momentum of sentencing. How does one respond to this in appreciative reading, test for its lessons, attend the inner energy of its kinetographic force? To ask this is only provisionally to demarcate one minor facet of literary response, to be sure, but one that may have an unexpected medial yield in any writer's (or reader's) strivenfor acclimation to the intricacies and grip, the sweep and flash, of prose disclosure.

Two clarifications, however obvious they may seem, no doubt deserve airing at this threshold of extended demonstration. The distributed weight of lexical choices, the cross-linked balance of syllabic sounds, the fluctuating pace of syntax in its various lurches and reversals—all of these, in their own temporal dimension, clocked over the length of an inventive sentence—are, at the same time, timed to the narrative material they deliver: synchronized with the themes for which their own material texture is the internal dynamic. And this, of course, in the same manner that, on the film screen, the camera is set in scanning motion, or its image shunted to some abruptly cut-in substitute, by the larger rhythms of plot, whose narrative (rather than plastic) thread depends on—while necessarily forgetting—the wheeling band of transparencies that spin out its action. I stress this bit of common sense about style timed to topic in literature (as comparably in film) because, in what follows, it is not always easy to explicate such connections briefly in a given fictional instance. And it is easy to see why. Layered, cumulative, vibrant or plangent or ironic, the full narrative scope that the power of a given sentence may compress, in whatever comparison to the film medium it may invite, will need sometimes to be taken more on faith here than on evidence—even with the generally well-known texts brought in for discussion. This book would be three times as long otherwise. That alone should sweeten this caveat about stinted literary *readings* in a chapter devoted instead to concentrated acts of reading.

In all this there's an important further premise (wrapped in a reiterated caveat) that may sound too much like apology without instances to illustrate, however loosely, its claim. For imprecision is precisely the point. A certain cut slack in correlations offers a further leeway for verbal apprehension. Parallels in this zone of transmedial comparison need a good degree of latitude, though not laxity, to be useful. Or put it the other way round—in the form of nagging uncertainties regarding a contemplated or boldly posited filmic equivalent for a given linguistic effect: Is that verbal maneuver really more like a match cut than a cross-fade? Doesn't that grammatical disruption or impasse, that choked-off rhythm, still feel more like rapid fade-out than stop-action? These hesitations locate the very point. The fact that there are no strict counterparts between medial devices is what most suggestively tests—along an always tentative, and instructively restless, axis of comparison—the uniqueness of the language event. Such is always the generative drama of wording in making (its way to) meaning—whether in the looping or jam-up of syllables, the parallelism of phrasing, the junctures of punctuated syntax, let alone the lexical cast of "image" in the literary mode of figuration. And here again the closely related caveat. In regard to the healthy looseness of alignment between phonics, diction, and syntax, on the one hand, cinematic engineering, on the other, it is crucial to insist—for this mode of stylistic rather that contextual analysis—that the writers taken up for study don't have to have seen movies, or even to have written in an age when that would have been possible.

Thomas Hardy stopped writing novels just before motion pictures arrived on the narrative scene, unless one thinks of him as one of their inventors. It is in this tacit latter sense that Terry Eagleton adduces the case of Hardy's novelistic perspectives—with their tragic diminishment of heroes and heroines—in connection not only, and perhaps surprisingly, with the satiric dwarfings of personality in comic writing, his book's topic, but with a cinematic model for them. Such, he writes, is the "double optic" one "finds in the fiction of Thomas Hardy, a novelist who will first park his camera, so to speak, behind a character's shoulder, then pull it back and broaden the shot to show him or her as a tiny speck crawling across a vast natural landscape."[3] The loophole of that "so to speak" is telling—and discussion to come will be trying, instead, to speak more directly to literary functions in the mode of such analogy. It's not that Eagleton's figure of speech for Hardy's narrative trajectories is wrong. For our purposes, though, it isn't wrung from anything specific about the prose. In Eagleton's trope, Hardy begins with a fractionally displaced POV shot (its over-the-shoulder approximation) and ends in a diminishing reverse zoom. Actual instances on screen are legion in computer-generated sci-fi sequences, for instance, in which the human subject, victim or avenger, is dwarfed by a pullback to the alien hordes or spacecraft armadas shrinking that figure by the relativities of digital scale, music swelling in correlation with the widening view. Not to mention, in TV or film adaptations of Hardy himself, helicopter shots of an exiled Tess Durbeyfield, or some other defeated figure, crossing the withering vista of a forlorn heath.

Or for a classic, predigital prototype, take this legendary (almost-single) take: beginning with the leftward pan that tracks a rushing Scarlet O'Hara, intermittently glimpsed behind and between limping soldiers and surgical carts (opening the most famous shot sequence from *Gone with the Wind*) on the way to—and then very much beyond—her shocked close-up at the edge of the railroad yard where the Confederate wounded are massed in agony. No reverse POV from her assaulted gaze, just a sudden (as if repulsed) cut, in immediately recoil, to a medium shot of her momentarily frozen dismay—and then the renowned pullback from ongoing lateral pan to bloody panorama. In this, even before dialogue spells it out, her private mission—to find a doctor for help with a childbirth—is rendered "absurd" (as the doctor eventually says) by the disproportionate scope of mutilation, pain, and death that encompasses her stumbling leftward motion. A motion that continues until we can barely pick out her figure from the ground of devastation spread beneath the flapping and tattered Confederate flag in overhead close-up, behind which her tiny form finally disappears. All the while the image's continued tracking, minimized by distance itself, is overborne by the lifting crane shot that subsumes her human movement to the scale of a gradually achieved (and, yes, Hardyesque) trivializing omniscience, with the Confederate banner fluttering in the infernal heat being a kind of title shot for a cause quite palpably gone with the wind. This is the sort of cinematic bravura that finds no immediate prose equivalent, except in a metaphor like Eagleton's "double optic." Published three years before the 1939 film, the closest Mitchell's serviceable prose comes to such a nightmare dynamic stepped off by widening lateral camerawork is when it seems to cue that first jump cut of repulsion with the delayed assonant clutch of its main clause: "As she rounded the corner . . . and came in full view of the depot and the tracks, she h*alt*ed app*all*ed."[4] There, in the echo chamber of a single recursive syllable, is the sound cinema of a sentence's own dissonant staccato music. Indeed, though period style prohibited, that internal stutter of *alt/all* might have triggered, rather than a distancing cut, in our terms a freeze-Fframe, where iterated photograms (rather than phonemes) might have been found running in place to sustain the very picture of sickened arrest.

What follows on screen, in scaling away from Scarlett's diminished figure, does indeed bear relation to both the tracking glides and overhead ironies of scale in Hardy's narrative "camerawork" of a heroine like Tess. His actual scene-setting prose can deploy a synesthetic blend of scent and newborn chirp as springboard for a camera movement all style's own: "On a thyme-scented, bird-hatching morning in May, between two and three years after the return from Trantridge—silent, reconstructive years for Tess Durbeyfield—she left her home for the second time." So begins, with the insertion of grammar's own dubiously recuperative pause, the third "Phase" of Tess's tragedy, with the play on a "time"-enriched animal fertility left behind—and this along a progression clocked by unresting determination: "She went through Stourcastle *without pausing and onward to* a junction of highways" (emphasis added)—a hasty phrasing in which the play of negated progressive and sheer forwarding adverb catches the emotionally forced march of her departure in syntax's own version of a rapid tracking shot. One inconsequential village succeeds another, as if in a further montage of dissolves. "Tess did not stop at Weatherbury, after this long drive, further than to make a slight nondescript meal . . .," where the temporal "further" seems fading off at once into the spatial farther-along of the next sentence's telescopic vanishing point in its rhythmically extended grammar, each semibreathless syntactic subordination ("in which," "that was") an extra widening of the perspectival lens: "Thence she started on foot, basket in hand, to reach the wide upland of heath dividing this district from the low-lying meads of a further valley in which the dairy stood that was the aim and end of her day's pilgrimage." When has "Thence" gotten so dynamically out ahead of a false and fleeting sense of "then"? When have nonrestrictive phrases ("dividing . . .") and clauses ("in which," "that was") been so dramatic in their unrolling freedom from punctuation? Or since when has a mild hendiadys like "aim and end" seemed less redundant? All contribute, step by step, to this progress marked by optic recession in the prose of a fateful long shot.

Still, any such actual filmic tension, as in the film version of *Gone With the Wind*, operating between close-up and long-take traveling shot within the "private grammar" of cinema (that phrase, again, from the stage version of *The Last Tycoon*), may nonetheless trigger not just the kind of "so to speak" indulged in by Eagleton but the further discernible sense of a certain shared reliance, in both media, on the pace of device and the cues of perspective, the angle of embodied vision and the encroachment of its scenographic surround. It is in this spirit that the examples ahead continue to be far more specifically *stylistic* than Eagleton's—though no less willing to entertain cinematic effects in the kinetic prose of writers, from Dickens and Melville to Hardy, who wrote before cinema. I have spoken about the limited exemplification available from a brief roster of examples. Selectively chosen, though, such passages adumbrate more than they can prove—or fully contextualize. To this assumption I hope my reader is already predisposed. As well as to the sense, before or after movies, that each instance of cinematographic prose, though not oxymoronic, remains medium specific in precisely its linguistic rather than visual dynamic. As we found at the end of the preceding chapter, Fitzgerald's Hollywood novel, *The Love of the Last Tycoon*, continued to do what *Gatz* had already done—with its literal voice "translation" in the "staging" of *Gatsby*—in highlighting, by contrast, what is so inherently literary, so figurative, about the author's style, even when it seems to be approximating cinematic immediacy, transparency, or scopic purview. It is this distinction between screen images in transit and either depiction or figuration in prose that will orient both evidence and investigation in the case to be made from here out.

Schooled by the Spool: Prose Montage

There is, to be sure, an internal build across these five chapters—not just a parceling out of emphasis. Language on the literary page, in the passage from eye to the "paging" of an inner ear; literary speech on stage—so far so good: the start of a rough verbal anatomy in a survey of the word's audiovisual ways, subvocal against intoned. And now a third facet of the question, its perspective falling somewhere between alternate common definitions of the term "screened": sheltered, hidden, camouflaged, on the one hand; broadcast, projected, put out for display, on the other. On the lookout for prose cinematography when taking one's seat in front of a novelistic page, how exactly, in yet a further sense, does one "screen" for such features? In this comparative exploration, the work of screening is a sifting, a filtering. So this is a chapter about literary language—scanned and sorted, winnowed—for motion picture analogues. And vice versa, as inclination dictates: movies rerun in imagination in order to grasp some machinated equivalents (and rough models) in screen pacing for literary prose. With the result that, in a certain laboratory (or classroom) version of this chapter's considerations, movies can be tightly surveyed—again screened, sieved—for "discursive" parallels. These intuited analogues in lexical or syntactic maneuver are formal counterparts best understood within a broad constellation of structuring increments and transitions in the shared narrative work of prose and motion pictures—complete with "grammatical" compounding and subordination, with modifiers and amplifiers, appositions and antitheses, inertial sequence and reversal—rather than narrowly construed according to the nonlinguistic codes of the editing shears per se.

One question above all drives these final two chapters: What is a cinematic sentence? No answer need be settled on in order eventually to have set a number of things straight—or at least to have set them going in an experimental mode of response. To begin with, the question of a cinematic prose soon devolves, productively enough, into discriminations—within the very idea of image—between the verbal metaphor and the photographic picture. And beyond that, the linguistic question is more pointedly syntactic. So—even with some likely contenders on record already—one keeps asking whether there is something not just discernible, but generalizable, that one could call cinematic in sentence structure, which is to say in its montage of words? Not a question about some mode of filmic syntax organizing a narrative moment on screen: that's indisputable. But a cinematographic articulation in language alone? What balance of focus and velocity, of angle and frame, even of aspect ratios perhaps, may be experimented with by the pacing of prose that might call up the dynamics of our long-dominant narrative medium? Aside from the vistas wedged open by metaphor, what is it about the gait of grammar, its starts (either sense) and arrests, its ambivalent overlays and reloads, that keeps us going forward, even when its own motion may in certain narrative instances seem rotary, even ironically circular? What analogous relation, in short, does the word as unit bear to the chain of photographic images spun into action by classic film, or, since then, transformed by pixelated frame shifts in the bitmap arrays of digital projection? Or is it more accurately the case that subsidiary alphabetic letters should be thought to precipitate, almost subliminally, the baseline of motion in their rapid aggregation into syllables, into words? And what difference would this clarified level of differentiation make?

Answers at this scope tend to be offered up, tend to *surface*, only in engaged reading. And then, caught up in just such a topographic metaphor, one finds oneself reading, or at least trying to conceive, the stratum they have been surfaced *from*. On the cinematic side of the comparative ledger, even before lexical sequences are closely engaged, distinctions are helpful going in. The screening that concerns this experiment in prose study, ultimately this roving tutorial, is not so much the continuous becoming of a film world in projection, as a traditional strand of phenomenological thought has it, as in writers from André Bazin through Cavell and Gilles Deleuze. Still less can this chapter or the next afford to settle for a literary poetics in which, according to media theorist Friedrich Kittler, it is only by the suppression of linguistic awareness, eliding the work of differential signification into a fantasized vocal continuum, that "poetry could let its film roll."⁵ On the contrary, the possibility of a cinematic sentence depends on film grasped not as a spun continuum but as articulatory *system*, its medial substrate at once variably spaced and paced, discontinuous from one microsecond to the next, and edited on the serial strip into a syntax of enunciation all its own. The only aspect of cinema that rolls automatically and unimpeded is the spool; everything on it is a manifest disjunctive construct, built on a palpably sequenced arrhythmic thread of optic data. The cinemachine manifests as a (dis)continuous shift of gears: an engine of signage in action. Once again: Fframe-advance.

The ways of the word, then, are retained as topic in what remains—but situated here by speculative comparison with the screening of visual text. It is in this manner that these closing chapters have one foot in film history, one in literary history—and its pedagogy. How would this stance, though, help teach not stories, but "writing" itself, inscription, across media? And why? Why, that is, take this line of approach? In my case—full disclosure—it was and is partly, and tactically, because my university's English Department had mounted a new creative writing major, limiting the number of elective courses in "literature and culture" that could be offered by a dwindling faculty. In order to teach cinematic analysis on a par with literary study as part of a culture of narrative expectations and medial formats, as I had repeatedly done, but in a way that would help meet and staff our new course demands, it occurred to me that I could float such lessons in a way that might directly appeal to apprentice writers in an age of dominant visual literacy. So here is the description that went up on the department website under that loaded lectographic title "Reading Movies for Prose Writers":

> This class will concentrate on the rhetorical and structural strategies, and nuances, of narrative cinema, both filmic and digital, as they might be productively mapped onto student ventures in narrative writing. Direct address and other ironies of "the fourth wall"; the syntax of parallel montage,

ellipsis, jump cuts, matches on action, dissolves, cross-fades, and superimpositions; flashbacks and flash-forwards; the closural grammar of freeze-frame and iris-out; plus the broader management of frame tales, depth of field, objective and subjective POV, other varieties of focalization and the optic equivalents of free indirect discourse—all this, as well as the potential yield of metatextual reflexes in the mode of self-commenting narration, will guide our investigations into established film techniques (always with ears to the ground for their verbal equivalents). Screen examples will range, in a variety of clips and full screenings, from silent screen comedy through the classic genres of detective noir and sci-fi to the genre-bending experiments of European high modernism and its influence on the so-called New American Cinema, including the latter's aftermath in the offbeat narrative strategies of certain indie productions and the recent trend in hypermediated laptop and Facebook narration, where silent film intertitles may be thought to resurface in formats related to electronic text messaging. The main focus will be on mastering the structure of screen storytelling—as a "reading competence" in its own right. But examples of cinematographic borrowings or parallels in major literary fiction, as well as essays commenting on them, will also be discussed in conjunction with frequent brief writing assignments meant to experiment with—from scratch or in revision of students' previous work—the potential dynamic advantages of a cinematic prose.

"A cinematic prose": whatever that is. I leave it for the enrolled students to ask, or to find out for themselves, slowly but—with luck—surely. Apparent from the start, though, whatever such prose might amount to, any viable sense of a kinetic writing would have to do with how word order—within the whole order of words—moves us to mold and pace our literary response from one unit of perception or conception to the next, spurs our cognitive production of the described scene in its unfolding phases, often involving their own irregular intervals of grammatical reaction time. Though far removed from any professional goal of writing for the movies, the point is to see how writing moves.

One further thing is clear, at least, on the side of the decidedly unintended. The goal of such a course isn't in the least to mine the movies for their two obvious "literary" yields: storylines and dialogue. Students have learned their dialogue—on and off the page, the very rhythms of their speech—from media anyway and already. Movies and TV can't help but continue their passive lessons in that vein, by cultural osmosis. What writers might stand to learn less intuitively from screen imaging, in an actual stylistic pedagogy, is how to "edit" their syntax at the compositional level, not just in revision: how to splice and diversify and propel and reverse attention, how to reframe and hold a note, a notation, a moment of notice—as well as how, and when, to sweep past, how to give a rhythm to syntax in the naming, and predication, of thing or event. Under instruction in such a spotty tutorial would be the very structuring of an inhabited narrative space according to shifting foci set by the tempo of enunciation itself, a world articulated as much as described. Such, then, where and when one comes upon—or construes—it, is none other than the cinematographic sentence. It is a unit of assumed (say provisional) authorial intent brought to the uncurtained display of its time-based content from the private theater balcony—and strategic mental vantage point—of sequenced audiovisual response: the perch of appreciative purchase in the headspace of materialization, of visualization, of temporal immersion. So it can't hurt to say again that none of this has anything to do with writing screenplays, only with the play of images on screen: moving pictures in their relation to grammatical momentum, an energy inherent to prose in any period, from the hand of writers as different as Dickens, who knew no movies, and Faulkner, who wrote for them. Such is the spectrum of my in-class examples—and here in this chapter as well. Analysis moves deliberately between committedly cineaste authors and earlier stylists with no plausible thought to automated image projection in the motions their prose inscribes even while describing.

Prose Machination: Beyond Nuts and Bolts

An anecdote, first, and in fact an incidental course yield. The second iteration of this seminar came round, in 2020, during the first academic fall of the COVID-19 crisis. Endemic to the broad constraints of this pandemic, instruction was as online as the syllabus, for which, at the last moment, I decided on an ironic epigraph—given the strictly video manifestation of the course this time out (if "out" is even the word): not to be confused, as the students often unwittingly do, with an "epitaph" for the whole venture in advance. I engraved in pixels, that is, an excerpt from E. M. Forster's 1909 sci-fi story, "The Machine Stops," in which he prognosticates a worldwide wired catacomb, if not "net," of attenuated screen sociality. Hoping that his title would not be an omen of the proverbial "blue screen of death" in my Zoom ministrations, I was certainly granting the dim prospects that my pointedly chosen quotation conjured for the vividness of instruction's audiovisual register—and here, ironically enough, in a course designed to inspire prose composition by devoted attention to just such a synchronized rhythm of image and sound in screen dynamics.

The Forster passage is about a musicologist giving a video lecture, in dull optical resolution, from her isolation cubicle in an underground future dystopia: "The clumsy system of public gatherings had been long since abandoned; neither Vashti nor her audience stirred from their rooms. Seated in her armchair she spoke, while they in their armchairs heard her, fairly well, and saw her, fairly well." Quite apart from my own speaking image, and however I would finally manage to handle the film evidence in this "interactive" mode of secondary rescreening, what I knew from the start that I'd be wanting the students to see as clearly as possible—and then to hear as well, at least fairly well, in their own thereby energized prose—is the potential drive and variety of what I wanted them to contemplate as a kind a cinematographic prose. For which their own literary study in other "classrooms," if now only numbered "courses" during the pandemic, would offer not only many a tacit model, for fictional style both before and after the invention of cinema, but the site of diverse analytic rewards in traditional critical essays. That's why these two chapters, unlike my syllabus, are less an exercise in pedagogy than in what I've taken, over the course of several monographs, to calling narratography. It is the kind of effect that Forster's own prose illustrates in the acid tact of that parallelism above, with its ironic phrasal echoes: the prose of what we might now dub interfacial reciprocity. Syntactic tact, with its sardonic adverbial echo. Elsewhere, phonetic syllabification answers Forster's call as well when the rhythm of discourse shifts deftly in that same story from parallelism to chiasm across a cause-and-effect pivot—this as the universal "machine" does indeed begin to stop. "The air, too, was *foul. Loud* were the complaints"—a clamor continuous with the fetid air that carries it. Call it, in dated cinematic terms, a phonetic "wipe." Call it an inverted match-on-sound. Either way, writing has the plasticity (without any present imagery) of cinemachination.

134   Chapter 4

But Forster is more openly "cinematic" yet, or say "mimetic," as students reared on sci-fi set pieces were quick to realize as they read on in the story. The "camerawork" involved emerges, redoubled, in a marked interplay between two passages that answer to, and animate, each other in no less than metagrammatical terms. First, a futuristic airliner rises in its mounting propulsion from the claustrophobic underworld of wired cubicles into the devastated upper atmosphere. It does so in a prose equivalent of the vertical pan for rocket launches—and the adjacent spatial details they outstrip—that sci-fi cinema had not yet invented (in its technical arsenal) by the 1909 date of Forster's writing: "Then the sides of the vestibule seemed to melt together, as do the passages that we see in dreams, the lift vanished, the Book that had been dropped slid to the left and vanished, polished tiles rushed by like a stream of water, there was a slight jar, and the air-ship, issuing from its tunnel, soared above the waters of a tropical ocean." From the passenger's eye view, here is a driven syntactic series in a literally escalating POV shot—with fast-paced clauses tracking the descriptive sequence as if filtered through the nervousness of the transported video lecturer caught in frazzled transit beyond her comfort zone. In what one might call again (as with the wind-fluttered remnants of Confederate iconography in *Gone With the Wind*) the "title shot" of the story's first (of three) subsections, "The Air-Ship," we move here, that is, not just on with the plot but as if upward, and do so with a genuine syntactic propulsion across consequentially linked clauses—though at first so loosely bonded as to seem like comma-spliced separate framings of a disorienting takeoff. Interrupted only by the subordinate clause of simile ("as do . . ."), a true serial grammar (recuperating the seeming run-ons) is finally confirmed by "and" before the sixth, last, and longest clause of motion, where "and the air*sh*ip, *iss*uing" lets off, as well, some extra sibilant steam at the swift juncture of its punctuated frame shift. Laying further stress on an accelerating and even phonetically propelled effect, the glide from "lift" to "left" ("lift vanished . . . slid to the left") is a fleeting part of that leaving-behind marked also by the twice-sounded fricative of "*v*anished." Under such lexical pressure, it is only through the extra progressive boost ("issuing") in the overdrive of that last participial phrase, with its further syntactic shove, that the final release, the ultimate liftoff, is achieved.

And what goes up must come down—here by that self-conscious grammatical mirroring alluded to above. The ship's previous vertical acceleration, pulsing across the clausal series of its quick serial reframings, is a narrative vector that finds its textual structure soon diametrically reversed. As the story's next section opens with the ship's scheduled landing, the previous rhythm appears played back in a condensed and narratively chiastic recap whose prepositional phrases, rather than clauses, click off one of the clearest cases in modern writing of reverse-action drama in a grammar of exaggerated inversion. Backpedaled in these precipitous cadences is the character's nervous approach to the previous embarkation: "By a vestibule, by a lift, by a tubular railway, by a platform, by a sliding door—by reversing all the steps of her departure," though with the clipped rapidity of the "by" grammar carrying as well, in recall of the previous optical sequence, a sense of 'passing by' as well as 'by means of'—we arrive not at 'Vashti arrived,' but more mimetic yet, in a final integral inversion, "did Vashti arrive at her son's room, which exactly resembled her own." Tracing the fulcrum-like grammatical economy of elevation and descent, this bifold example—a mirroring syntactic diptych—was especially useful as illustration early in my rebooted course "Reading Movies for Prose Writers." But no such pictured motion is needed in motivating the cinematic analogy to motion picturing in any number of other passages called up by such an approach, where the closely tracked cellular units, or constituent frames, of phrase and clause are caught in the act of generating narrative's inherent perspective—and this in the conflated sense, micro within Macro, of its overall, and everywhere coterminous, Fframe-advance.

Half a decade before cinema with *Tess* (1891), a decade and a half after its invention with Forster: the difference makes no (material) matter in the texture of prose. With both authors, and many more, their writing, their inscription, can be equally cinematographic. One of this treatment's premises, again: that the urgencies of moving-picture writing get out ahead of any actual chronology in screen technique. Building on that twice-ventured course syllabus in this chapter, analysis is now duly concerned, amid the many ways of the word, with language being "screened" in itself after all: not in adaptation but in primary activation, not just sifted out for examination but enacted as quasi-optic prompt in the mind's eye—or, of course, its ear as well, given the arrival of sound cinema as further kinetic model. By filmic analogy in such an undergraduate writing course, one does indeed end up attending to the serial pace of words synchromeshed with meaning in the filing past of their organizing grammar. Through the earned aperture of decipherment, we screen the prose spool into its designated virtual reality (its phenomenological parameters) by the unreeled means of wording's incremental momentum: a process often indiscernible bit by bit—as, on screen, frame by frame, and since then by the flux of digital bytes. But some lexical and even sublexical features of this subliminal continuum do surface to consciousness as operable verbal pivots, part of larger "shot" patterns and overlaps: developmental phases—incremental facets—in the phrasing of a depicted discursive scene. So another way to put the question behind "Reading Movies for Prose Writers": If all writing is screened in one sense, projected as scenic material for an inward eye and ear, what can some particular writing—in its letteral, then lexical, then full textual scope—stand (never quite still) to learn from actual celluloid or pixel sequencing in an alternate medium altogether? The issue is in part a matter of scale: of reading's virtual world versus its linguistic infrastructure, turning again on the renewed and specified question from page to page, paragraph to paragraph: What is cinematic about *this particular* sentence? Or about *these* as well, hard on the heels of the last?

At the lower level of Fframe-advance, of course, any analogy between script and film—not between novel and film script, but between two kinds of imprint, alphabetic and photocellular (or pixelated)—is bound to highlight the discontinuities of the signifier in lexical inscription, including the alphabetic slippage and sound play to which literary fiction can be made prone. Hence prose's most compelling bid for occasional correlation with film's sliding means: namely, and by a burst of syllabic simulation on my part, with cinematography's engineered method of eliding exactly the frameline's punctual rips in the amassed trip of each strip's serial transparencies as pulled past the aperture by sprocket clasps in the apparatus of apparition. Language, too, discloses under attention, in short, its own mechanism of succession, with separate but equal powers—and recuperable vulnerabilities—in relation to those of cinematic automatism. It is therefore no exaggeration to say, as borne out in examples coming, that any number of "cinematic sentences"—when trained on the screen image as topic—can even find ways to trace the default of the image(d) track itself in certain of their own syntactic lapses and jam-ups.

So let me make perfectly clear what was to be expected of that curricular experiment, "Reading Movies for Prose Writers," even as its guiding emphasis is, in turn, experimentally transferred now to a discursive chapter with no illustrative frame grabs, let alone clips, but those of prose itself. Absent all home screenings or in-class DVD excerpts in these pages, what remains of the cinematic homology for the motoring drama of prose is left—and no bad thing—to the writing alone, where I'm trusting that a latent instructional aura, the potential for a certain learning curve, persists beyond any actual curricular setting. Even there in class, though, in dialogue with matriculated creative writers, learning by transmedial example is not proffered as an applied method, just a practiced disposition toward the temporal flow of story. Modeling in this broad sense is not imitation; it can come by immersion, indirection, approximation, say even inspiration, not by a rigorous agenda. Moreover, a curricular enterprise like that course's venture in an inverted "visual literacy" is after something less programmatic yet: a freer permeation of fine-grained cinematics in transfer to the fabrications of prose kinesis.

It is for just this reason, nonetheless, that both of the deliberated rectangles in question, page and screen, benefit from a concerted "technical" attention to their machinations—if not from the categorizing terminology that usually backs and braces it. Without insistent theoretical extrapolation or specialist vocabulary, still the "technical" is our access to technique. Where less is never more; where "overdoing" it, in the reach for transmedial equivalents, might resemble exactly the therapeutic do-over that a given stylistic effort of the student's own may thrive on. Everything depends on bearing down, zeroing in, listening up. In any such workshop environment, the goal isn't, in the long run, to channel master modernists like Woolf or Faulkner, let alone earlier grand stylists like Dickens or James, and certainly not the dated lather of Thomas Wolfe's prose, let (further) alone the notion of writing Spielbergian or Kubrickian or Tarantinovian or even Hitchcockian prose. The overarching assignment—as a stage-managed assignation between media—is simply to channel regard itself: close notice, that is, rather than awed respect. Channel it toward what might be learned, piecemeal but cumulatively, from the audiovisual faceting of any such achieved prose when attended, and rerun, in the same imaginative theater as comparable montage art. It's a matter of taking heed before heading out on one's own, battening on possibilities before testing potential. The paradigm—the imperative—is an old-fashioned one in writing programs, and all to the good: read before you write, and here in particular look before you leap. The why is obvious, but, to borrow a phrase out of context from James, it "concentrates the mind wonderfully" to know what one is reading (or looking) *for*. Hence the sanction for such a specialized classroom experiment in discerning, both remarking and parsing, the cinematic sentence—which may turn out to be not so specialized after all, but quintessential in its microdynamic rollout.

Moving ahead two decades from Forster's classical prose symmetries of phrase and syllable, in their lexical dynamics and syntactic reversal, to an even more hypervisual episode in prose from the heyday of Hollywood narrative, we catch the eponymous tempi in the open-ended finale of Thomas Wolfe's *Of Time and the River* (1935).[6] This concluding episode begins with what might be imagined as a kind of slow zoom, from the POV of a young woman waiting to board a bulking ocean liner, a pointedly framed view that eventually locks in on an elaborated ocular perusal of the loner shipboard hero, Eugene Gant, leaning out from the deck above, "lone and lean and secret, on the rail of night" (890). Even "rail," as nautical architecture, is canted away to metaphor for this border state on the physical brink of a temporal boundary. Eugene's fetishized solo form is the center of gravity for a now fixated optical register—amid almost two dozen "and's" in her gathering impressions of his person and imagined persona, including conjectural epithets that escalate into the sheer abstraction of a figure "wild and young and foolish and forsaken" (890). Suddenly, however, and climactically—from his photogenic perch above—the woman's wide-eyed stare is intercepted and returned. Yet no subsequent reverse shot forecloses the fantasy in an embodied reciprocation.

The funneling of the look is more complicated, it is fair to say, than in any Hollywood production of the period. The pattern of exchanged glances in the standard shot template well established by then in Hollywood editing—the structural engineering of desire that one might well expect to be triggered here—is in fact truncated by the hero's own activated but self-absorbed longing. And with an extra psychoanalytic shove, at that. Picking up on the last syllable of her framed view of the looming youth—"how like my wild lost father who will not return!" (891)—we encounter, before the hero's answering glance, a kind of syllabic "match cut" that translates us, after a paragraph gap, to exactly the present-tense "turn" (rather than spectral "re-turn") that alone remains possible, however much under an Oedipal cloud—or imprimatur. Coasting in on such an instantaneous residual trace of formative desire at this moment of pivoted focus, the elating return glance we expect is immediately transfigured by a further (and loosely echoic) motion—ultimately inward—on the hero's part at the break (//) between paragraphs: ". . . will never *return*! // *He turn*ed, and saw her then, and so finding her, was lost, and so losing self, was found, and so seeing her, saw for a fading moment only the pleasant image of the woman that perhaps she was, and that life saw" (891). Though rooted like a fascinated glimpse of optical recognition, Eugene's returned look quickly oscillates instead into a kind of narcissist reciprocity of vision and self-image (as if introjecting, rather than meeting halfway, the yearning purview of the other). Latent with the axial reversals of a meet-cute moment of transformative eye contact, like something out of a DiCaprio/Winslet ricochet of glances in the 1997 film *Titanic*, here the ensuing "subjective shot" isn't fully other-directed, being no more a matter of aroused sight than of precipitated self-insight. Whose eddying momentum, more than emphatic parallelism, crests on the undulant shift of "so" from the sense of "therefore" ("and so finding her, was lost") to "thus" or "in that way" ("and so seeing her"). The moment entails only a final last thought bestowed on objectivity: directed, that is, to what "life saw" in her. Life, somewhere outside of the hero's introvert stream of consciousness, is at one with an omniscience ("life saw"—not unlike the aerial "long shot" ascribed to the überproducer in *The Last Tycoon*) into which Eugene's own introvert POV has sliced for a moment at an acute angle of mostly inward recognition. In effect: in place of the never returning father, he turned, returned her gaze, and in seeing her, saw (found) himself—until this last pocket of see/saw solipsism ("and so seeing her, saw . . .") explodes into the novel's happily-ever-after rhapsody of a lifelong bond.

Though with culminating imagery not a fraction more strictly pictorial than *Gatsby*'s downbeat nautical apotheosis, here too, even before the liner has left the pier, we are swept away upon a rapid flash-forward and slow fade-out—with its lifelong vanishing point in the *ruling passion* (an idiom one almost hears played upon with "governance," and then echoed in the sentence's last syllable): the enduring passion of a partnered life to come, replete in "that immortal go*vernance* and unity *of love*" (891). The purple rhetoric of this peroration, like the rest of Wolfe's novel, has never lent itself, unlike Fitzgerald's fiction, to screen treatment. In this respect, it is worth wondering whether sentences can be too cinematic for screen use: too kinetic in their own lexical edits to brook cinematographic reconstitution. Yet to decide as much is hardly to minimize film's contribution, dubious or not at times, to the tools of prose momentum. Nor to downplay the axis of comparison itself in analysis. That open paragraph "cut" at Wolfe's climactic pivot—between her seeing her father in him and him seeing both her looking and himself found at last in that look—illustrates unmistakably (I trust) a case of lexical Fframe-advance in which the internal disyllabic rhyme of "return"/"He turn(ed)" effects at syllabic scale the macroreversal in pictured sight-lines and response.

With that closural novelistic example of a diverted (introverted) shot/reverse shot from Thomas Wolfe in mind, or the perfervid close-up on female flesh that opens Fitzgerald's *Tender Is the Night* at the end of the previous chapter, it seems important to stress again that any apologies for imprecision in these alignments of medial technique would be somewhat beside the point. The more prose examples one brings forward that seem to be taking on loan, or say on spec, the patterning of film shots in relation to possibilities for literary wording—even while exposing in the process the differences between the two media—the more one sees the real point: that the cinematic sentence is still a sentence, not an image cluster, and that its mobilities inevitably contrast with, even when evoking, the automations of camera movement. The ways of the word may involve tracking and zooming and tilting, the equivalent mobile perspectives to those of cranes and dollies, the punctuated syntactic correlates of cutting and pasting, but only *so to speak*. In what follows, as apparent so far as well, the difference from Eagleton's version of this hedge ("so to speak" in regard to Hardy's camerawork) is only one of scale and resolution, the effort here being to subdivide any overall notion of prose's shot plan according to its lexical constituents under syntactic disposition. And it is worth stressing that any such figurative speech, even in a trivial idiom like "so to speak," is the province of writing, not film. Even an unequivocally "cinematic" set-up of convergent sight-lines, as in Wolfe, verging on the intercut gazes of standard Hollywood grammar—and caught, in the process, transforming the very idea of invested visual focus into a kind of empathetic inhabitation of the desired other in a new view of self—can serve to italicize by contrast the suboptical interiorities, we might say, on which literary kinetics thrive. Where spectacle can revert to introspection in the split instant of second thought. The more fully probed, the more forthright the disclosure: namely, that anything like a full-blown cinematic sentence is only one minor mode, however exemplary it may be in lexical or syntactic terms, of verbal motion at large.

Syntactic Time-Lapse

If nothing privileges twentieth-century writers in claims for a cinematographic style, certainly nothing should argue against recognizing such effects when they happen to seem spilling over by linguistic association from explicit cinematic allusions, let alone when recruited to describe the medium itself in operation. Certainly, with few consequences for the actual technique of prose, many a novel may call up cinema as its cultural context or backstory. But sometimes the rubber of allusion hits the road of representation with an unexpected traction. In Vladimir Nabokov's deliberate prosecution of cinema among the pop-cultural subtexts for *Lolita*, some devices of rhetorical irony are explicitly lifted from film, or interpolated into the text as cinematic asides. When Lolita happens to pause in front of a "rogues' gallery" of wanted posters in her narrator's pedophile road trip with her across the American landscape, Humbert's *projected* identification is unmistakable: "If you want to make a movie out of my book," he says to an anonymous reader in breaking the fourth wall that prose fiction in fact shares with film, "have one of these faces gently melt into my own, while I look."[7] The fluid internal variables of syllabification in that effortless adverbial transition, in the modest assonance of "gently melt" and its equally fluid chiasm (*tl/lt*), hardly constitute, even as they contribute to, the blurred superimposition otherwise evoked: a histrionic lap dissolve that—to speak anachronistically—would *morph*, or say transmute, Humbert into the spitting image of a criminal deviant. And in his own as well as Lolita's or a jury's eyes. But sometimes the imitative filmic syntax waxes more dramatic than in the spectral delicacy of "gently melt." Sometimes—make that often—and even elsewhere in this one novel.

The explicit filmic touch of dissolving face recognition, as it were, in those wanted posters has recently been compared to another, less explicit, cinematic nod in this same novel—but with no further comment on the technics of prose that convey it.[8] Amid the narrator's many overt allusions to star cults, Hollywood screen images, genres, and camera movements, this later and more specifically *filmic* callout—also guilt-driven, and ridden all the way to parody as such—involves Humbert's mordant take on the unmentioned mechanism, not of screen editing in general, but of the inset "montage" compendium of classic narrative film. The borrowed device is tacitly deployed in an accelerated distillation of an unachieved future in the star-is-born mode. Humbert realizes that, without his damaging presence, Lolita, with her fine tennis form, might well "have become a real girl champion." The internal filmic montage in question: "Dolores, with two rackets under her arm, in Wimbledon. Dolores endorsing a Dromedary. Dolores turning professional. Dolores acting a girl champion in a movie" (232). Such juxtaposed images of Humbert's imaginary flash-forward are serial, exponential, and in every case mediated by the publicity "vehicle" of screen dissemination in quick-cut biographical acceleration. If this isn't a close technical approximation of classic time-lapse, in its preternatural speeding-up of the frame rate itself, it certainly does leaf through the frames of a life-not-lived—and does so in a manner derived from the pre-cinematic flip-book so often rehearsed in elliptical screen narratives of this sort. Each "period," each punctuated epoch, marks a counterfactual narrative phase in itself, spanning between episodes of celebrity ascent—and resembling in turn a kind of newspaper montage of captioned photos tracing the juggernaut of fame. In this brand of condensation, fragmentation argues the forged continuity of the unstoppable.

With the mass-media paradigm perfectly understated—and understood—in its stylistic blatancy, no reader could process this without sensing the editorial work extruded by the prose itself. But to further the transmedial *sensibility* to which such recognition might lead in a student's rhetorical arsenal, some closer parsing of this *Lolita* passage is advised. Disjoint syntactic cameos are set in motion at first by a mere noun phrase ("Dolores . . . at Wimbledon"), its modification set off by commas, but then further animated from this snapshot logic to something more, beyond implied newspaper coverage, like the sweep and shuffle of newsreel footage—entirely unspoken but syntactically phrased—on the way to an actual fiction film ("a girl champion in a movie"). Hollywood is both the model of the prose and its incarnate destiny. In each of these later moving-image glimpses, the action is conveyed by participial progression in a "reframed" absolute construction (a grammarian's category for the collocation of noun and verb but with no predicated tense structure, as in "Dolores endorsing . . . Dolores turning . . . Dolores acting"), all in this case part of the onward spread and fallout of fame. The cross-sectioned slices of this snowballing celebrity come to rest only with the break from the participial cinematics of those progressive absolutes, those autonomous serial film clips in mass audience release, when reverting to the slack compound grammar of another snapshot-like fixed frame—and eliciting there a final alliterative fantasy of sports star and her legalized marital trainer: "Dolores and her gray, humble, hushed husband-coach, old Humbert" (232). The very salience of that iterative syllabic wording, with exactly the kind of palpable phonetic drift (and deflation) unavailable to film optics, is symptomatic. The montage aesthetic is caught ceding deliberate ground again not just to the fixed-frame two-shot but to a huffing phonetic excess that—hard on the heels of those jump cuts into eventualities unachieved—reaches through, reaches back and down, to the insinuated undersong of prose itself. Dolorous in all the lost possibilities it records. To summarize otherwise: the planar negotiation of tense is exactly the malleable stratum of representation that is both maximized and collapsed in the cinematics of temporal condensation, even without an actual fast-forward time-lapse.

In the relation of prose to the edited and projected film image, or its video derivatives, imitation may be one form of flattery, but it need be no more sincere than it seems in certain satiric treatments—as there in Nabokov's black-comic send-up of media notoriety in headlined, or otherwise visually newsworthy, escalation. Catching the tone of such writing, along with the technical allusion, is crucial. A recent scholarly book on America's dream of literary "immediacy" in writing's contest with emerging media, from photography to video, makes note of the way Robert Coover's account of precipitously dashed hopes, in his famous story "The Babysitter," explicitly travesties—and in ways worth examining more closely—the happy-ever-after montage of a movie broadcast or its derivative in Hollywood-trained TV editing.[9] Watch it wash past, as the babysitter does, if only out of the corner of her eye, when noticing "a man . . . singing a love song on the TV": "He loves her. She loves him. They whirl airily, stirring a light breeze."[10] In its quick-cut, then perhaps cross-fade, logic, think of these short sentences from Coover as beginning with a shot/

reverse shot treatment of some screen couple's loving gazes, yielding place to dreamy two-shots of their ongoing bond. But in that romantic twirl, whether in small-screen movie rerun or directly pillaged TV technique, more is spun round than their magnetized bodies: "They whirl airily, stirring a light breeze," where even that whoosh of internal rhyme (*irl/airl/irr*) impels, with an extra giddy flurry, the remaining images. The montage goes so far—from all credibility—as to close with the noun "wisp" transfigured to an ersatz, kitschy, and illicit verb form, as fake as its evoked effect amid this kinesis of embodied romance in "a landscape of rose and emerald and deep blue"—where "her light brown hair coils and *wisps* softly in the breeze" (209). No such verb, no such believable event. In contrast, for the woman employing the babysitter, an ensuing fast-forward replay of her own life—by relay through the TV image we assume only the sitter might have noticed—shatters the sedate grammar of uplift into fragments (or fast-forwards) of erosive decline: "He loves her. She loves him. And then the babies come. And dirty diapers and one goddamn meal after another. Dishes. Noise. Clutter. And fat" (209). The discrepant teleology of "fat" added as temporal effect to the ongoing pressure of mealtime chores answers to the capstone artifice of the preceding screen musical, a sylleptic phrasing that immerses the hero "in" his own outflow across the separately ironized manifestation of something like "vocal sincerity" when, instead, in forked phrasing, "He smiles in a gushing crescendo of sincerity and song (209). I had said above, regarding Nabokov's syntactic irony and its montage "condensation," that "fragmentation" of that sort "argues the forged continuity of the unstoppable." As of course it does, too, in the swifter precipitation of Coover's second, antithetical montage of biographical decline. Across these contrasted passages in Coover, paradigm and parody are slammed together in an unmistakable node of debunked media clichés shared by film and TV.

This is the same Coover who, a decade and a half after this landmark story, will turn to more explicit versions of "montage" manipulation, and to even subtler, less explicit equivalents in their prose conjuration, for the opening chapter of *A Night at the Movies*. Called "The Phantom of the Movie Palace," this tour-de-force passage unfurls one absurdist gesture after another in ways that double, quite incidentally, for a useful classroom checklist of cinematic techniques—and in some cases their mimetic phrasal equivalents. A lone projectionist in an abandoned theater mixes reels and projectors, "creating his own split-screen effects, montages, superimpositions,"[11] with that unpunctuated series netting something of the disjunction and overlap it rushes to sum up. Similarly: "Or he uses multiple projectors to produce a flow of improbable dissolves, startling sequences of abrupt cuts and freeze frames like the stopping of a heart, disturbing juxtapositions of slow and fast speeds, fades in and out" (22), where that last pair of technical terms is, one might say, superimposed upon (almost mimetically) with a fleeting present-tense sense of the compound phrasal verb *to fade in and out*. Sometimes "thick collages" show car crashes and battling soldiers, cowboys, gangsters and "mating lovers" all, in the narrator's sexual pun, "banging away in unison" (22). And sometimes it is only sound collage that the projectionist attempts, when he "leaves the projector lamps off altogether and just listens"—as we do to his own phonic recurrences, verging on the onomatopoeia of plop and shriek, in "the sounds of bl*ob*s and ghouls, r*ob*ots, gall*op*ing hooves and s*cree*ching tires, *crea*king doors, s*crea*ms" (22). And in a further test of our eared attention, there is a final paced run of ellipses—"fists hitting faces and bodies pavements, arrows targets, rockets moons" (22)—that seems again to volatilize noun forms ("targets," "rockets") toward the flash of inoperable phantom verbs.

Sprocket Tolls

In searching out the manifold options of the cinematic sentence, as mentioned, no priority is owed to its signature practitioners. And yet such manifest test cases are certainly instructive. Salman Rushdie's breakthrough novel, *Midnight's Children* (1981), which quickly became a poster child for magic realism as genre, was shot through, often as part of its brandished magic, with cinematic references in its scene changes and "camera angles," even its aesthetic "perspective" at large. In fact, a skeptic's epistemological *view* of "reality" finds itself crystallized at one point by a cinematic metaphor that turns out, from the novel's incipient digital vantage in the early 1980s, to apply as well to the pixelated, as much as to the celluloid, frame in digital imaging's granulated internal composite: "Reality is a question of perspective," Rushdie's narrator asserts, and the proposition is afforded an immediate filmic analogue in a direct reader address reminiscent of Nabokov's frame-breaking asides: "Suppose yourself in a large cinema, sitting at first in the back row, and gradually moving up, row by row, until your nose is almost pressed against the screen."[12] The result, carried on the crest of the same repeated adverb: "Gradually the stars' faces dissolve into dancing grain"—like the lexical dissolution incurred at the slippery ligature of the phrase itself ("dancing grain") in its pelleting molecular fallout. It is in this way that "tiny details assume grotesque proportions; the illusion dissolves"—as if enacted (across some backward undertow of those last two words) by a kind of fused lexical *disillusion*—"or rather, it becomes clear that the illusion itself *is* reality" (189). The prose track is almost as unstable as the screen resolution, together with the disruptive ontological emblem, it depicts.

Seven years later in Rushdie's work, in *The Satanic Verses*, cinema has come to the thematic forefront, with prose following suit. An invented adverb—the compacted "downdown"—captures in progress the impossibly survived fall of the Bombay screen-star hero, Gibreel, along with a fellow actor, from a jetliner exploded by terrorists over the English Channel in the opening chapter.[13] That both iterative and compressed adverbial coinage opens one of the gathering paragraphs of their magic descent, whose extremity is projected like a GGI spectacle of cosmic zooms and particle effects, their bodies slashing through aerial strata of mist and ice crystals: "Downdown they hurtled," unhurt as yet, but as if fate's eventual collision with the earth were crammed latent into the "Down(e)d" of that compound. Acceleration itself is given the cellular weight—and drop—of syllabification as sonic metonymy. Soon: "Speed, the sensation of speed, returned, whistling its fearful note" (8). And next this raced syntactic series: "The roo*f* of cloud *f*led upwards, the water-*f*loor zoomed closer, their eyes opened" (8)—with its alliterative variation on aeronautic lingo for the atmospheric "ceiling" (the passage deploying "roof" instead). To sustain the syllabic funnel of this plummet, what is *sped* away from them in their fall is echoically recast as "fled" upwards in the vanishing space of descent.

This is only the beginning of syntax's play with transience in the inaugural chapters of Rushdie's novel. Once the falling star, Gibreel, is presumed dead and "in fact" reincarnated, in this fantasia of magic realism, the uncanny drop from the sky is matched in the second chapter by an uncanny fading away of his image in both publicity and projection—even while sustaining the inferred astral metaphor of a doomed radiance exploded in dispersal: not, this time, in the "dancing grain" of an unresolved close-up, but in an explosively dissipated "supernova" (16). Along with his "mammoth cardboard effigies" on promotional billboards, the "portraits" of Gibreel "on the cover of movie magazines acquired the pallor of death, a nullity about the eyes, a hollowness" (16). Call it, in premature erasure, a magic exacerbation of the proverbial *faded glory*, with glossy visual presence leached away across the leveling alliterative run of that tripled "ll" cluster ("pallor . . . nullity . . . hollowness")—and then deftly stressed in this further time-lapse image of photochemical decay: "At last his images simply faded off the page" (16) like the kind of backwards Polaroid resolution that is part of the reverse-action irony of Christopher Nolan's 2000 film, *Memento*—and might well have found a place in Martin Amis's *Time's Arrow* (1991) as well. In Rushdie, the time-lapse of fading and erasure finally reaches a description of the dimmed star's projected iconic face, where the kinetic screen image also bleeds away. "Even on the silver screen itself, high above his worshippers in the dark, that supposedly immortal physiognomy began to putrefy, blister, and bleach" (16)—as if, we might guess, and even in the puckerings of its plosive alliteration (*p/b/b*), from some of the same rapid chemical decomposition suspected with the defective "ink" of the published photographs.

But there is more—with a turning-point phrasing very much more cinematic yet in its ambivalent slipping of grammatical gears. After a semicolon, we get, at one and the same time, a further version of this projected evanescence, enacted by syntactic accident, as well as a diagnosis of its cause. It is here that prose rises most ingeniously to the cinematic occasion—or, more exactly, its cognitive lag time to the crisis of filmic snag and dissolution. If only momentarily, syntax itself is disconcertingly thrown off track along with the image: "projectors jammed unaccountably every time he passed through the gate, his films ground to a halt, and the lamp-heat of the malfunctioning projectors burned his celluloid memory away" (16). Three clauses linked in an *and* series, perfectly grammatical, each with its own subject (one of them the personification of the star's celluloid image as "he" in motion) are nonetheless swept ahead by syntax as if the first two were so causally related as to be comma-spliced in an illicit (or say mimetic) run-on apposition: "projectors jammed unaccountably . . ., his films ground to a halt." Grammatically it's smooth enough as two clauses;

descriptively it skids, skips a beat in a kind of technological redundancy. The sentence, that is, could have ended with "halt" by another syntactic logic as well—with "his films ground to a halt" offered as an absolute of past-participial finality ('having ground') rather than a simple intransitive past. But that subliminal possibility isn't enough to override the specter of a comma splice on the run.

Instead, as the overlapping grammar quickly sorts itself out, the clear point is that no sooner do projectors clutch up than the image stalls, only for that microsecond halt to be detailed further by the third *and*-bonded clause about "lamp-heat." Track the flickering of serial cues this way: 'Projectors jammed every time his image passed, his films [thus] halted, and the lamp-heat incinerated them.' One may at this point recall the famously jammed and ignited celluloid close-up in Ingmar Bergman's *Persona* (1966), even while such an incendiary glitch finds specification in Rushdie—after a final colon at the end of this unraveled sentence—as the apt fate for a musical screen celebrity: "a star gone supernova, with the consuming fire spreading outwards, as was fitting, from his lips" (16). A case of "gone" in overlapped senses ("turned," with the faint afterimage of "removed"), where kinesis coincides finally with its cause in the vanishing cellular track of a spooled film and its contingencies. In the meantime, however, in that overrun of the second onto the first clause in the preceding sentence ("projectors jammed . . ., his image ground"), syntax has broken the pace of its own punctuational sprocket holes. Framed precariously on screen, the star shines only until the underlying default of Fframe-advance fires him into oblivion. And sooner yet than previously remarked, since one way of catching the syntactic drift in this staggered flux, by a quick rethinking, would be to assume an absolute construction first off, as soon as a separate clause licks at its heels: "Projectors [being] jammed unaccountably every time he passed through the gate, his image ground to a halt. . . ." The snare is already in progress, and its searing glare, however we read.

Syllabic Flips, Expanded Spans

I spoke of the flip-book model—like the prototype of the thumbed photo album—in connection with Nabokov's fast-forwarding through Lolita's balked and thus unrecorded, thus merely fantasized, future. There is a recent and more explicit orchestration of this precinematic format, and with reverberations for prose's own segues, to whose ruffled whispers we should listen. Sometimes the match of grammar with explicit cinematic analogues can be just short of complete—and, in the minor width of difference, all the more revealing. We have looked before at what novelist Richard Powers is able to "highlight" simply by rear-view citation in the closural dynamics of Willa Cather's prose, and we will return to this tendency toward revelatory embedding with a later novel of his in the epilogue. But it is the particular kinetic cast of his own writing that comes through, under thematic emphasis, in his most recent, Pulitzer Prize–winning novel, *The Overstory* (2018)—as something like the precinematographic understory of his epic ecological plotting in its first chronicle phase. Inspired initially by the Victorian optical toy known as the zoopraxiscope, three generations of Iowa farmers in the novel's first narrative sequence preserve the monthly "ritual" of photographing, on a fixed tripod outside the family farmhouse, the growth of a beloved chestnut tree—even as foreign-borne spores, eventually reaching westward from their first Brooklyn infestation, will blight millions of these trees across the American landscape. The original patriarch, when his daughter had tired of her postbellum toy, "kept playing with it" on his own until—in the parallel participial grammar of progression itself—"those squadrons of flapp*ing* geese and parades of buck*ing* broncos that come alive when the glass drum spins animate his brain."[14] Unpunctuated, the predicate density at "spins animate" is sped—spun—past at its own syntactic pace, with the latter verb figuratively transferred from cartoon animation to triggered idée fixe. And in the process, the alliterative iteration of the "bucking broncos," catching in its own phonetic right the optical abutments of the specular technology invoked, is preceded even more tellingly by the marginal lexical (rather than ocular) fusion (the flicker effect of differential Fframe-advance) in those closely sequenced "flappin*g g*eese."

Once the man's brain, too, is sprung into motion by the plan inspired by such piecemeal visual seriality, and he has assembled in a stack the first year's black-and-white images, he "riffles through them with his thumb" (11)—in the manner of that other precinematic optical toy, the flip-book: in this case, the predecessor as well of time-lapse effects. The "riffling" is sustained across the double prepositional phrase itself (*th*rough/*them*/*thum*[b])—even while, in the verb's clearest possible distinction from its near alternative "rifle through," its fricative force makes good on the *OED*'s speculative sense of the chosen word's fused derivation from "ripple" and "ruffle" together. In any case, the innovator's son is soon to inherit this photographic legacy and obligation, and it is at this point, as he continues the regimen of dutiful monthly snapshots, that the chestnut infection spreads its way west toward their homestead. Always west, but also south, at which point the photographic, turned cinematic, waxes metaphysical: "If God had a Brownie, he might shoot another animated short subject: blight hovering a moment before plunging down the Appalachians into the heart of chestnut country" (14), with "heart" against "chest" a kind of biological intensification of a humanizing figuration in sympathy. And few wordings could be more subtly mimetic. After the syllabic telescoping of "shoot" to "short," the word "blight," nominalized as it is in back-formation from its use as a verb, governs the subsequent teeter of present participles, linked in their inevitable sequence by assonance as well as literal (rather than just letteral) contagion. Shot held, poised in negative recognition, thumb on the trigger, then the fast-forward flip. In "hovering"/"pl*u*nging," the mere audial slide of the "uh" sound operates a momentary phonetic levitation before the spreading, the descending, the perceptibly cadenced, extension of the epidemic threat. In this second flip-book of riffled movement, Powers's lexical cinematography is brought into unusually close correlation with his filmic trope. And, further along in this generational declension of arboreal record, when the aggregated photos, over two hundred by now in a "five-second flip," are said to have inspired the early graphic designs of the great grandson, it may feel like those "penciled dreams" (90)—instead of just 'pencil dreams' (given that wonderfully unnecessary past-participial *ed*)—have borrowed the blur of minimal difference, the essence of lexical succession itself, from their flickering counterparts: via "reams" of sketches, no less, in a time-based ocular shuffle. Or listen this way: in that split-second phonemic flip, we hear, as it were, the flutter of prose's own drawing in words.

But we must now stand back, widen the viewfinder. Partly to return the scope of discussion to cinematic effects not narrowly linked to explicit cinematic allusions, even prefilmic ones like that elicited by Powers; partly to give an even more striking example than Rushdie's of a tacitly cinematographic comma splice in prose, one that never resolves into normal grammar, but only into a specular wonder of exactly the sort that is jammed in Rushdie's vision of the botched, blotched, and blistered screen icon; and partly to round out this section on "time-lapse" (whether in the dissipation or the consolidation of an image)—we turn back now, over half a century, from Rushdie to the lyrical transformation of a bleak and commercial landscape that closes D. H. Lawrence's *The Rainbow* (1915) through the focalized vision (and visionary elation) of his heroine, Ursula Brangwen. The gradually materialized prismatic crescent, emblem of a cleansing social renewal, is then reprised three sentences later in the novel's last line, with its spiritual as well as architectonic sense of the titular configuration "fitting to the over-arching heaven." In a kind of dispersed etymology of this matrix syllable as linguistic *arche*, there is the last sentence of the preceding paragraph, playing between—amid other syllabic play—the bracket "arc" and "arch": "The arc ben*ded* and streng*thened* itself till it arched indomitable. . . ." That wording has installed a markedly obsolete past participle (instead of "bent") that in its own right bends the expected phrasing out of shape—or stretches it out toward the "ed" of the stronger coming participle in this rhapsody of ocular and visionary aggregation. It is across this syllabic sequence—and now in reversion to the hard *c* sound after the distention of "arc" into "arch"—that the misted sky is seen "ma*k*ing great ar*ch*itecture of light and *c*olour," where the softened *ch* also slips back in—or say accretes phonetically if not alphabetically—in the texture of "tecture" (*tekchure*) itself.

So the sky is seen, yes. But from what camera position exactly in the heroine's heavily subjectivized POV? The very question, even in its final irrelevance, situates this as a perfect test case for a cinematics of prose. Because it doesn't matter whether you think of this, or were to film it, as a steady low-angle shot of the sky's panoramic expanse or as a vertical pan up to the apex of the luminous formation. The real kinetics are lateral: horizontal in the sentence, even as cumulative, layered, and subtly differential in the manifold curvature itself, which builds without moving. So listen as you continue to look, auditing the exponential, seeing things in the very look of words. Immediately preceding the syllabic massing of phrases just quoted (*arc . . . arch . . . architecture*), there at the inception of this vaulted span of transfiguration is an adverbially tracked chromatic impaction that comes out of the grammatical—as well as the aerial—blue. The clausal layering is remarkable, even for Lawrence: "Steadily the colour gathered, mysteriously, from nowhere, it took presence upon itself, there was a faint, vast rainbow." By this double encroachment of phrasal and opalescent phenomena, we are caught up in a compressed and naturalized version of time-lapse imaging across the prose's unabashedly comma-spliced progression, where again (as with the archaic tense structure of that dictional choice in "bended") grammatical usage is strained in transition, this time in the form of a momentarily equivocated vernacular turn ("colour gathered"). Idiometrics again. A 'crowd,' for instance, *gathers*, in the intransitive sense, as well as 'momentum' in the transitive—if that crowd is in motion, that is. But not usually "colour"—unless in some strange way it operates as a plural noun, which of course, with the lustrous striations of this accreting, gathering rainbow, it does. Grammar quickly explains itself, this time in a clear reflexive syntax, with the appositional "took presence upon itself." But this clarification only triggers a further elusive dynamism.

Once more, no particular camera angle need be imagined. So look yet again at the wording—and listen in. More tightly aligned with the immediate cinematic valence of the episode, it is as if the terraced lambent bands of this composite rainbow were under imitation by adjacency per se, translated from prose lineation to iridescent sedimentation. This happens—in that sentence still monitored before us in its grammatical license—when the phrasal conjuncture "mysteriously, from nowhere" either divides in half, attaching backward and forward at once, or wavers ambiguously in the superimposed phases of consolidation. Wavers by hovering, both over and across—and so by nudging—the double comma splice ("the colour gathered, it took presence . . ., there was . . ."). This is the wording, the phrasing, that rounds itself out—in the syntactic as well as cognitive mode of before-you-knew-it—in the fulfilled modest euphony of "th*ere* was *a faint, vast rain*bow." The image's blended, bended manifestation seems in part phonetically generated through a crucial fricative pivot in that inward wavering of long and short *a* sounds mounting across the verbal rather than atmospheric arc—a kind of layered syllabic diffraction in its own right—in *er/a/fai/va/rain*. So it is that words, too, take presence upon themselves. As a side note, but also a sign of pertinent transmedial distinctions, the fact that Ken Russell's 1989 film of the Lawrence novel ends with a blatant special effect of multicolored superimposition, rather than some serendipitously captured atmospheric phenomenon on just the right rain-swept day, is only all the truer to the mystified figurative, rather than strictly specular, manifestation at hand in Lawrence's final paragraphs. There can be no doubt that prose at this pitch of mimesis, under horizontal pressure, has arced into shape the symbolic omen out of the rarefied thin air of its own enunciation.

Over half a century and a world war later, the 1973 novel by Thomas Pynchon, *Gravity's Rainbow*, that famously begins with the present-tense alliterative evocation of an incoming rocket bomb during the London Blitz—"A *screaming comes across* the *sky*"—has later etched that pending curve, that clarified "parabola," as an overarching existential parable. It has done so in a run of what one might call subsonic *ru*-mbling across adjacent sentences. Narrative and stylistic, along with human, fate appears inexorable in "moving toward that *pur*ified shape latent in the sky, that shape of no s*urpr*ise, no second chance, no ret*urn*."[15] In the unreeled syllabic track of description, iteration, distillation, "purification," the *ur/er* reverb spans expansively the next sentence as well in that arcing of syntax that Pynchon might well have learned from Lawrence, including at the cross-word bridge of the rainbow's very naming via direct article: "Yet they do move fo*rev*er und*er* it, res*erv*ed for its own black-and-white bad news c*er*tainly as if it *were* the *r*ainbow, and they its child*ren*" (212). Even the understood elision of the second unmurmured "*were*" seems hovering by a subsyllabic chiasm in that last word "child*ren*." And even before that, in the revving up of this second sentence with the crisscrossed assonance (*oo*) and alliteration (*v*) of "*d*o *m*ove fore*v*er," we hear released—as inoperable verbal residuum, and all the spookier for ghosting the wording with no syntactic role to be had—the yet more ominous lap dissolve of "doom" in "*do m*ove forever" (a word making a dozen "actual" appearances in the novel). Like the parabolic rainbow in this passage, as a "shape" only "latent" in human history, so is this suboptic afterimage of a single word.

Splicing: Comma vs. Montage

Several examples of the pesky absolute construction, so elusive for students, have come into varying degrees of unstable focus so far: Nabokov's in accretive fragments ("Dolores endorsing a Dromedary. Dolores turning professional"), Rushie's in uncertain deployment ("his films ground to a halt"). Let me give a student example of this syntactic option and, in the process, better late than never, one upshot of this whole pedagogical agenda as a creative writing initiative—what we are now told to call an "outcome assessment"—before returning to published evidence. As predicated on the syllabus (though forewarned is not always forearmed), my class on "reading movies" began with a few weeks of basic grammar exercises in the reading of prose itself—and its writing: somewhere between remedial and adventurous. For a while, the semester seemed on the verge of becoming a term of terms, and one of the hardest for students to master or activate, it turns out, was (without that fragmentary *Lolita* example above, found since, either to help or to further confuse them) the absolute construction: that form in which, typically, a noun plus participle (past or present) hovers in freestanding adjacency to a main clause, levitated in place by commas. *One exercise or conversation after another stalling over this format*, I finally learned why students were surprisingly shy of it, *its utility being so obvious it would seem hard to resist* (to give two flagged instances of it right there). For several members of the class, it appeared to encroach on the dreaded territory of the punishable comma splice, threatening to collapse into the ungrammatical run-on sentence, as, for instance: 'Students stalled over it [students having stalled], I finally learned why.' That (without the implicit bracket) was the feared transgressive paradigm that needed to be overcome in getting them to exercise this wonderfully malleable option.

To help with this problem, and in continued pursuit of microlevel alignments between camerawork and grammar work, I showed the class an extended YouTube video by nonacademic German "syntactician" Friderike Hirsch-Wright, on the pleasure of sentence parsing. In it, she happens to introduce a passing filmic comparison, in her favorite sentence from *The Great Gatsby*, for the "so-called absolute construction" used by Fitzgerald to tuck in a typifying detail about the women's hands after the unorthodox adverbial opener: "Slenderly, languidly, their hands set lightly on their hips, the two young women preceded us out onto a rosy-colored porch. . . ."[16] For starters, students would have to learn not to be haunted by the punitive shadow of a finite grammar (requiring more than a comma), like "their hands sat [rather than "set"] lightly on their hips," in order to warm to such an independent syntactic effect. But more to the point, the appreciative video about Fitzgerald's sentence isolates the hands-on-hips effect as the equivalent of a "cinematic zoom shot": a kind of grammatical "inset" detached from the main syntactic skeleton, a sudden anatomical close-up. Just right, in this case, that filmic analogue.

This exercise did help, I think. In any case, a demonstrable payoff from our worrying over this issue came later in the semester, when one of the students, outside of any specific grammatical prompt, used the absolute perfectly, and twice over, in an assignment asking the class both to describe and (at the same time) to rhythmically evoke—via a kind of screen ekphrasis—one of the many cinematographic tropes of montage in *Citizen Kane*. At stake in the offered example that so cannily deployed this elusive construction—not showy like the screen episode itself, but immediately telling—is the famous lap dissolve from banker Thatcher's manuscript, in his memorial library, about first meeting Kane in a Colorado snowstorm. It is read by one of the newsreel team in an angled shaft of light like a projector's beam—as the camera, drifting to the right along the line of longhand script, gives way to the young Kane on his sled literally tracking back to the left, scoring the snow as he goes. With inked cursive doubling for filmic inscription in this lateral pan, here is fade *out* in flashing *back*: releasing an independent scene to speak for itself. And here, to boot, converting memorial to memory, is a rare case of Fframe-advance grasped by analogy at the alphabetic level itself in the text's s/crawl forward into the past.

The fluent student sentence capturing this could be singled out as a textbook example of the grammatical absolute in cumulative action, with the cinematic cross-fade situated aptly, as if effortlessly, in a continuous present tense: "As we read what is written on the page, snow begins to fall against the white background, the page transitioning into a blanket of freshly fallen snow, a young boy sledding down a hill obscured by white." The avoided comma splice is precisely what makes for overlap rather than run-on. In a rudimentary nuance of mimetic syntax, part of the charm of this grammar's precision entails its use of the prepositional vectors we'd also been practicing on and off in the course, as involved in the kinetics of wording, here channeling the very sequence of superimposition. There is the choice, first, of "against" rather than "on" to grasp the spectral snowfall that is interfaced, filmy as well as filmic, with the manuscript paper in a metamorphic zone between interleaved granular surfaces, page and screen frame. And then (boy and hill together, in fact) "obscured *by white*" (rather than, say "by the falling white")—again with the shared rectangle of white straddling the paper backing of handwritten text and its framed screen visualization in an exchanged syntactic independence, an "absolute" separateness, even in (trans)fusion, of incommensurable script and scene: "the page transitioning" over against "a young boy sledding." This classic device of graduated scene change (with, in Coover's unsettling plurals, its "fades in and out"), here heavily thematized, might be thought of as the opposite of the freeze-frame, so common—along with the blackout—in screen treatments of death's arrest.

The onward thrust of wording like this points us forward as well into a further chapter of examples. And not least because what is so quietly effective about it, so filmic—though readily arrested, retraced, and "diagramed" for pedagogic demonstration—slips past in a lockstep rhythm just as immediately legible as the screen's own overlapping grammar. And yet, unlike the *Kane* effect when projected in a theater, it must be stressed that this prose evocation is—for any reader (as well as any writing instructor)—immediately available for rescan and analysis, as I've just reproduced here. Hence the need for a renewed *Laocoön*—this time circumscribed within the realm of time-based shaping—to distinguish, *in view of* reception, the serial media of literature and film, the latter operating, long since Lessing, as poet Vachel Lindsay's famous "sculpture in motion." However we might invest in the idea of a cinematographic prose—let alone some broader, looser, and less interesting notion of a given author's cinematic style—any *reading* of such writing, as mentioned earlier, and as apparent above, enjoys the uniquely literary freedom of instant replay. Such reading is not, that is, constrained the way unaided screen viewing is when removed from any remote device: not left to the immediate assimilation of effect by plot, where narrative perception must submit to the trans(i) tory. For any given workshop in creative writing, or its creative reading, cinematographic attention takes us back in imagination not to the author's desk but, instead, either to film labs or to the digital workings of industrial laptops. It is there that we intuit, by prose analogy, certain generative processes of mechanical or electronic editing in comparison to the imagined craft of a writer's own adjusted wording. Slowed in this way to the conjured time of studio production rather than motorized theatrical consumption, what you see in appreciating a turn of cinematic prose, unlike its equivalent on screen, isn't all you get. You're seeing how it got there as well. The looking harder involved in this, in its specialized mode of close reading, yields not some immediate grasp of structure, but rather a patient reconstruction of its build. Such mobile reading tracks the work of succession per se: the way of edited motion in words as well as images.

5

Fframe-Advance

Little things composite the big picture. The ingredient matter of wording activates semantic pace, including the interplay of time frames in the orientation of narrative structure. The different linguistic scales at which the ways of the word were found deploying even the grammatical mainstay of tense, in the analyses of chapter 2, spurred an explanatory "aside" concerning the comparable relation of alphabetic sequencing to the double work of the cinematic strip, both in the teeth of projection and in on-screen action. That issue has by now come home to roost—as integral to the cinematics of part III and its Macro/micro (F/f) template.

Fframe: as this inaudible orthography suggests, the one module always hidden inbuilt in the mobile composite, with all visible motion, camera movement included, thrown to the screen from the broken-backed cells of the strip's masked discrepancies and elided framelines. Any continuum is only achieved, vitalized, over the dead bodies of transparent still photos. Letters, phonemes, syllables: these, roughly, the clustering equivalents of enchained photographic cells. Such a proposed comparison is blinkering, again, only if tracked without sufficient latitude. Analysis has no reason to cling to a rare cognate instance in terminology; the shared nomenclature for celluloid splice and comma splice, for instance, shouldn't mislead us into narrowing the pertinent analogy of syntax and optical machination to the microsecond—the cell-splitting breach—of timed transition. But no reason to miss or minimize this, either, when sentences have their own way, for instance, of overriding cuts as junctures. Or of laminating one wording over the trace of another.

The Romantic poet Keats speaks of Newtonian positivism starkly "unweaving" the rainbow; stylistic parsing of either its prose description or its poetic equivalent does far less damage. In the incremental bend and bow, the build and lilt, of the rainbow's horizontal syntactic spectrum in Lawrence, as "disbanded" in the last chapter's penultimate exhibit, wonder is maintained at the level of style's own layering, shades of purple prose included. A transfiguring Frame—a discursive field of view—is advanced from within, frame by frame, in the "gathering" together of this depicted chromatic spectrum, its accrual evoked by the very pace of syntactic escalation. So, too, if more rhythmically than pictorially, with the mathematical abstraction of gravity's bowing force in Pynchon. Dynamism is the shared term: intrinsic to the comparable passage(way)s of the two media.

Entrained Phrasing

Not just cinema as a training ground for contemporary writing, then, but filmic sequence as an interrogation of narrative motion itself: that's where evidence has been headed. So far: syntax commanding a kinetic technology whose differences from cinema are never more obvious than when evoking that alternate narrative medium. And on the other end of the conceptual spectrum, to be noted in immediate contrast and clarification: whatever we end up wanting to decide on this intermedial point, motion pictures did in their own right, across their early history of silent narrative, screen for their audiences many sentences that were not in the least filmic, even in their deliberate vehicular use as the carriers of plot. Nothing exposes the exactitude, as well as the connotative range, of cinema's own grammar, the tonality of its rhetoric, faster than our transported glance—not across cuts between image frames, from one scene or another—but in that jolting reversion from image plane to the bland, perfunctory truncations of explanatory bridging intertitles. Routine in the packaging of silent cinema, these are the discursive placeholders that, above and beyond transcribed dialogue, tend to summarize with flaccid succinctness what is unfolded across a more complex visual syntax. And these deflating title cards tend to be no more cinematic in their literary energy when the whole screen treatment is drawn from literature, even from poetry. The Victorian laureate Tennyson, we'll soon be noting, writes a cinematic verse at times, but not D. W. Griffith's team in drafting the intertitles for the director's 1908 adaptation of Tennyson's narrative poem *Enoch Arden*, a film under the title *After Many Years* singled out for "syntactic" explication in a famous essay by revolutionary Soviet director and montage theorist Sergei Eisenstein. But it will be useful to look first at Dickens's prose, a more definitive benchmark yet for Griffith as well as for the teleological prehistory of film in Eisenstein's account. From these Victorian forebears, in verse and prose rhythm by turns, we will then move to a quite different stress on the latent aesthetics of film in a critique of traditional silent narrative by Virginia Woolf.

Merely to name such names from the cinematic century as Eisenstein and Woolf, in respect to film commentary, is to suggest, straightaway, that regarding the interart confrontation between movies and books—camerawork versus prose, montage versus grammar—students of the cinematic sentence needn't go it alone, just by the seat of their pants in the screening room or in laptop privacy. From canonical responses to contemporary critical debate, a packet of assigned readings and a library reserve list are easy to produce. More broadly, of course, there are rich further materials in the scholarly archive on the competing media, literary versus screen narrative, as well as on their mutual reinforcements over time. But one divergence of opinion is especially generative for the question of prose style and its montage analogues. That's where the crux—and aesthetic break point—of the realist (photographic) image in cinema comes in. From major thinkers about narrative form across media—and from opposite sides of a postwar watershed in screen innovation that entails the consolidation of classic Hollywood and the counter-cinemas of the European avant-garde—it is of signal relevance that Sergei Eisenstein, writing in 1944, excoriated in hindsight the kind of antirealist cinema that Virginia Woolf, two decades earlier, had celebrated for the embryonic possibilities it seemed to hold out.[1] In Eisenstein's view, the expressionist grotesquery of *The Cabinet of Dr. Caligari* (1920) was nothing but a "barbaric carnival," a rampage of "destruction" for the "healthy human infancy of our art" (203), whereas for Woolf, writing a few years after that film's release, and relieved by its extravagance from all the inert literary adaptations she was impatient with, its pictorial anomalies suggested the use of motion pictures for something more vital than the picturing of human motion in theatrical exaggeration. Rather, she saw cinema's potential for metaphors of emotion in new ocular form: not scary actions, say, but rather images of fear, which she sensed in *Caligari*'s chiaroscuro abstractions. For her, rightly, that instance of the Weimar fantastic was some kind of harbinger. Indeed, it presaged exactly what Eisenstein saw as a mistaken fork in screen practice, including the "chaos of superimpositions, of over-fluid dissolves, of split screens" (202) that came later in the 1920s, both after *Caligari* and, in many cases, even after Woolf's passing appreciation of that Weimar fantasy in 1926.

Eisenstein valued instead the rudiments of montage worked out by Griffith, in a photographically grounded cinema, precisely so that—a point never quite laid out in this essay—they might be disrupted into new syntheses in the prosecution of his game-changing dialectical montage. His emphasis is on what Griffith rightly learned from Dickens about the Victorian prose equivalent, for example, of "optical quality," "frame composition," and "closeups" (213)—including also the rudiments of traveling shots and superimpositions in his list of Dickensian evidence—as part of an overriding "plasticity of treatment" in the Victorian novelist's prose. This is the very plasticity that Eisenstein had so potently argued for between—rather than within—frames: a bending of entrained pictures to the will of a consolidated storyline rather than the warping of individual frames with geometric distortion in a search, valorized by Woolf, for some new vocabularies of visual symbolism. Woolf had no interest in filmed Dickens—or in literary adaptations of any kind, dismissing their fossilized derivation from another aesthetic altogether. Where for Woolf the motion picture's hopes were solely optical, lying only in forging for itself, and on its own terms, a new visual and stylistic rather than discursive art, for Eisenstein, instead, cinema's true inheritance was the legacy of narrative. Woolf thrilled to an amorphous, squirming shadow encroaching on the space of plot in *Caligari*, and distracting us from any story in its engrossing abstraction. Such impinging, wriggling form installed for Woolf, one might say, the vision of creepiness itself, not an image of approaching danger. For Eisenstein, in contrast, the true imagery of cinema, its metaphoric force, was generated between frames, via an antithetical tension: one that depended in the first place on the micromanagement of a realist narrative progress across photographically rooted shots.

Hence Dickens as tutelary spirit. Eisenstein's longest quotations come from the panoramic cityscapes of *Oliver Twist*, but there are better examples yet of depicted motion having penetrated to the very mechanics of Dickensian wording. In coordinating parallel vectors of advance in fiction, syntactic and representational, explicit vehicles of passage (boats, carriages, train cars, later automobiles and airplanes, of course) tend to sponsor such kinetic effects with a unique immediacy (or call it an italicized mediation)—as is the case, for Dickens, with the newly debuted railroad in particular. Looking to such exemplary *logomotion* in Dickens, then, we find it manifested, in his 1848 novel, *Dombey and Son*, by the rush of certain *railroaded* words in the depiction of a famous and withering train journey. Right away one is reminded of the latently cinematic character of adverbs and prepositions, respectively, in their modification of motion and their interrelation of spaces. Technology has brought the railroad to midcentury London in this tour-de-force scene, and the embodied engine of progress has cut its swath relentlessly across a series of adverbials—in a propulsive grammar of both progressive participles and often compound prepositional shoves—that send it "burrowing among . . . flashing out into . . . mining in through . . . booming on in . . . bursting out again." The force of those impacted tandem prepositions is both unprecedented and explosive. Under this sustained and extraordinary phrasal pressure, it is as if the train were gouging open the very t(er)rain of damage through which it moves. By such means does the cultural and physical upheaval with which locomotion is associated plow its way across a despoiled urban space, so that "tearing on resistless to the goal," in the second iteration of the participial phrase, seems to suggest a ripping as well as a racing urgency. As this passenger train barrels on through the torn night, only its own speeding light—intermittently cast on a dank wet wall—reveals to the racing passengers the "fierce stream" of their own progress. As it might well be said to *scream* past, the train is accompanied by the descending vowel cadence of the "shrill yell of exul/tation" (*il/el/uh/ex/ul*). The unnatural personification entailed here is partly marked in its aberration by that formal and abstract term of Latin origin (over against the harsher Germanic derivations of "shrill" and "yell") with which the phrasing turns breathlessly polysyllabic in those final four syllables—as if, further, and in the combined shriek of whistle and screech of rails, the prose were incurring, in a contorted failed anagram, its own as well as the train's wailing 'exhalation.'

In any event, this whole mobile audiovisual panorama transpires—and, in the reader's silent enunciation, respires—en route to a climactic moment in the ongoing participial juggernaut of "roaring, rattling, tearing on"—where, in the process, stunningly, and from the focal point of the passengers still, the train is found "sometimes pausing for a minute where a crowd of faces are, that in a moment more are not." After all those motiveless headlong prepositions, here predication alone captures the velocity of a vanished landscape in a kind of split-second stroboscopic flash. At this frenetic clip, "where" has no time to become *there*, nor does "are not" necessitate—from the midst of its elliptical negation—any expected wait for the recursive adverbial "are not there." Rather, each determinate locus is being obliterated by speed, place itself eclipsed by time. With all motion compressed within the precipitous present tense (rather than "in a moment more *were* not"), even the grammar of number as well as of tense abets this rending progress. The minor solecism of giving "crowd" a plural verb (no particular requirement, then or now, of British English) seems more mimetic than sloppy here. In the speed of passage, it appears (almost apparitionally) that the one and the many were blurred, fused, crammed into a plurality no sooner glimpsed than neutralized across the toggle of minimal and obverse predication: "are . . . are not"—little more than a vanishing phantom presence under the impress of speed per se. Cinematic not least in its own on/off modular momentum, the wording is all the more so if one thinks of the entrained window frames of the railway carriages—though a blur from the platform's point of view—securing the Fframe-advance vanishment of the station/ary crowds. In any case, the sense of stroboscopic oscillation is transferred to the prose's own grammar of posited presence under immediate negation.

Scenic Dysjuncture

Exposed in the *Dombey* passage is an entire verbal infrastructure of engineered functional correlation between the train's rotary motion and that of prose—an ironclad route, so to say, forged in tandem by grammatical tense and number, participial syntax, diction and its divided etymologies (abstract and Latinate), and fissured connotations, all of it necessary to keep such Dickensian sentences going in precisely what Eisenstein would call their audiovisual montage. Other, more nuanced effects, if not as brilliantly strenuous, operate in Tennyson from the same mid-nineteenth-century period, in verse rather than prose—and as brought, if only tacitly, into the discussion of cinematic equivalents by Eisenstein. We can see this in triangulating his reading of D. W. Griffith's version of Tennyson, concentrating on the screen treatment of a famous poem, with an argument literary critic Julian Murphet, in *Multimedia Modernism*, builds on the same nexus of alternating shots (Eisenstein's sense of rudimentary montage).[2] This alignment of poet and later screen theorist arises as part of Murphet's effort at placing Griffith's raid on Tennyson over against Pound's too sweeping dismissal of his Victorian poetic forebear. It is an argument that can take shape only by proposing, as Murphet does, a deeper link—in the "media ecology" of modernism—between popular screen technique and the resistant compressions and obscurities of Pound's imagism. We are therefore returned, if only indirectly here, to the vicinity of our introductory discussion of Pound's "How to Read" (a work not adduced by Murphet), where no clear break could be made, we saw even then, between his three orders of poesis: aural, pictorial, and lexical.

Whatever Pound ultimately meant to rope in, and cordon off, by those primal demarcations in "How to Read" (again, melopoeisis, phanopoeisis, and logopoeosis), the third category of word art, it bears repeating, is not wholly accounted for in the melodic sounds made—or images made visible thereby—across the activation of lettered text. Wording undergirds the work—but is given up to contemplation by it as well. So what place does his ultimately metalinguistic category, logopoesis, have in an imagism devised and promoted by Pound that would seem, at least by name, to prioritize the phanopoetic frame of visualization? The question isn't soon to let up under investigation. Yet regarding Pound's schematic triad—a poesis harmonic, imagistic, and hyperlingual by turns—and in light of his avowed disgust for Tennysonian melodicism, it is certainly worth observing the paradigm shift involved in the translation of the Victorian laureate's narrative verse and its syllabic nuance to cinematic intercutting at the hands of D. W. Griffith: in short, noting the new syntactic (and therefore quasi-logopoetic?) rather than strictly pictorial dynamic that results. But this same emergent agenda of a more abstract rather than wholly representational image regime, before taking us back to Tennyson's protofilmic lexical succession, takes us first to the movies.

Murphet's literary history is meant to pave its own way to the screening room. The effect that his "media ecology" wants to build on Eisenstein serves to isolate pictorial frame from plotline, tableau from flow—and in this manner (Murphet's further point) finds the Tennysonian optic less divorced than ordinarily thought (pace Pound) from an imagist aesthetic in postimpressionist modernism. In Murphet's account, and with Eisenstein's analysis specifically in mind, Tennyson's pivotal narrative effect in the *Enoch Arden* verses, viewed against Griffith's treatment, involves its own kind of protocinematic imagism. Murphet sees Annie Lee, bereft and forlorn, looking out from a deserted shore in the direction of her husband Enoch's departing ship, in a manner that incarnates just such a plot-arresting image—and not merely in Griffith's close-up but (this being Murphet's main intervention) in Tennyson as well. Eisenstein's interest here centers on Griffith's original and path- (as well as frame-) breaking cut, not on any oblique source in his Victorian prototype. (For Eisenstein, Tennyson is no forebear like Dickens is.) The Soviet theorist's attention is spent entirely on the unprecedented 1908 screen close-up of Annie long after Enoch's exile, first severing head from body (in a most Dickensian fashion, according to Eisenstein), and then her entire space from the distant scene of shipwreck and desolation into which we are tossed, thousands of miles away in the associated but disjoint next shot (Eisenstein, 225). As if only half anticipating the eventually established syntax of shot/reverse shot in the later eyeline intimacies of Hollywood practice, this crosscut exacerbates distance rather than elides it.

Engaged here is not a true "suture"—as analytic vocabulary would come to characterize the stitching-in of the viewer's invisible access as intermediary between seamed shots in the reciprocal gaze of character interaction (to be discussed with further exemplification from Tennyson below)—but more like a trope of telepresencing. The psychological paraphrase might run this way, as a cue to disjuncture itself: 'In her abjection could be glimpsed its cause. In her face you could almost see what she was thinking (of), fixating on in her mind's eye, the husband far and long gone.' In Annie's italicized close-up, that is, expression becomes itself expressive of its own content, but not entirely contained by subjectivity, by memory or desire. The ensuing syntax of omniscience gives us, as well, the man she is thinking *about* in the presumed real time (codified in later years by the secured protocols of parallel editing) of his answering desire and brutal separation—as if they were each looking into a reversed void, hoping to bridge the gulf by the kind of disembodied imaginative projection that film technique is at this point exemplifying. By inventing.

As laid out again by Murphet, the gist of this rigorous shot analysis is all there, to begin with, in Eisenstein. In his third chapter, "Figure, Image, Thing," what Murphet expands on Eisenstein's account of this breakthrough moment in film technique to argue, regarding a systemic competition across media, is that more of it is there in Tennyson as well—the detachment of freestanding image from the forward drive of plotting—than a denigrator like Pound would be inclined to acknowledge. Whereas Eisenstein stresses the filmmaker's debts to Dickens, for Murphet, Griffith might well, even if unconsciously, have found(ed) this very effect of resonant disjuncture—this narrative suspension bridge of affect—in his reading of Tennyson. The mere description of Annie stationed immobile on the beach alone, wrenched from narrative time, from all continuity and future, shows her immobilized in the flow of poetry as in the diurnal pace of life. That's what Murphet thinks Griffith, too, elicited from his recourse to Tennyson's sentimental narrative—and knew how to capitalize on. In regard to on-screen results, Eisenstein had already archived this moment for film history, as we've seen, with Murphet then productively importing it into the register of modernist literary debate. In his transmedial argument, the "cuts" on Griffith's screen that sever image from image amount to slices of space-time in calculated ruptures forded at first only by intercutting and its metonymies of association: grieving/shipwreck; abandonment/exile. Telescoping space within the reciprocal sightings (rather than actual scenes) of desolation, temporal abutment alone reads out as distance. In Griffith's inaugural deployment, the explicitly Dickens-inspired cut, the breach, the gap, the woeful lacuna (characterize it how you will), is a disjunction distended to oceanic scope, reverting in the process from optics to tropology—from image to *imagery*—for this overleapt abyss of separation in the register of affect alone. Innovated here is a dialectic image in embryo (as Eisenstein half implies)—awaiting the third term that would release it from bathos into conceptual synthesis.

But what more to learn from such moments, such pressure points of medium-specific technique, about their plausible prose equivalents—let alone their poetic precedents? If there is to be a cinematic wording in prose, there must just as clearly be a filmic enjambment in verse: a seedbed for eased transition, for delicate balances and transacted pivots, for, in a word, lap dissolves as well as jump cuts. So, in a moment, back to Tennyson—and to the time-based flow of language—rather than, for instance, what might be understood as the simultaneous time-lapses of Whitmanesque prophecy in the previous decade, imploding—as we saw in the arrested "Crossing" of "Brooklyn Ferry"—the energies of flashback and flash-forward upon the empty center of textual premonition. According to Murphet, the shot exchange just scanned in Griffith is a case of film building on Victorian language in its unwritten pictorial codes, where verse wording can be found subtracting the image from one narrative stream in order to syncopate it with its answering idea (rather than shot) in another: syntax subsumed to rhetoric. That clean-edged and historically unprecedented Griffith cut between Annie and Enoch—a mutual but disjoint optic, a verging without merger—is, Murphet would imply, despite Pound's recoil from Tennyson, a kind of technological imagism in defiance of strict narrative logic.

What to learn, one asks again, from such cross-medial claims—and, perhaps more to the point, from the cited evidence they are mounted on? The answer, it barely needs saying, gravitates toward more than a classroom sales pitch: more than the mere collective payoff from some systematic colloquium in the mode of "cinematic" writing. To spell this out for potential students of prose, as even the most modest of caveats, is to dispel, once and for all, any (however unlikely) false conceptions concerning these final two chapters. The tactical logic, as already stressed, isn't one of imitation, but rather inhabitation. For any aspiring writers into whose hands, between keyboard sessions, this book may fall, the effort—half-intuitive, half-analytic, or instead more like the two inseparably—could only be to reside in the prose, or ride it home, and sometimes its verse equivalents, until their rhythms have induced something like a muscle memory in the potential rhythms of your own way with words. The idea certainly isn't to *do* George Eliot, or Henry James, even Salman Rushdie, let alone Tennyson, but to see—and hear—*how they did it*. To keep ears peeled until your fingers might twitch with the itch to write something not like it, but as intensely likely, however surprising, of your own—in a feasible contemporary idiom.

In just this spirit, then, I suppose the immediate premise of this chapter can benefit from re-emphasis. In turning the page, as it were, from screen editing to verbal syntax, the exercises in comparison broached here can be imagined as the verso to the curricular recto of any course syllabus, like that of "Reading Movies for Prose Writers," focused so centrally on sampled screen grammar—and its rhetoric. If creative writers stand to learn from filmic inscription about the variables of narrative advance, there is no reason to think that the same lessons might not be educed from accomplished writing that has, in its own way, either learned from cinema or even, in a preceding century, anticipated its advent by the kinetics of its own phrasal succession, its disjunctures, overlaps, elisions. In the activation of any such pedagogy, students sampling clips from Griffith to Godard, Keaton to Kubrick, Fritz Lang to Francis Ford Coppola would of course also be reading, alongside such moving images, any number of "filmic" predecessors and descendants in timed-based representation from Dickens to DeLillo, even Tennyson to Pound in the latter's famous quick-cut metonymic montage from 1913, the colon changed to an even more disjunctive semicolon in the 1916 standard edition of *Lustra*:

> The apparition of these faces in the crowd;
> Petals on a wet, black bough.

Such is Pound's surgically spliced film strip of a parataxis, complete with the demonstrative immediacy of its *these/the* slide in the frameline flickering and descriptive shift of its decisive match-cut semicolon: one shot, then its figurative equal and conceptual as well as phonetic rhyme (*ow/ough*). Pound's "In a Station of the Metro" owes nothing directly even to Dickens's locomotively scanned "crowd of faces," any more than to Tennyson, except—and no small thing at that—the inner dynamic of transient linkage in the grain of verbal inscription per se, of imaging as wording.

Lexical Panning and the Ripple Effect

Last we looked, Murphet had trained our gaze, in his descriptive clip from *Enoch Arden*, on the discrepant shot pattern of Annie Lee's syntactically answered but technically (logically) unreturned gaze, detaching image from narrative grammar altogether in its raid on the supposed fixed framings of Tennysonian rhetoric. Yet here one needs to draw a line—by looking more closely at the Tennyson lines behind this mode of innovation. Only a case in point can test this claim, and it might as well be Murphet's example, taken one notch further (as well as four lines back). He looks earlier in the poem than does Griffith for the kind of cinematic prototype too quickly downplayed by imagism. He finds at the opening of a crucial stanza from *Enoch Arden*'s departure scene (quite apart from Griffith's later interpolation on the score of prolonged exile) an image isolated from the narrative rhetoric that at the same time washes over it and sweeps it up. It behooves us, however, to pick up the narrative peripety just before—at the close of the preceding stanza, where, with Enoch setting sail, Annie tries, so to speak, *to see him off*. And to this virtual meme of shoreline valediction in the epic literary mold, Tennyson brings new micronarrative energy. The syntax is precipitous, with Annie's nominating pronoun hurtled forward—across the choppy thematized delay of a periodic grammar—into an attempted sentimental prosthesis in the rhyming to come: "She when the day, that Enoch mention'd, came, / Borrow'd a glass, but all in vain." The grammar seems almost as internally layered and self-encased as her telescope. Even as that collision of the verbs around the enjambment at "came, / Borrowed" has a propellant force all its own, speeding us under extra pressure toward the day of days, it turns out, when the time so rushingly comes, that she couldn't focus after all, perhaps through teary eyes. Ensuing from this failed ocular linkage of aided eye and vanishing object on the horizon, the next line "cuts" on the colon (and its caesura): "She saw him not: and while he stood on deck / Waving, the moment and the vessel past"—and precisely in that anomalous phonetic elision of the past tense "passed" typically favored by Tennyson, as if already to anticipate the temporal result of the spatial motion it names. Just before, enjambment rounds the turn of disappearance as if Enoch were waving goodbye to the very chance of valediction (a hope as if 'waived' by fate)—and this across the self-parted grammar of time and space in the passing of "the moment and the vessel" together: two nouns dividing the lost opportunity between them, via parallel but disjoined predications, in a redoubled downbeat of the irreparably elapsed. (Couched here is the grammatical obverse of a more openly splayed logical forking like 'She lost sight of him and her chance of a returned wave at once.') Syntax has slid out from under itself as if, yet again, slipping the sprocket holes of its own rotation.

There may seem no reason to force the cinematic analogue at this turn, this familiar Victorian turn of phrase in forked compounds. Seriality reigns definitive here, with tempo noted only, as with Dickens's locomotion, when operating in some kind of default or overdrive. That might have been enough to say. Yet Eisenstein has a keener sense, elsewhere, of the actual grammatical paradigms involved in such parallel tracks of enactment (with manifold instances in Dickens, though unmentioned by his later Soviet admirer): grammatical parallels split down the middle and divided logically against themselves. What we encounter in the cresting of this Tennysonian verse wave, its peak and drop, is the motivated and poignant equivalent of the strained and strictly functionalist parallelism castigated by Eisenstein in the kind of parallel editing he illustrates (and parodies) as "Came the rain and two students." Tennyson's effect is, in contrast, reverberant rather than swiftly serviceable—and puts us in mind of those later sylleptic forkings, long after Dickens, in the acquired English of Conrad, Nabokov, and Brodsky considered in chapter 2. In "the moment and the vessel past," a bitter simultaneity is continuous and consequential, a cinematic panning and a plangency at once, pivoting around a kind of internal syntactic watershed. And turning further, at that, on the latent play, in this grammatical context, tipping an understood "pass'd" over into the adjectival "past" that would dislodge the intransitive grammar into its own hovering absolute ("the moment and the vessel being past")—there where his waving can only seem bitterly ironic in the face of the very waves ferrying him away.

All this is suspended in operation with an odd extra sense of lexical superimposition—or perhaps "match cut"—in the shift from forestalled nautical valediction to this very different, nongestural wave motion. If I seem to be fishing for cinematic terms in these verse waters, that's in the nature of this whole experiment. But it is the waver of the text itself, not in my floated screen equivalents for it, that I mean to characterize as a "rippling" shimmer at both the syntactic and even, as we're about to find, the phonetic level. The filmy lapping of Tennyson's grammar (vessel passed and the chance for valediction with it; boat and opportunity lost sight of, both now past) is more than an irrelevance in the vacillations of this enjambed *passage* (both senses, once again, of paced transit). And at the almost microscopic (or microphonic) scale of alphabetic tremor and fade-out as well, the far and vanishing glimpse of the ship (if not telescopic, her borrowed "glass" unavailing) will come to be focalized, as it were, by phonemes alone.

In the now familiar homology of levels in the operation of Fframe-advance—mobile panorama, say, and its subsidiary serial articulations on the strip—it is indeed tempting to associate these fluctuant effects in Tennyson with the ripple wipe of subsequent screen grammar: in the literary case, one frame of reference, so to speak, elapsing by dissolve into another in an adjacent crest of sense (rather than, as with cinema, in the emergence of a whole separate scene). So here is yet another case of syntax "screened" for the motion effect of its own inner roll and undertow. At the grammatical level already cited (and dimly sighted)—"the moment and the vessel past [pass'd]"—we are engaged not with tableau alone, then, as Murphet would stress in the lines' proto-imagistic split from narrative, but with the ruefulness of the off-frame in a swift departure past the embodied aperture of vision. Even at this stage—and staging—of the marital separation, the language is every bit as cinematic, in the ship's edging from frame (passing, passed, past) as it may be thought to be, on screen itself, in any later exchange of fixed shots after the vaster and more drastic severance of the couple. And it grows more so yet, more cinematic, and in this same passage, at the lower end of the Fframe scale. Following the line break and stanza gap, as marking its own version of an affective gaping wound, the moment of lapsed opportunity—at exactly the point where Murphet begins his citation and analysis of an image supposedly sprung free from narrative—is prolonged by something less than a full reverse shot. We don't see Annie beached and still fumbling with her spyglass, but we have narrated for us instead, along the very horizon of a syllabic pan, the vanishing object of her gaze—yet entirely from her perspective: a kind of free indirect optics that might on film, in a later mode spawned by Griffith, have been handled by a rapid exchange of shots. In what I am terming instead a lexical ripple effect, here is the epitomizing line from the renowned "ear" as well as pen of Tennyson: "Ev'n to the las*t dip* of the vanishing sail / She watch'*d it*, an*d dep*arted weeping for him." Not only is there a chiasm of exits in this transition, his away from and hers back home, its opening phrase lends it an extranarrative valence in transitional overlap with the preceding stanza after all. Given "vessel past" on the preceding side of the stanza break, there is a thin antecedent continuity established, then broken, with the first line's grammar above, as if it were attached backwards by a loose enjambment ("vessel pass'd / even to the last dip . . .")—until the adverbial segue is registered by inversion, instead, as completing the delayed object ("it") of the verb. But that hardly exhausts the subject/object dialectic of this waving/gaze switch point, which has penetrated to the crevices of its own lexical inscription. Through the ubiquitous synecdoche by which "a sail on the horizon" signals (signs) a ship, part for whole, the 'last tip' of the receding sail can hardly be said to go unspoken by its drifting over into "last dip"—transitory cause to the shrinking effect in this visual residue of departure, even while the *d-p* ripple returns in the slant rhyme (and cross-word acceleration) of "an*d dep*arted." A precinematic blink of wording results there from the editorial scissors of poet rather than filmmaker.

Whereas the inertial momentum of *Dombey*'s railroad journey rammed through its own flickering jump cuts—or swish pans—so that transient images "are there, that in a minute more are not," Tennyson's slower, wavelike drift swallows time every bit as markedly in the ligatures of syntactic gradation. So if one wants to think of Tennyson, along with his coeval Dickens, as being there at the conception of cinema, long before its birth, such small-gauge verbal events are ready to be brought into evidence among the cellular developments, the embryonic molecular bondings, that vitalize the word as differential image. This is what we might dub a long nineteenth-century perspective in the ways of the word—mastered for narrative prose by Dickens, as for narrative verse by Tennyson, and willed by divergent lineages through Griffith's Hollywood technique to the recoil of Virginia Woolf and, in contrast, the later approbation of Eisenstein in his own modernist aesthetic agenda. It is a perspective that soon takes us also to Woolf's further (unacknowledged) refinement of Griffith's intercutting in the prosecution of her own cinematic sentences.

Syntactic Suture

But before Woolf's stream of consciousness, there is the very agon of consciousness in the cognitive labyrinths—and entangled dialogue—of a daunting modernist stylist considered too cerebral, in the true lifeblood of his syntactic involution, for cinematic translation, despite the many screen adaptations that skim the supposed cream of his plotting. Halfway between the birth of cinema and Griffith's recourse both instinctively to Dickens and more specifically to Victorian verse narrative—for not just the outline, but (as Murphet would have it) the whole quasi-imagist inspiration, of his *Enoch Arden* film—falls the last novel of the great transitional modernist Henry James, including its own use of a loaded marital crosscut in its closing dialogue. Where a radical severance of desire is triaged by the same grammar that diagnoses its forced rapport.

Now, the last thing one wishes to instill in student writers is the tortuous involution of a Jamesian sentence as their go-to option, even when such a sentence may be thrillingly alive with an erotic drama of emotional blackmail and psychic entrapment. But striving for a similar contemporary effect with the Lesson of the Master in mind, there are ways and there are ways—all within the waywording of syntax and its reversible foci. I should still certainly pause, anyone should, before introducing *The Golden Bowl* as even a potential modeling exercise in a chapter sharing the interdisciplinary spirit of an undergraduate writing curriculum. Yet modeling, as stressed above, isn't really the issue, the procedure; it's a matter of syntactic consciousness-raising. And that much James is eminently good for under apprentice eyes. This we've seen in the introduction when a single strained idiomatic compression, a single skewed turn of the phrasal screw—"to encounter also herself" (in lieu of 'for herself')—spins the whole phrasing out of true into an uncanny premonition of the supernatural itself.

Eminently good, James certainly is, at exemplifying such functional aberrations of the norm. And with what uptake for modern writing? The routes of assimilation can be richly indirect. And what might seem cinematic about them always equally so. Inspired by the renowned and thickly layered mise-en-scène of *Citizen Kane*, for instance, one doesn't (anymore than when imagining the camerawork that might translate a given syntactic knot in James's description) set out to write a "deep focus" prose, each sentence crowded with receding details concerning the furnished space of action or dialogue. Imagine an effort like this (in my ad hoc approximation) as a wrong way to learn from *The Golden Bowl*:

> In this moment of last hope for their frayed marriage, behind them as they spoke into each other's fixed gazes, their urgency oblivious to it, dropped away in perspective all the luxuriant décor of their isolated life together,

polished tabletop antiques of modish chinoiserie in the foreground of their conversation, fading away past eighteenth century marbles and Etruscan statuary to indiscernible mere objects across the richly furnished chamber of their commitment and their imprisonment alike, its vanishing point, like their fate, all sheen and blur.

Like the imagined setting, this is too precious by half. There is, however, a quite cinematic pairing of sentences about the similar last-minute recoupling, and in the lap of a comparable cloying luxury, in the actual novel by James, whose closing impact falls very far from Hollywood theater. Yet whose phrasal counterpoint is so deeply filmic in its ocular interchange that I once included, as introductory evidence in book of mine on screen theory, an extended "shot analysis," including a vectoral diagram, of its ingrown grammatical alterations—under the subheading "Suture 1914."[3]

Scanned a good deal more briefly here, this climactic exchange from *The Golden Bowl* begins in response to the heroine's slightly patronizing idiom ("don't you see?") about the situation of the couple in the enforced maintenance of their marriage. The gist of its cinematic dynamic can be given fairly succinctly. Here's the grammatical interface in question (the counterweights of its syntactic fulcrum italicized), with the second sentence entailing its own internal reboot (at the ominous "but . . .") in a subsequent full clause after the semicolon. The initial subject of the sentence is the inferential weight of that idiom itself ("don't you see?"):

> It *kept him before her* therefore, taking in—or trying to—what she so wonderfully gave. He tried, too clearly, to please her—to meet her in her own way; but with the result only that, close to her, *her face kept before him*, his hands holding her shoulders, his whole act enclosing her, he presently echoed: "See? I see nothing but you."

Before this ironic foreclosure of the suddenly literalized look, this reciprocal episode of inhabited attention has, in the axis of vision, traversed the tacit rhyming close-ups of hero and heroine in a palpable, indeed claustrophobic, shot/reverse shot, capped by the first of three absolute constructions (with its elliptical verb force): "her face [being] kept before him" in that viselike reversal begun with "kept him before her." All but cauterized by dramatic irony in this case is the suture that temporarily heals the marital wound at the expense of the world. Suture: the theoretical term in cinema studies, again, for the stitching together of shot and its answering shot around the disavowed void of camera position itself—as if the viewer were impossibly slotted in to alternating points of occupied view. In contrast to the narcissistic reflex of the returned erotic gaze in *Of Time and the River*, James's finish gives us a true correlate to this cinematic mainstay. Between whose phrasal about-faces—in the very grammar of "faces" and persons "kept before"—we may even sense shaken loose, in an insidious final irony continuous with the syntactic clampdown, the deflected undertone of 'keeping face' for a marriage compromised by adultery and accommodation.

At first, the strictly rhetorical "don't you see?" is the hook that, in a thin rhyme, "kept him before her therefore"—there and therefore, as it were. Kept him (which is all she wants): kept him there . . . until "he presently echoed"—echoed not just her previous idiom but his own clenched speech in redoubling it, first as metaphor, then in the objectified form of a facial vanishing point—"See? I see nothing but *you*." There the gaze stops, all else occluded in this connubial myopia. Just here the previous tactical back-and-forth is fulfilled in a syntactic flange of blinkered, interlocked sight lines—just the kind of ocular exchange rendered hypertrophic, at the end of Wolfe's text, by the interknit eyeline stare we saw supposedly rarefied into subjective reflex, spiritualized, in a briefly met, and then radically internalized, erotic gaze.

Three decades earlier, however, one certainly doesn't need to say that cinema's intercutting inspired this kind of construction in James, not least because its techniques of close-up and reverse shot had not yet been regularized except as optic potentials of the new medium. None of this discussion, then, is compromised by anachronism. (Nor can it be off-loaded onto the Merchant-Ivory film version of this novel, which handles this closing marital exchange in a flattening two-shot). In the reading of the original James passage, we need only grant that, over a century later, a novice contemporary writer's sensing something similar, and potentially suggestive, in an actual shot plan when visualized on screen, having perhaps nothing to do with a Jamesian text or temper—or entertaining a sense of the cinematic in another such sentence from James, James Joyce, Joyce Carol Oates, anyone—might be onto something. Take it where you find it. Suffice it to say that noticing the focalizations enforced by syntax across the least torque of a given word template—like the unfolded matrix of "kept before" in its dizzying flip of predication—is no bad way, in its mental stretch, if not its actual strained rhythms, of seeding a potential grammar of a student's own in the aftermath of both attentive movie watching and rapt novel reading. All the more so if one's feel for the dynamic pulse of such alternation traverses the entire scale of effect from tagged dialogue exchange to the disjunctive shot plans of simultaneous montage inherited through Griffith by prose's own parallel temporalities and interlinked scene shifts. And traverses also, at the same time, and even in the same process, the full gamut of Fframe-advance in the range from depicted space to the lexical wrinkles—or ripples, and sometimes psychic riptides and undertows—that articulate it.

Picture vs. Vision: Imagery beyond Image

We have deferred long enough our return to Virginia Woolf's critique of mere literary adaptation on screen—as in fact it is lent weight, and not parodically either, by her own most cinematic sentences. Given her aesthetic instincts, these are more satisfying on the page, at their tightly contoured verbal scale, than is a more obvious "literary moment"—slavish borrowings especially—on the narrative film screen. The forced marriage between literary fiction and film—unfulfilling, she finds, to both parties—is of no interest to Woolf. She doesn't want translation, but abstraction, as befits a medium definitively visual but potentially nonrepresentational. Not someone identified by title (or title card) as Anna Karenina, a figment in black velvet, as she mocks such an impersonation, but some other audiovisual topography of the troubled self—or, as in *Caligari*, the amorphous shape of fear itself rather than images of the fearful. Not Garbo, one might say, but the optic garb of hopelessness. Woolf's is a call, unidentified in so many words, for medium-specificity in the aspiration to art. And it pivots implicitly around two separate senses of "image," tropological versus optical. Shakespeare's tropes, as she celebrates them in this same "Cinema" piece, bring sensory images to mind by layers of lexical connotation. The motion picture has no such vocabulary. It must work from the visual image toward the figurative. But instead, it is regularly trapped in the literal, the merely photographic—and especially in its treatment of the literary. She wants, instead, the indirection of art, not the immediacy of technological reproduction: poetry not visual theater, as of course she tries for in her own prose.

A year after publishing her "Cinema" essay, Woolf has, as it happens, not only composed one of her most "cinematic" scenes (a kind of parallel montage welded by a reversible structure of unsutured gazes) but has embedded within it that brand of emblematic abstraction (championed by modernist aesthetics) that she would hope cinema could absorb, not from literature but from the other arts. And then in turn, though without saying so, with inferences—drawn from that apogee of climactic painterly abstraction in *To the Lighthouse*—for what fiction could learn from film: not so much in narrative finesse as in the abstraction of its ideas in a further aesthetic resistance to Victorian realism. We don't know if she had seen Annie Lee on the shore of amorous separation as well as Anna Karenina in escalating despair. Likely not. But the same "blind" exchange of the gaze in Griffith, between beached desire on the mainland and islanded isolation abroad, is there at the "intercut" finale of *To the Lighthouse* to figure the opacity, within the abiding force, of empathy itself—and its aesthetic fallout in transmedial representation, literary and painterly.

As the suddenly widowed Mr. Ramsay, in these last pages, leads a recuperative excursion—with his two children—to the lighthouse beyond their island home, no sooner has he looked back with his "long-sighted eyes" (a clinical description turned figurative) than the tracking of vision splits: between his daughter's subjective guess about his POV and her own blurred eyeline imaging. Open to view is an inner cinema, we might say, of the speculative rather than the specular, where "perhaps he could see the dwindled leaf-like shape standing on end on a plate of gold quite clearly. What could he see? Cam wondered. It was all a blur to her." A more dramatic quick cut then returns us to the island, to Lily Briscoe the painter and Mr. Carmichael the poet, both fixated—in a kind of transaesthetic fellow feeling—upon the unseen arrival of father and children from the artists' removed pair of strained and indeterminate points of view. The vectoral "to" of the novel's title (a directional prominence in the angling of sight lines as well) concludes with the adverbially inflected landing of Mr. Ramsay in a sprightly final clause, when both children "rose to follow him as he sprang, *lightly like a young man*, holding his parcel, on to the rock"—"lightly" as befits, beyond any semantics, his destination in the lighthouse itself—where the internal modification (my italics) seems matched, all but exactly, to the brief time of the jump. To the lighthouse, and onto (on to) its rock, he has come.

Then, immediately, a more dramatically contrastive jump cut in this parallel montage. From her perch on the distant island lawn, Lily's own attempt at far-seeing has been a strain both optical and subjective. For as we return to her exploratory gaze in description, the "lightly" of Ramsay's spring is answered—in the very next sentence—by the heavy slump of her being "suddenly completely tired out": a flagging of energy on the backs of adverbial echo itself. From within her contemplative stare at the technically unseen, she can only presume, not observe: " 'He must have reached it,' said Lily Briscoe aloud." No other sense but sound, her own in the rhythms of monologue, offers confirmation. "For the Lighthouse had become almost invisible, had melted away into a blue haze, and the effort of looking at it and the effort of thinking of him landing there, which *both seemed to be one and the same effort*, had stretched her body and mind to the utmost" (emphasis added on the conflation of subjectivity and sight line). Looking and thinking are simultaneous, equivalent: here and, of course, in fiction itself, especially in the channels of free indirect discourse. But again she speaks out, in choric fashion, on behalf of this exaggerated ceremonial (almost sacrificial) closure, so that internal monologue has become soliloquy: " 'He has landed,' she said aloud. 'It is finished.' " Not in fact hearing her, the arriving poet Carmichael also voices his confirmation out loud, phrased in the future perfect—and thus at one further remove from imagined visual proof. Call it poetry's sense of events outside of language: "They will have landed." Again, the grammar of tense inflects the inner lining of a narrative trajectory.

In the failed resolution of any lighthouse sighting, the scene is now firmly—or not quite firmly—returned to the island lawn. The ocular logic of the description is again pivoted around adverbial pointers, vague at first until leashed to her painting: "Quickly, as if she were recalled by something over there, she turned to her canvas. There it was—her picture." From "over there" to "there," the arc of a rapid swish pan in a simple slide of demonstrative grammar—with the pertinent inference, soon confirmed, that the "canvas" and its achieved "picture" can be differentiated—and especially at this pending moment of achieved form. The eyeline gaze remains for a moment restless, in transit: "She looked at the steps; they were empty; she looked at her canvas; it was blurred." The nearby household steps are only an aesthetic stepping-stone. The gaze is triangulated. In a lateral return to her painting, the blur it shares with the seascape beyond, and the lighthouse landing, is now to be rectified by the decisive insert—as at the end of any novel, this one included, of a fitting last "line"—a line displaced here, in compositional terms, to the canvas plane: a single line "there, in the centre. It was done; it was finished." The linear cascade of empty steps isn't rendered, as if by photography or film, but abstracted to a single mere *delineation*, indeed a medium-essential stroke of the brush.

And one that seals tight this closing passage at an almost subliminal level of echo and connection. The trisyllabic rhythm of "suddenly completely," converting an odd sing-song measure to the gravity of exhaustion in the first rendering of her response, is now transferred to the tighter downbeat of assonance (in a cross-word *e/i* latch): "Yes, she thought, laying down her brush in extreme fatigue, I have had my vision." At degree zero, with the described insertion of a single (but doubly figured) "line," both literary and pictorial, Woolf's sustained minimalist ekphrasis of Lily's unframed abstract work in progress has met completion. Just as cinema can't get at the essence even of realist literature, in Woolf's view elsewhere, it is also the case that such visionary prose as she has come to execute in her fiction must of necessity escape the strictly pictorial. Lily's painting exceeds, defies, and evacuates ekphrasis. From "they will have" (landed) to "I have had" (my vision) is, in effect, the spaced duration of closure for a novel whose double "finish" plays between a highly cinematic treatment of low-fidelity optics, in a mimesis of eye strain and its reciprocal "blurs" in parallel montage, and an abstraction of finality that resembles a final freeze-frame on the as yet unframed but just perfected canvas. What Woolf has conceivably borrowed from "realist" camerawork in the sight lines of parallel event—the limits of its clarity, its shifts in focus, the adjusted lenses of its registration—all converge in this last abstract stroke. Here is an "edited" ocular plane that—as Woolf wishes for cinema in its own kinetic precincts—strives less for a moving picture than for a distilled vision, whose optics are themselves imagistic rather than documentary.

Focalization: Point of Audition and Its POV

But then screen picturing in its own right—not in the silent completion of a painterly rectangle in the days before sound film, but later in cross-medial history—can offer a symphonic orchestration of image in prose form.

180   Chapter 5

If Woolf in *To the Lighthouse* seems, almost despite her best instincts, to incorporate the full flowering of a Griffith-style montage across no longer untraversable waters of distance and projection in the moment of the look—only to revert to the ekphrasis of a painted canvas rectangle in embedding her own counter-realist aesthetic emblem—it goes without saying that many other options for prose picturing exist elsewhere in an equally cinematic vein. In her own prose as well, to which we'll return for a more melodramatic and violent example of the mobile POV shot. And beyond her particular mode of fiction, of course, options proliferate. There are, for instance, focal managements that can actuate a full battery of "cinematic wording" from within the fixed frame of a single audiovisual long shot. On certain pages, that is, the eared and the screened converge—in precisely the play between sonic momentum and grammatical focus.

I had written, a chapter back, that the concerns of such discussion have nothing to do with "writing for the movies." Faulkner, however, did indulge in such screen-writing, famously, lucratively—and in his own fiction wrote scenes of graphic spectacle worthy of filming. The twain might even meet at times, but distinctions remain. For it's the prose too, as well the histrionic action it sometimes motivates and realizes, that has its own internal drama—its focus pulls, its off-frame tension, its variable resolution and adjusted perspectives—as here, for instance, in the conflagration that engulfs the dynastic mansion at the end of *Absalom, Absalom!* (1936),[4] a fire set in mistaken panic by Clytie (née Clytemnestra) in a symbolic scourge of the Sutpen dynasty. If, in its climactic melodrama, if not its southern gothic extravagance, it recalls the burning of Atlanta from *Gone with the Wind*, it does so with no relation to the prose of that novel from the same American year. All transpires at this point in Faulkner's text under an omniscient medium-long shot in wait for an arriving ambulance. As the scene explodes from the fixed remove of our observation, the idiomatic "roaring" fire (Germanic origin: "imitative") is conveyed by a subvocal soundtrack that pits it explicitly against the emerging noise—from within this vista of inferno—of an inarticulate human moan caught by a distancing syntax that removes this baffled tragic chorus-of-one from all visibility. As the doomed House of Sutpen is swallowed up in rampaging flames, the overwhelmed dwelling is at first expanded by apposition as a "monstrous tinder-dry rotten shell seeping smoke through the warped cracks in the weather-boarding as if it were made of gauze wire and filled with roaring . . ." (300), that last word a freestanding gerund in capture of sound's own congealed ferocity. The open-ended ellipsis of mine that suspends attention at this point leaves something else, in a moment, to reveal—as the uninterrupted grammar does in the normal, but jolted, pace of one's reading. So far, in this soundscape of a raging maelstrom, the choked *o* of "monstrous" is distributed among, or say ignites, the muffled *o* of "rotten," the gaping *a(h)* of "warped," the long *oa* of "boarding," and the softened *au* of "gauze"—all in a spreading vocalic firestorm transmitted to diction's own roiling turmoil. As if it were some uncontainable syllabic spread of arson's *awful roar*.

Here, then, is the quintessential eared page of a preternatural cacophony that suddenly, in this vision of incineration, layers its own grammatical perspective, and rhythm, with that of a different cognitive register altogether. This results from a sudden stress on what cinematic technique would identify as "point of audition" (by analogy with POV, the point from which a sound is heard) as it operates in tandem with the encompassing optical shot—and with all that its fixity leaves unseen, unpursued. The reader's grammatically calibrated access to the devastation now seems drawn inward, if invisibly, from the conjoined elliptical phrase "as if it were . . . filled with roaring" to its further reverb, aural and grammatical—summarily cut off the first time through, for emphasis, by my own ellipsis. As we resume the sentence in its original tempo, syntax pushes through to a less subjunctive separate clause that trails away toward some kind of audial vanishing point—as if broken loose from the preceding cumulative grammar into its own lumbering coordinate, then subordinate, extension. The ancestral mansion persists only momentarily now, silhouetted against its own incineration, as a thing "made of gauze and filled with roaring, and beyond which"—with the *on* of "mo*n*strous . . . shell" returned more neutrally, at least for a moment—"beyond which somewhere something lurked which bellowed, something human since the bellowing was in human speech, even though the reason for it would not have seemed to be" (300). It is, we realize, the addled, maddened cry, the inarticulate "speech," of Jim Bond, spurned offshoot of miscegenation and violence. In the recessional space of this whole nightmare (one "which" is caught dropping back to another layer of removed anguish in that second subordinator), we hear, that is, the identified cries of the unseen outcast as they will continue to emanate in his frenzied retreat—straight past the end of the novel—beyond the borders of the razed plantation and the plot alike.

And in this tapering back of narrative, beyond image, to its unfinished finale, we note a power of language that differs, almost by definition, from film rhetoric. At the height of the conflagration, Bond's is an unsourced wail ("something somewhere which bellowed") raised in concert with the surrounding thunder of the blaze. Situated by our point of audition, it propels this crescendo of violence with a force that we might call in-scene but off-screen. Yet at the same time, by a scarcely raucous play on words in that same sentence, the twice-enunciated dead metaphor of "bellows" (in its etymological relation to the overheated breath of "blows") is obtruded in inescapable lexical association with the fanned fires of historical revenge. In this audiovisual mayhem, it is as if the derivative verb were haunted by back-formation from its noun source—or vice versa—in an inflamed synesthesia of hearthside tool and useless misery. The irony hovers, lingers, incriminates. The bellowing of this mentally incapacitated victim of inbred generational cruelty cannot be doused along with the cinders of ancestral fatality. And if a filmed version of the scene could be imagined to approximate the overlap of the two oxygenated "roarings," human and chemical, this would bear pale comparison to the double valence of the punning "bellows" in the language itself of the fiction.

Fade to black. Fade, cut, iris out. Who's to say, since the prose doesn't? So I don't want any such mere similes from screen optics to imperil the point. On the scent of the *cinematic* sentence, no metaphors are needed except the one, in that admittedly figurative epithet from film practice, that sponsors the pursuit all told. The torrent of assonance across those evoked surging flames in Faulkner, the compounded syntax and its further grammatical lurch into lexical irony ("bellows") and a subsequent expelling distance (the superbly telescoped syntax of "and beyond which lurked somewhere something which"): these are cinematic (in our laboratory sense) precisely because of what is linguistic in their execution, no "as if's" about it in the fudgings of analogy. So a teachable moment: principle again emerged from instance within the literary register itself, when strictly observed. The grammatical hierarchy of subordination can unroll in syntactic time as a tracked motion, whether in one direction or another or both at once: here a straining forward to hear, an encroachment of noise from an occluded depth of field.

With no undue stress on comparison, let's say simply that what the least curiosity about potential medial correlation—or better, what a merely incipient transmedial instinct—might have "screened for" in this climactic moment from Faulkner's masterwork is nothing more unlikely than the prolonged "wide-angle establishing shot" of the blazing mansion and the searing "acousmatique" force of withdrawn off-frame rage. Same in Woolf, or same difference under analogy—with the occluded mutual vanishing points of lighthouse and island residence in link with the two-dimensional "freeze" on the inset picture plane and its final-line culmination. Nothing cautionary in any of those scare quotes. Such heuristic metaphors, if only provisionally entertained, are not likely to get in the way of wording so much as to "rerun" productively (there's another one), for functional appreciation, its actual pathways.

So let's circle round to Woolf again in her dream of a cinema beyond plot: an image system cleansed of pictorial explicitness, a motion picturing of idea rather than event. I spoke of the closing eponymous phase of *To the Lighthouse* as "one of her most 'cinematic' scenes." And in the lockdown on Lily's canvas at the moment of its finishing touch, perhaps, cinemato*graphic* in extremis. But there is another and earlier example in Woolf's fiction, more "graphic" yet in its mobile optics—as well as in its phonetic mimesis. And certainly in its violence. Woolf's own fiction was hardly drawn exclusively to the kind of rarefied abstractions advertised by Lily Briscoe's foursquare canvas, or to the sfumato of distance in the blurred lighthouse sighting. So that in contemplating the filmic Woolf, one does her prose no full justice in singling out only the sedate equilibrations that bring *To the Lighthouse* to a close by resting on a two-dimensional symbolic field like a lineated page rather than a world. In contrast, another of her most famous scenes is, we might say, punishingly three-dimensional. In *Mrs. Dalloway* (1925), there is a moment more nearly in sync with the jagged, stabbing set designs of Weimar gothic, all acute angles and fractured affect—erupting from the center of an existential comedy of manners. But this effect hardly approaches the geometric abstraction she praised in *Caligari*: a cinema of visual poetry rather than pictures. The famous scene in question is so far from visionary as to be an ophthalmic trauma of overexplicit identification: a lethally plunging body seen from the inside out by delegation to the emotional telepathy of a participant witness.

Into Clarissa Dalloway's party has barged, as regrettably invited guest, a famous doctor, with news of his doomed patient. In her hypersensitivity to pain, Clarissa's is an instinctive shudder of recoil. But the stream-of-consciousness prose is anything but instinctive in its closely calibrated, bludgeoning force: "He had killed himself—but how? Always her body went through it first, when she was told, suddenly, of an accident; her dress flamed, her body burnt." The punctuated choppiness there, in the grammar, chimes with the rehearsed shock of impalement now burst into consciousness: "He had thrown himself from a window." Her initial question—but how?—may seem to have been answered. The means, at least. But now the more palpable "how" of it, its bodily feel, launches her into the annihilating scene itself in her projective imagination, where adverbial inversion (and a borrowed "focalization") seems to make the street-level railings rise rather than the body drop: "Up had flashed the ground; through him, blundering, bruising . . ." We might expect the participial alliteration, broken off there in my paced rerun, to be attached backwards to the plunging body, blunderingly bruising itself in its leap, but instead the stabbing instruments of death turn out to have been faintly personified ("blundering," fumblingly blunt) as the grammatical inversion lifts them into penetrating view: ". . . blundering, bruising, went the rusty spikes." Until a minimal grammatical inversion (rather than 'he lay there') is all that's left to fixate the inert: "There he lay with a thud, thud, thud in his brain"—as commonplace a noun, in repetition, as the slant rhyme "blunder" was a verb, and in each case suppressing, even while obliquely summoning, any glimpse of spewed *blood*. A modicum of protective censorship accompanying the otherwise gruesome tenor of Clarissa's free indirect discourse may seem to be working overtime—so that the spurting blood is, as it were, only made audible across the syllabic flow of its grisly off-echoes. All this—"and then a suffocation of blackness," with the abstraction "blackness" being both cause and effect of this choking off of consciousness.

The sequence feels ineluctable. Flash insert to the obtruded brutal scene, fast-forward vertical zoom, pounding short-lived soundtrack, rapid iris to black, then, in effect, the close-up reaction shot in a return to internal monologue at the party: "Thus she saw it. But why had he done it?" When all is said and done, done by being said, one can sketch the cinematographic storyboard of this effect without beginning to exhaust its internal lexical and grammatical scenario in the performed routes of wording. To admit as much is to highlight again the means by which one "screens" such a passage, not just in imagination, but for its strategic medial analogues: the shock cut, the subjective POV flashback, the returned implicit close-up on the unanchored gaze of sympathetic penetration itself. One does the originality of the passage some justice even in risking the suggestion that its true cinematic equivalent has become almost a cliché of optic counterpoint on the modern screen: the internal montage that erupts with the involuntary return of the unsuccessfully repressed, whether from a lived past or an imagined death. If cinema in general finds it hard to eschew the vividness of dramatic narrative in favor of the visual metaphor Woolf's criticism coolly favors, so, at the same time, does Woolf's prose find it hard to renounce a syntactic melodrama built on the dynamics of ocular focus.

In probing the literary equivalent of screen camerawork—including many a reworking of captured image in the transformations of the lab—what, then, we might well ask again, is a cinematic sentence, a cinematographic clause? What *isn't*, one might answer—under the right serial tension of adjusted focus, convergence, disjuncture, transit, swivel, iteration, discharge, and correlated audiovisual release? What kind of prose dynamism doesn't permit thoughts of cinema—even cinematic thinking—in anything from the idiomatic appositional redundancy of optic recognition and implicit fixity in "there it was—her picture" (Lily's epiphany) to the receding depth of field in "beyond which somewhere someone bellowed" (Bond's agony) to the clairvoyant stabbing reprise of the assonant "up h*ad* flashe*d*"? In the mental cinema of writing's wordstrips, it is repeatedly the case that their rips and trip-ups and reversals, their projected latchings and detachments, serve to bring out the ways in which the edited camerawork of prose, its pace and focus, works us as we read.

A Postfilmic Sentence?

In my closely illustrated insistence (across four books on motion picturing in the transition from photographic to electronic imaging) that the narrative medium has not gone postcinematic, but only postfilmic, the place—and parallel evolution—of televisual editing only confirms, from a different direction, the norms of cinematic camerawork retained by video. Certainly Don DeLillo is no stranger to cinematic timing in the pace of his sentences. And by no means restricted in this to a "cinema-themed" narrative—though one of his early narrative exercises has milked this possibility with blistering irony. In his 1978 novel, *Running Dog*, following such incidental mentions of cinematic technique as in the distracting static of "overlapping dialogue" at a crowded turning-point reception, we finally close in on the silent film itself, toward which the whole plot has been driving. This is the recovered last footage of Hitler in his bunker, though the material is not what underground rumors predicated. In all its nitrate fragility, it was assumed to be the record of some last degenerate orgy. Instead, when secretly screened, it turns out to be one of Eva Braun's lackluster home movies, a crude document including in this case the simulation of a simulation: footage of Hitler, in a deranged spiral of inauthenticity, impersonating Charlie Chaplin, who had parodied the Führer himself in *The Great Dictator*.

This macabre pantomime homage is revealed only after a number of inert establishing shots of the assembled restive audience. Finally, the described camera becomes "active," and prose follows suit, moving first laterally, in an explicit pan, across the normal run of a paragraphed sentence in italics, as if to capture in prose the "foreign language" of cinematic emphasis: "*In a long slow panning movement, it focuses eventually on a figure just beyond the doorway. A man in costume. After an interval of distortion, the camera, starting at the man's feet, moves slowly up his body.*"[5] To capture that unidentified vertical "tilt," optical reverse of the literary formula of head-to-toe description, there follow eleven paragraphed (or itemized) noun fragments of the Führer in costume, not as himself, nor even as in his uniformed doubling by Chaplin, but in tatters as his slapstick alter ego in the latter's iconic Tramp persona: a camera lift, that is, from "*Oversized shoes, turned up slightly at the points*" all the way up to "*a battered derby*" (234), then down and up again, as if in a second reproduced optical (if not mechanical) scan, from cane to "the famous moustache"—famous as the signature look of the demonic cult figure and the star alike: a deranged and monstrously compressed episode of tragedy replayed as farce.

Shot analysis need not, of course, be anything as explicit in fiction to catch the eye. Nor need the cinematic sentence have actual film footage in its narrated sights. Nor, for that matter, need the inscription of prose's own alternating filmic frames, as a return briefly to Dickens will shortly remind us, have film process even conceivably in mind. All that aside, the last phase of this chapter's "cinematics" has set out by wondering, not if there might be a genuinely kinematographic prose (as so bluntly overdetermined in that Hitler film ekphrasis), but if there is something like a postfilmic or video *writing* as well? If so, it certainly wouldn't be so closely leashed to the celluloid archive as in the case of that Nazi nitrate spool. DeLillo again, then, but over a decade later—where, in *Mao II* (1991), it is nonetheless the cinematic model that remains in place, even in TV transposition. In an almost digressive episode of media-savvy depiction, inherited patterns of camerawork are reframed on the small home screen in what amounts to—comes down to, at the syllabic level—a phonetic ekphrasis of epic TV coverage watched with the sound off. Mute, if only to dial up the phonetics of the cinematic sentence itself. Unfolding on the screen is Ayatollah Khomeini's vast funeral cortege when tracked by the steady lateral march of the camera in its documentary Fframe-advance (both verbal scales again). Depicted twice over is a classic, if frustrated, panning of the mortuary panorama across the documented course of the burial, its phonemic and monosyllabic increments italicized here in one possible tracing of its scan(sion), curtailed by scope itself: "The camera could not absorb the full *breadth* of the crowd. The camera kept panning but could not *inch* all the way out to the *edge* of the ang*uish*ed mass. On the screen the crowd had no *edge* or limit and k*ept* on s*pread*ing."[6] Even the recurrent letteral clusters in the second and third sentences can seem to be edged forward from within, by their own advancing alphabetic borders, across a sequence only finally breaking free—*ch/dge/ish/edg*—with a tauter echo, and further phonetic stretch, in the shift from "ed" through "kept" to the fully graphic but not phonic dilation of "s*pread*ing." Even that very word sound is heard rounding back as well to the "breadth" its horizontal sweep is meant from the start to address. This is the DeLillo, familiar from chapter 1, who likes to match word endings—beginnings and middles, too—all part of the prose poetics of his internal rhymes: likes to pair, to liken, and even at times to dramatically mismatch, syllabic matter. And for effects less symmetrical at times than more disruptively kinetic.

Kinetic, temporal—and even in the form of an implied reverse action next, in an effect reminiscent of the retrogressive sequencing in Amis's

Time's Arrow. What we find enacted here, in this mortuary panning shot from *Mau II*, is a video return from the historical past—via a nonetheless instantaneously archived live broadcast—that involves its own would-be optic wrench, within the depicted scene, into an arresting present tense. Two directionalities, two vectors, those of time and the camera, coincide and ironize each other in this closely calculated effect. As the TV footage continues sliding sideways in an always outstripped pan, what it ultimately tracks, and is magnetized by, is a frenzied attempt at reversion. In this footage of mass grieving: "The living beat themselves and bled. They ripped the funeral shroud and tried to take the dead man into their tide, their living wave, and reverse the course of time so that he lives" (189). After wedging open the bland assonant idiom 'tide of time' by edging it into an appositive amplification across the "wave" motion of syntax's own undulation, this televisual sentencing arrives not at 'lived'—in mere counterfactual continuity with the narrative past—but at a show-stopping alternative. Aligned with the masses' wish-fulfillment delusion, DeLillo's prose "coverage" offers up the present-tense "lives" of grammar's own backpedaled temporality, not in medial immediacy but in reverse-action fantasy.

Silent home movies in prose approximation, cinematic camerawork in TV remediation. All par for the course, even in their strenuous capture by literary device alone. But DeLillo is perhaps more famous yet, at least recently, for his engagement with digital rather than cinematic or video imaging. Even here, though, he might be thought, in the flicker effects of his descriptive coruscations, to be adapting the still essentially "cinematic sentence" to new computational occasions. In his 1997 novel, *Underworld*, named in part for the cyber grid of contemporary existence, even aerial imaging by computerized scans gets access to the stylistic underside of such shimmer. These are the riveting "Landsat photos" in which satellite overviews are adjusted to translate topographical data into color-coded image, including the sibilant zing of "sizable cities pixeled into mountain folds."[7] The sound play—the word shuffling, or say the pressure of words on meaning—is even more phonically marked in recognizing "how sweeps and patches of *lustrous color*, how comp*ut*er f*usch*ias or ror*sch*ach pulses of unnamed shades" (415) might elucidate nonvisible information.

Nonvisible, but captured in the literary (rather than algorithmic) code by graphonic inference—and syllabic interferences. The pixelated "underworld" (pic-cells; originally pic-el[ement]s) of the digitized image, in transfiguring aerial landscape to luminous data grid, has found its objective correlative in the conversion of syntax into phonemic "folds" and their own aural topography. A phonic mosaic acts upon semantics—acts up from within it—as digital processing does in the case of aerial imaging: exaggerating the pulse of its increments, including the echoic labial play, turned plosive, of the "the*rm*al *bur*sts" that name them. So that when "Photo mosaics seems [*sic*] to reveal a secondary beauty in the world, ordinarily unseen," we hear its stereophonic equivalent in the appositional, say, ex*u*berance of "some hall*u*cinatory fuse of e*x*actit*u*de and r*a*pture" (415). If DeLillo admits, as we earlier saw, and all else being equal, that "I might want rapture matched with danger"—in the chime of antimony, presumably—who can deny that here, in *Underworld*, he's found some sensory equivalent for the bliss of precision in the pulsional pull between distinctness and ecstasy, "ex*a*ctitude and r*a*pture," four syllables purified to two, while shadowed in the process (in predetonation by the building long *u* of "hall*u*cinatory . . . f*u*se . . . exactit*u*de") by the last off-echo (yet teasing eye rhyme) of "tude . . . ture"? To speak of the postfilmic flicker of the legible reading thread in such effects is more metaphoric than anachronistic, and pardonable either way I trust, in summoning the bitmap grid of phonetic reticulation in the differential substrates of prose.

Yet one might also be forgiven for thinking differently about an abiding cinematic model. Elsewhere in *Underworld,* where DeLillo's narrator is embroiled in estimating the entirely postcinematic webwork of fiber-optic streaming—in the relay of pixel-destined data, rather than in the projection of film narrative—the attempt to compass this global infrastructure retains a montage force that has gone to school in the editing procedures of screen rhetoric and its own quaint and dated metonymic links. Take, famously, the negative rhapsody, and latent paranoid flash point, of digital entanglement at the end of that novel, where global linkages—a potentially strangling web of them—are evoked perfectly, precisely as regards their discrete nodes of entailment, in the flexions of standard literary phrasing in its tested syntactic dexterity. As opposed to the satellite overworld and its pixel delectation, though even there it is the syllable that carries the day, the cable undernet is syntactically webbed in manifestation with a rapid "shot exchange" familiar from certain high-velocity cinematic sentences: "Everything is connected. All human knowledge gathered and linked, hyperlinked, this site leading to that, this fact referenced to that, a

190   Chapter 5

keystroke, a mouse-click, a password—world without end, amen" (825). So "connected" is everything that the severed noun phrases in the threefold cadence near the end, in loose metonymic link to the establishing grammar, lend their tripled article "a" to an ironic desanctification of "a/men," just as "pass*word*" seems all by itself to have generated the adjacent vestige of a scriptural "world" made mock of by the overriding underworld of the WWW.

Even before this, an immediate disconnect, not quite comma-spliced but discontinuous in focus, separates the copula of predication in the first sentence (the connectedness that "is") from the extended grammatical fragments to follow, almost paradoxically unraveled in their own entanglement. So deeply connected they need no conjunctions. The whole sequence is fashioned from that kind of absolute construction we saw amassed in Humbert's montage of Lolita's celebrity future as tennis star in the last chapter: those subclausal syntactic increments crisply self-contained, autonomous in tense, suspended halfway between noun and verb phrases, bearing subjects but no finite predicates ("Dolores endorsing a Dromedary"). Call it wording doing double duty for reference and grammar at once. And thus readily enlisted as the phrasal equivalent, to vary DeLillo's network trope, of cinema's own way of managing "this sight [rather than site] leading to that," often "hyperlinked" in the montage nexus to a different spatiotemporal frame (capital *F*) entirely.

In DeLillo's ironic peroration, then, a disembodied adjacency—with no tense beyond simultaneity, and indeed "without end" in the circuits of cyberspace—is electronically archived in the very moment of transmit. A grammatical template comparable to that in Nabokov's treatment—one that catapults us into a cumulative future in almost a time-lapse fast-forward—is deployed here instead ("this site leading to that," etc.) as a spatial and/or temporal montage: a trans-synchronic mapping of global parity and interpenetration, of dependencies unglimpsed in the syntax of webworked dispersion. This entails a snare of broadband filaments, not film broadcasts, but ones already netted in a prose of serious transmedial street cred in its previous "cinematic" incarnations. To be more specific yet about the cognitive constellation enacted here: though couched to disclose an underworld of invisible electronic connections, the quick-cut shot-plan of this passage, its performed site links, deploys its isolated and self-contained syntactic nodes—finally reduced to an association of mere nouns like "keystroke" and "password"—as if they were propelled by jump cuts or rapid cross-fades from one interactive scene to another in the subservient zones of a universal algorithmic fix.

Flip such worldwide unease to its opposite in private nostalgic euphoria—with another textbook-worthy version of those absolute constructions—and you can better appreciate the instructive common denominator between an evoked global entanglement in DeLillo and an alternate elegiac rhythm, shot by adjacent shot, in a pastoral rather than paranoid montage from Dickens's *David Copperfield*: "I never hear the name, or read the name, of Yarmouth, but I am reminded of a certain Sunday morning on the beach, the bells ringing for church, little Em'ly leaning on my shoulder, Ham lazily dropping stones into the water, and the sun, away at sea, just breaking through the heavy mist, and showing us the ships, like their own shadows." All is suspended in the amber of an iterative grammatical present. With no break there between the main clause of passive predication ("I am reminded") and the fourfold facets of the memory that independently fill out the flashback (bells ringing, Em'ly leaning, Ham dropping, sun breaking and showing), here is another case where "everything is connected"—but in the mental levitation of reverie rather than in the radical impersonality of networked filiations, where all is unseen alliance and exponential reliance. In each case, screening this latest grammatical contrast as we've been doing, one almost *sees* the structure, can almost picture the difference involved.

The comparison has nothing to do either with influence or even finally with rhetorical common denominators; it registers, instead, the shared ways of the word in the syntax of intersection. Wording can work quite opposite wonders. In Dickens, on the one hand, a prose sequence "vertical," synchronic, its abiding aspects stacked all but simultaneously together in the uploaded lyric immanence of romantic retrospect; in DeLillo, on the other hand, yet according to a similar grammatical format, aspects dispersed in a spreading international horizontality. In either case, the sentence—whether cinematic or not, or videographic, but how better to appreciate it?—is offered up, in syntactic form, as a primal unit of interdependence. And not least when deployed in summoning just that coalescence, whether under the sign of prelapsarian harmony or "underworld" global imbrication. Summoning it, and, as noted, eliciting its suggestive verbal symmetries.

From Dickens to DeLillo, then, and call it cinematographic or not: the kinetics of a graphically realized system of narrative enunciation in the linkages of prose—a more generative field of intermesh and resonance than in the reductive computerized case of 'this fact referenced to that.' Writing exceeds computer script precisely, one might add, in its ability to evoke, simulate, and satirize the latter's own uninflected tentacles of connectivity. In and beyond this process, it is language in its own right that seems frequently to emerge as the appointed, not just implied, indeed the virtually anointed, hero of DeLillo's storytelling. In *Zero K*, whose dystopian linguistics we touched on in the opening chapter, DeLillo's narrator is confronted with evidence of a coming cryogenic future characterized by the forfeit of all known languages in the reformatting of human ontology itself. In glimpsing discovered signs, both gestural signage and sounds, of the strange tongue that will replace us at the root of our identity in language, the narrator recoils from the intricacies of computer-derived messaging, "the involutions, the mind drift"[8]—or the mind rift—that such a future expression portends.

In particular, with communicative agency reduced to an entirely new phonemic basis for posthuman speech, the memory of literary language as we know it will come only as electronically implanted. And, from DeLillo's narrator, we get a typifying instance of this—and of what, signaled by enlivening wordplay, might well be lost in the process. The contemporary writer who, as writer, avowedly authors sentences first of all—rather than paragraphs or scenes or books, and in this way maximizes the recurrence of syllabic matter in subtextual patterns—has his narrator channel him at one point in *Zero K* by allusion to another such author, Ernest Hemingway, and the natural flow of his benchmark prose. But you—the apostrophized future subject, in effect, addressed by proxy in the nonperson of a character adrift in suspended animation—can't be expected to have seen the intertext coming, since the canonical name is deceptively withheld until the end of the relevant clause, deferred by metaphors that invite a deliberately literal misreading. "With nano-units implanted in the suitable receptors of the brain, all culture is rewired through you"—including, at the close of this very paragraph, a chance "to revisit the rivers and streams . . ." (72). For a split second, across the heightening syllabic splits of *re/vi/sit* and *riv/ers*—like a step-time lap dissolve at the microlevel—the dystopian passage may appear briefly stabilized in a kind of ecological nostalgia, whether for such pastoral experiences in literature or in life.

Not, as I say, for long. Not even for the length of its own syntactic arc. For installed there, in more than a mere alliterative flip of syllables, what we stumble into—as grammar aggregates the rest of the sentence—is the "flipped switch of hallucination itself" (72). Artificially triggered by the synapses of electronic prosthesis, what can be jolted into retrieval by the hypercharged mind is not only Hemingway's setting or theme in a given story, recovered by cortical download, but even the vividly traced ways of his wording. The nanotech option here imagined, projected, by the narrator at this inner sentence turn—once we have let the iambic grammar breathe freely in its full syntactic span, and so let it finish executing, in effect, its horizontal pan—is the chance to "revisit the rivers and streams *of sentences in Hemingway*" (my emphasis on the rounded-out clause). The cyborgian desideratum is indeed ratcheted up, from within the unorthodox pace of phrasing itself, from nature to metatextual culture. Not settled for here is the forked path of some big two-hearted river (from one of Hemingway's titles), but instead—though still trapped in this computer-wired parody of reading—a cued neural path through the digitized units of recovered syntactic byways, the very rivulets of prose evocation. Not sentences about streams but the inward stream of one sentence into another.

Novelistic prose, including the timings of its alliterative syntax, outplays cryoresuscitation on the latter's own described terms. This is a still-human prose whose phonetic ripple effects, channeled by banked constraints, can best be mapped, via technical specifications quite apart from digital implants, along the palpable vocal grooves of prose lettering—in all the frequent "exactitude and rapture," again, of their lived (because subvocalized) linguistic rhythms. About the audio tracking of just such prose intensity in other contemporary fictional settings, and in the context of other cybernetic approximations—as well as in a return to such forebears as Whitman and Melville—it is time, there still being space, for a further (never final) estimate in the epilogue.

Instantaneous Iris Out

But time and occasion before that, in closing off these two chapters aimed at screening prose for its cinematographic grain, for one final and extravagant example (to return to a previous subheading above) of "focalization," both audio and visual, in a contemporary prose more closely aligned with the melodramatic frame-advances of classic film than with digital codes and their relays. Having written one book and a separate chapter in another, respectively, on the death scene in literature and film (*Death Sentences*, "Deaths Seen")[9]—taking up the limits of subjective representation, figural and audiovisual, at such parallel narrative impasses—I still wasn't prepared for their closely orchestrated medial convergence in the tour-de-force suicide scene of Jonathan Franzen's 2015 novel, *Purity*. If Franzen didn't in fact have *Mrs. Dalloway*'s "up had flashed the ground" in mind, or Woolf's own rendered "suffocation of blackness"—where the optical aperture is instantly irised or just blacked out (who can say?)—the prose of *Purity* tells us he might have.

A more widely heroized version of Julian Assange in Franzen's plot, the brilliant German hacker guru and political leaker Andreas Wolf, holed up at his mountain-rimmed compound in Bolivia, is consumed—in the penultimate volume of the novel, called "The Killer"—by the memory of an earlier brutal murder committed by him during his time in the former East Berlin, with the killer instinct now overmastering his personality to the point of a recognized suicidal drive. Eavesdropping on the world until this point, in an unchecked tech network of intercepted voices and their texts, finally he realizes that he's never really been listening to others after all, except as functions of his notoriety—has always been emotionally severed from the web of community. The man facing him now on the edge of a cliff face, one of the few who know his homicidal secret, and once his only friend in the world, refuses to shove him off the symbolic "pinnacle" where he has hoped to stage his relief from torment, and so Andreas must take the leap in full admission that the killer *within* has won. Three aspects of the literary death scene I once, long before Franzen's novel, anatomized under the headings of displacement, transposition, and epitome—the death that projects consciousness onto an outside force, transposes realist representation into metaphor at death's epistemological limit, and figuratively sums up a life in the process of expunging it—all operate in close coordination here. The Killer has become someone other to himself entirely, who can no longer hear an actual human plea (the silent scream of his antagonist)—only nature's ambient, impersonal noise instead, which is transfigured at the last moment into a synesthetic rush of distant vegetal thrashing registered as sonic force. All this goes to suggest—in its narcissistic distillation of death by epitome—that Andreas Wolf dies in the burst bubble of an isolation lethally true to form, a kind of death to others all along.

Before quite unmistakable cinematic effects are engaged, the scene builds by its own brand of schizoid dialogue, summed up in Andreas's advice to his alienated friend Tom: "If I were you, I'd kill me,"[10] which captures the canonical death scene's frequent psychic displacement, here in a crisis of grammatical shifters. When the suicidal protagonist is instead collared by his betrayed friend, Andreas no longer seems his own agent, but a second self looking on from the recesses of internal monologue: "Tom tightened his grip on the collar. *Someone* took hold of his wrists" (544; emphasis added). That "someone" is the Killer, now the would-be self-slayer, cogently suggesting that it would be less incriminating for Tom to shove him off the cliff than to strangle him. And again the displaced agency: "Someone went close to the edge of the pinnacle," asking to be pushed. Self-destruction is already transferred to a kind of out-of-body option, the fate of some doomed other. Accused of wanting to do it in a further desperate exchange, Tom refuses, until the diagnosis forced from him at this point of no return, explicitly delivered in the novel for the first time, articulates the split in Andreas's consciousness as a death trigger: "No. You're psychotic, and you can't see it because you're psychotic. You need to—" But the paragraph is over. No more room for the infinitive mood of posited counteraction. All is finite now—and fatal.

Immediately: "The sound of Tom's voice stopped. . . . Tom's mouth was still moving, and there was still the distant rush of water, the screeching of parakeets. Only human speech had ceased to be audible" (545). Silent human cinema obtrudes within a technicolor cacophony. The final epitomizing thought looms in a cornered version of free indirect: "Had the Killer always been deaf to speech?" In this "mysterious selective silence," transposed from psyche to scene, even though a dimly echoic "scr*abb*le of feet on the gr*ave*l" is heard in Tom's lurch to prevent "someone's fall" (545), the latter's panicked gestures come with no words. And now, in Andreas's toppling forward, the scene's panoramic lens enters upon an exponential traveling shot in POV, naming no action but the space of a rapidly evacuated cognition. The only human sounds are those of the prose's own mordant assonance: "He turned back to the precipice and looked down at the *trop*ical tree*top*s, the l*arge* sh*ard*s of *fall*en rock,"

196   Chapter 5

with "the green surf of undergrowth crashing against them" (545)—that last image transferred in its hallucinatory metonymy from the sound of distant, unseen waterfalls, so that implicit *waves* of foliage heave up an unwritten 'turf' into a sound-drowning "surf." The only immediate physical "crash" is still pending.

From here on, vanishing distance is measured in the adverbs of intimacy rather than height (these topographic details, trees, rocks, undergrowth, moving "closer" rather than "upwards"), so that the accelerating Newtonian onset of obliteration arrives along the descending cadence of a single sentence: "When they began to drift slowly closer, and then moved rapidly closer, and more rapidly yet, he kept his eyes open wide, because he was honest with himself" (545). Because indeed he himself was, is, the Killer: the now dominant "someone" within. And because this fall must sustain its hold on the aperture of a wide-eyed objective shot: nothing subjective about this POV, in a vertical tracking turned zoom, except for the subjectivity it is momentarily to eradicate. The rapidly telescoped long shot has lasted only until the next and last sentence of the paragraph, chapter, and volume alike, closing on a parodic apocalypse of global telecommunication for this morally deaf hackmeister—and preceded by an unnerving, disjunctive syllepsis collapsing space and time together: "In the instant before it was over and pure nothing, he heard all the human voices in the world" (545). No remission implied in this received universal transmission, this final effacing noise.

But what about the adverbial temporality of the wording per se—even beyond the internal phonic undertone and hinge of "be*fore* it was *over*"? The equivalent of a mediated "over and out"? At once "over and nothing"? Deliberately awkward? Brutally abrupt? Radically precipitous? At this instantaneously truncated mortal vanishing point, any syntactic characterization sounds stupidly euphemistic. In the harrowing Fframe-advance of this plummet, the narrowing of vision operates the differential calculus of extirpated consciousness. With the surveillance genius infinitely plugged-in at the instant of going off-line forever, there is no time for a grammar like 'before it was over and there was then pure nothing,' with its rational parallelism. Cut loose from any antecedent, the "it" (life, the moment, anything, everything) is effaced even as mentioned. The syntax at this climactic turn of *Purity* thus divides, or more like implodes, across a subordinate clause ("before it was over . . .") and some version of a perverse title image in an elided phrase: any beforeness—effaced too fast for grammar by speed itself—now simultaneous with an arrived "*pure* nothing." The instant no sooner come than gone. After the dilated iris view (the eye's rather than camera's) of facedown (and faced-up-to) annihilation, the passage's heavily cinematic cancellation comes with that final implicit synesthesia of universal audition: the blinding blood roar of brain death. In wording's comparable terms, cut (not fade) to black.

And not only is this perhaps the most undebatably cinematic "shot" in our prose samplings so far, but its grammatical apparatus can help round out—even as the exception that proves the rule—the admittedly unstable homologies between screen sequencing and prose sentences with regard to their time-based mediations. For no matter how often we might slow down and reread (as I have done with the Franzen many more times even than the preceding analysis would serve to reenact)—and, in rereading, have worked to slow that weirdly elliptical phrasing ("before it was over and pure nothing") to the remote control of virtual frame-advance, one lexeme at a time—the effect of its portrayed fatality is always just as inextricably fast and final in any coherent reading as its film version could ever be. Such is this prose's semantic shock effect before silence slams it shut. Without the reflections of these last two chapters behind it, that phrasing might seem to offer a misleadingly rare point of convergence between imagined viewing time and actual reading time. But, stressed in its full histrionic anomaly by the "variably paced" examples that precede, let it stand as limit case until further remarks on the literary soundtrack, appended as epilogue, can help contextualize such writing one level down in the field of medial comparison.

The fact that I first "read" Franzen's novel in audiobook form on a long car trip, and replayed these last sentences as soon as I safely could before getting my hands, a few days later, on the print version (as when returning from the National Theater, mentioned in chapter 3, to the e-text of Shakespeare)—the fact, in other words, that remote streaming is a digital affordance shared by visual and audial media these days—only quietly secures the link between the edited sentence, whether or not orally transmitted, and the edited screen image when the latter is "read" (the quotation marks again) in analytic backtrack. And the added literary fact that attention, in the form of retention and return, may pause (over) a single shaped word rather than a spaced phrase—in a syllabic freeze-frame on phonic fluidity itself within or between syllables—is a condition of reading, though well evidenced so far, whose elusive bandwidth deserves some brief final, and finer, tuning.

TRACKED

An Epilogue on Aftertones

Via deeper review—in probing further beneath the media interplay of part III—a word more on wording's sensory difference from screen montage is in order. The given: that the leading elements of literary inflection in the weighting and aiming of the word—diction, syntax, and figuration—have, up to a point, their plausible filmic counterparts. One prevailing difference, again: that the latter can register on screen, short of remote intervention, only in passing (even if remembered, meditated on, interpreted), rather than by that braking and back-up of immediate retrace everywhere available to both the hyperalert and the easily distracted reader of written text. On screen, visual puns within or between shots, by graphic symmetry or match cut; metaphors that liken the look of one image to an optic pattern in the next; "syntactic" ambiguities of shot change that dissolve from one incipient expectation to a corrective picturing along the (unlineated) lines of a wavering retinal "enjambment": these are commonplaces in a cinema maximizing its medial possibilities. In being "borrowed back," or rebrokered, by prose—in writing that experiments with the quasi-filmic dynamism of narrative description—devices of this sort might be understood alongside the similar *acoustic* figuration of audial bridges between scenes, overlapping dialogue, and overt sound matches (even sonic puns) across shots.

But what these remaining pages need to consider—again across the temporal divide between cinema's automated sequence and reading's (or at least rereading's) entirely variable pace—is a more foundational analogy. This is the comparison that subsists between, on the one hand, the time-based alignment of a differential image track with its adjacent sound track in the apparatus of screen projection and, on the other, what we might call the *double tracking* of graphemes and phonemes, the elements of diction and their running activation, in the silent projection room—but resonant auditorium—of the read page. This latter dual channel locates the ultimate *way of the word*—with its only subliminal visual counterparts in the oscillation of screen imaging: the word's *passage* into consciousness, and from there into narrative action, only through inhibited speech muscles . . . where, just for instance, the more thorough recap promised at the start of the preceding paragraph may articulate at some half-formed level as well, via phonetic flutter in the promissory phrasing "via deeper review," a cross-syllabic hint (true enough to the argument) of the "deep preview" already seeded in such pliable phonics.

What remains to be said is indeed readily anticipated. Literary phrasing, we've recognized more than once, is never over till it's over. Wording may linger into its own rethinking, floated on aftereffects syntactic and lexical alike, grammatical and syllabic, each cueing us at different scales to the structuring—and sometimes straggling—work of words. The former effects, as noted, operate by grammar's forkings and redoublings; the latter, also by routes now familiar, through a slippery give in the phonic grooves of wording's syllabic generation. These latter effects can amount to something like a sounded alphabetic afterimage, even while recuperated as internal to the lexeme in process. Think, by ocular parallel, of the spectral traces manifest on screen in the lingering cling of certain images slow in giving way to their successor shots. Such effects are suggestively modeled on—and actually achieved at this level in the lab or computer as well—the defining microslippages of the celluloid or digital image file: constituting the yield (both senses) of one original photogram or bitmap scan in transit to the next. So, too, do phonemes—as much as photograms or pixel grids—typically disappear in(to) the "images" they catalyze. At either scale of literary recognition, syntactic or alphabetic, operable lexical aftertones (as scripted afternotes, either bold or ghostly) can be thought audialized, even while still inaudible, in that textual playback mechanism—and subvocal tracking system—known as reading.

Can "be thought audialized": assumed to be, and ruminated as such—often via just the kind of ambivalence called-out in that predication. And beside, or alongside, such phrasal flickers, the cross-fade within a single word: together those reversible semantic afterimages—and (as here) sometimes phonemic after-rims—that keep attention on edge. By cinematic analogy or not, each piece of evidence ranged and sorted across these chapters can be understood as a kind of sliding cognitive repercussion—and instantaneous regrouping—in the siftings of decipherment. What has been tabled until this endpiece is only a need to take some further, brief, and expressly comparative testimony on those two major facets of such time-release articulation, phrasal and phonic, in the wily byways of the word. This amounts to tracking them again—but less in the cinematic mode of the last chapter than in a no doubt unexpected final convergence of the locomotive and the phonographic models of such unfurled action, rotary and lateral in combination.

But first, a final clarifying crane shot of the terrain so far covered. And I use that cinematographic trope advisedly—since only by achieving a considerable distance on this book's launching motives did its developing method become wholly clear, even to its author. Only, that is, in drafting part III of this study—on cinematographic prose as frame/d display and displacement—did it dawn on me what its true modus operandi had not become but been from the beginning. Sequenced diction under interpretive depiction as language act: that was the self-assigned task. Yet other recurrent work of mine was not set aside here but turned inside out. In my critical writing on the plastic arts of painting and sculpture as well as on the time-based images of celluloid film, digital cinema, and conceptual video, the need has frequently arisen—either absent a budget for full illustration or when having to settle for the mere stilling of montage in frame grabs—to face the challenges of ekphrasis in (by common definition) the verbal description of a visual artifact. This book has evolved, I belatedly realized, by reversing that procedure. In order to think about the ways of the word—in both its assemblage of, and its passage across, a given kinetic if arresting syntactic field—new descriptive protocols have been called for, and thus called up in various engagements with literary writing. In order, that is, to think about wording per se, not just to think its meaning in the words given for it—attention must, if only intuitively, and as odd as it sounds, attempt something like the ekphrastic rendering of a verbal rather than a visual artifact.

In mounting some useful *picture* of a sentence at work, one sets about terminologically redoubling the *phrasal*, the *phrastic*, in a kind of topographic closed circuit with the more straightforward yield of designation. More simply put than it can often be practiced, this entails silhouetting the patterned shapes of wording, at once syntactic, lexical, etymological, syllabic—and, first of all, phonic—in a quasi-spatial schematics of language: language not just in process but in its structured and structuring form, its outline, contour, and gradual reshadings. Its terrain—as well as its variable duration and internal velocities. This is the approach I began gesturing at in chapter 1's discussion of Willa Cather's prose as stressed by highlighter within Richard Powers's novel. Falling certainly at the low-profile end of any kind of cinematic spectrum for the kinetics of wording, still her grammar's subtle self-adjustments seemed easiest to envision as recursive "loops" in the renewal of a forward thrust. Not like the video loops of GIF or TikTok, but graded, progressive, part of a larger sentence rhythm. It is through the lens of such visual analogies that one may come to see the shape of wording rather than just eye its words. Even subvocal enunciation benefits from such "picturing" across the lapsed traces of its graphonic dimension. And this in analogic—as well as analog—relation to the "optical sound track" of predigital cinema, where graphic traces on celluloid were, in projection, "read off" as sound waves, rather like phonemes from graphemes.

But to what, now, do this book's episodes in the imaging of wording add up? That's only for given readers to say: my readers still, for a few further pages, but, more to the point, those curious readers of fiction and poetry who might take leave of these pages more disposed than before to deliberate over a particular stylistic inclination or lexical incident. Incident, lexical event: always involving the retraced *way*, rather than mere semantic destination, of wording's cumulative action—in all its ingrained and inextricable phono/graphy. In which spirit, we'll next have recourse even to the archive of vinyl disks and their progeny for a quick set of illustrative tracks. Yet always, even in direct audition, outlining in the mind's eye the word's shaping pressure on its neighbors in the chain of sense.

Microphonics

The kinetoscopic filters through which the ways of the word have been closely screened in the last two chapters are of course thoroughly audiovisual already, even when retrieving the phonetic (as well as imagistic) Tennyson as prototype for silent cinema. It was Keats, though, in the earlier generation of British poets, whose pun puts it best—in his "Grecian Urn" allegory of script's silent piping lute, exceeding the "sensual ear." This idealized music involves a hearing "more endeared" than audible. And, right there, recognition sets in, even before the full syllabic play on "ear," when the very prefix carries with it—into our own sense of undertone, and immediate afterthought—the etymological aura of all things *end*emic to the mental life of reading, *en*tailed by decipherment, *en*tering our inward ear from the rotated, low-relief frieze of verse, *end*ued throughout with a noninstrumental music. Or, switching centuries and emblems again: all things coming to notice from the nontransparent strip of reeled-off text. For just this reason it is worth insisting on the quasi-spooled fiber—as well as inherent tracked timbre—of wording, in prose as well as poetry, always in its close fit with the propellant script of syntax. Propellant, but crucially discontinuous. Each word-border and boundary-crossing becomes a potential crux in some semantic skew and overlap: potential in manifestation, definitive at base. Even more endemic an en-d/ear-ment than in the Keats—here almost corporeally realized, though in the inner vacuum of unappeasable regret—is heard when the persona of Gwendolyn Brooks's poem "The Mother" is found hopelessly addressing her aborted fetuses as her "dim killed children," achingly knotted up in rhyme (*ill*[*e*]*d*/*ild*) with their own stilled possibility.[1] Theirs are the lost natural cries heard in the "voices of the wind" that, by the very turn of the line, it may for a moment seem—sound—like she has closed her mind against when "I have eased / My dim d/ears . . ."—but only, as momentarily spelled out, "at the breasts they could never suck." The counter-"sensual" respite of 'dimmed ears' can't be so easily achieved—and would certainly be no less transitory than its phantom phrasing in the line.

To speak of such linguistic slippages in certain cases as language's constitutive undersong is so little an exaggeration that we can even be helped to recognize this function, to hear it, by convergent instances of so-called pop vocals in the postwar American songbook—where the reverb of a syllabic note, like the afterimage induced by a lap dissolve in film, edges segue toward thematic consequence. In "the lyric," broadly speaking, rhyme is among the unequivocal sites for everyday linguistic recognitions—rhyme and pun as well. There, if nowhere else, unschooled audition hears the divided ways and parallel tracks of wording lifted from mere vehicle to inflected medium. Enunciated at the pop microphone, even if slurred over a bit, softened, buffered, a certain mode of overt melodic rhyme is only the "poetic function" (Jakobson) in showcase reduction to the unmistakable, even when just a little off-kilter. In the first paired exemplars I have in earshot, the rhyme word shared by each is that song staple—but rhyming hurdle—"love." When Nat King Cole, in "Too Young," imputes to the censorious adult world the accusation that the monosyllable "love" is a word that he and his girlfriend are "too young to know the meaning of," one may almost associate the falsely claimed frailty of their passion with that slack and dismissive half rhyme. By contrast, in the later pop hit "What the World Needs Now," the stronger, broader rhyme—on the already emphatic "love, sweet love" with "what there's just too lit*tle of*"—allows its cross-word skid to sound out the complaint, one extra time, with its own backdoor reparation. In this second case, a passively transformative aftertone loans out its fragile rhyme to a lending—and blending—of syllabic matter in the unexpected lilt, and tilt, of juncture itself, as one word leans into its phonetic complement and lexical completion.[2]

The way of the word here, shadowed in advance by its keynote "love," is an after-trace of mere adjacency. Love, one may say, is spoken a third time in that refrain without quite being said. Which is also to say that the power of attraction at play is more than romantic, more even than semantic, but also alphabetic: melopoetics (Pound again) subsumed to logopoetics. In another fleeting triad of repetition, from an earlier lyric in the American songbook, there is the refrain from the original version of "Time after Time" (Sammy Cahn and Jule Styne, not Cyndi Lauper), where the title phrase is completed with "I tell myself that I'm"—narrow idiomatic dodge of *telling the time*—"so lucky to be loving you." Especially in legato delivery, time lays its own claim on the grammar of identity (the contracted "I am") in an internal rhyme ("tha*t I'm*") serving to deliver a third aftertone of the line's own iteration in "time after time." Overriding mutability from within its own phonic accidents, even an ode to persistence benefits from the niceties of local timing.

In this same vein, popular movie titles as well as pop lyrics can be marked by such syllabic slippage—whether tacit in the 1988 extraterrestrial thriller *Alien Nation* (the alphabetic other within) or explicit in 2018's typographically knotted BLACKkKLANSMAN, that extra *k* like a nervous catch in the throat. In the spirit of ekphrasis as a late-stage methodological recognition in this volume, one might picture the effect of such phonetic oscillation, in that sprocket-snagged rebus, as that of a Necker cube: alternate phonetic and alphabetic shapes claiming priority in the gestalt of reading—an effect certainly rare by comparison with the strictly phonic glides of enunciation in a musical lyric. In a proudly promotional vein—as opposed to the suppressed, choked-back, KKK of Lee's title—there is the ingenious and uniquely *internal* syllabic rhyme (on that fertile word *love* again, phonetically bridging an alphabetic gap with its echoic "uh" vowel) in the Israeli beachfront logo TEL♥IV. Without enunciating the elisional wit of this pictorial glyph as a monosyllable rather than an emoji ("luv" rather than "heart"), such an extreme graphonic music would be lost altogether.

Apart from the rebus punning of such nomenclature and the vagaries of the pop microphone, there are, of course, microauditions that inflect poetry at every turn, not simply at the rhymed turn of a line. When engaged with the paradoxical tense structure of Whitman's "Crossing Brooklyn Ferry," I had promised a return, here in the epilogue, to the "eddies and drifts of Whitman's wording." Unnoted at the time, a thematized case was even there before us in the original quotation from Whitman's text. Just as the forked grammar of split predication (Tennyson's "the moment and the vessel past") can seem a scaled-up version of phonetic wordplay at the syntactic level, so, too, with another related figure from classic rhetoric (hendiadys rather than syllepsis, as exemplified by Hardy's "aim and end" in chapter 4)—deployed in a loosened-up fashion by Whitman in the very lines we were examining, with the double play of "just as," both temporal and comparative: "Just as you are refresh'd by the gladness of the river and the bright flow, I was refresh'd." Distended, and thus muted, this remains an instance of that marginally illogical phrasing (delighted in by

Shakespeare, and first diagnosed by William Empson) in the *a and b of c* format, where related aspects of an impression are segregated for remark. First metaphoric (the transferred personification of the river's "gladness"), then glossed by its source in the literal ("bright flow"), together these attributes ('the gladness and bright flow of the river'; its 'glad bright flow') correlate a projected affect and its precipitating fact, effect before cause. It is, if one comes to think of it this way, its own kind of cinematic superimposition across psychic and pictorial registers, thrill and shimmer at once.

But the eddying spread of language in Whitman's poem can be measured more narrowly, an instinct attested to by a similarly disposed contemporary poet when turning to reflections on his American forebear. This is the analysis once put on hold—until its phonic ramifications would have their fuller context in this volume as a whole. The phonetically adept Geoffrey G. O'Brien—who, in an online poem called "Three Seasons," enjambs in apposition "the followers, / the flowers" and later, in a phonetic *self*-embedding, "wildf*lower*s, litt*le wars* / at their center"—has thus prepared himself, in his own way with wording, for what he finds at the end of "Crossing Brooklyn Ferry." It is there, for O'Brien, that the flaunted bardic immortality depends on "having no body but staying in the earthly heaven of text," on a "boat" that is "permanently crossing between two shores."[3] What's more, he adds, "there *are* two shores reached at the end of the poem but they are sounds not places." This happens when "the last two lines say 'furnish your parts' enough times, twice, that we can cross from *furnish* to *your* until we hear the 'shore' formed in the crossing and the open 'your' inside it" (98). Along this fungible shoreline of Whitman's "Crossing," reversibly past and present at once, are words that divide and fuse at their own sedimented borders, indiscernibly coming or going, approaching or receding, in "the now of text." Whose bardic temporality is of course serial and cross-spliced in the continuous thematic emergence of *the/n/ow*.

On this account, Whitman's imperative is said sufficiently often— "enough times, twice"—to be saying something else at the same time(s). Enough times to be its own micro-equivalent, again, of a filmic loop effect, though minimally rerun—and with a flickering difference. Is this the difference iteration always potentially installs? Asked otherwise in the same familiar zone of comparative speculation: in the Fframe-advance of Whitman's crossing, is this push-pull between words (here with the internal 'shore' of nondivision at "furni*sh your*") a case of slow motion or fast-forward, or perhaps a vertiginous tracking-reverse zoom shot (in the manner of Hitchock's *Vertigo*), in and out at once, warping the focal length of reading itself? Or another Necker effect of gestalt reversibility? In any case, it is a hint accomplished, one might also suspect, with a further reverb of visionary *sureness* (again "furni*sh your*") in the phonetic bargain. Bargain—or wager. In any sensed eddy of the *sh* phoneme—O'Brien's, mine, in either case latently Whitman's—an aftertone turns internal to the increment it remakes, assimilated as catalyst in the precipitated new wording.

To say the least, in continuity here with the preceding two chapters, this is very much *not* what Friedrich Kittler means, in his dismissive sense of media blindness in nineteenth-century Romantic verse, when insisting that poetry "could let its film roll" only by denying its own linguistic structure, supposedly given over to the natural flow of a mimed temporality. The poetry O'Brien writes, and hears in Whitman, is instead decidedly a language, as is the case as well in many of the prose passages we've been screening: a language that, always as such, lets its strip sputter in a jam of fluctuant aftertones. To phrase this at the far edge of this book's argument, such is a wording so vehement as such that it loses obedience to individual words, letting them loose to their own phonic shadow play, projected in fluid levitation between the alternate grounding shores of eye and ear.

Verbal Entrainments

As highlighted by our brief return to Whitman, the cross-weave of verse and prose in this epilogue—including song lyrics (pop so far, classical next)—represents a natural point of convergence for this study in the poetics of the word. Irrespective of genre or mode, attention has been trained on those ways of the word whose enjambments can be internal to phrasing in formation, whose grammatical distentions require no meter but the measure of syntax itself, and whose resonance, whether in verse or prose, is equally the work of lungs, thorax, tongue, and teeth under the rule of suspended breath and the auspices of the inner ear. Not to mention whose "montage aesthetic" is not finally determined by narrative momentum so much as by syntactic machination: a sense of tracked grammatical impetus for which, at many a point in literary history, locomotion—or, again, logomotion—emerges as a guiding trope, along with, for instance, the wave motion of nautical passage. Regardless of figuration, however, such processes involve an internal gearing of the word by which, in its further cinematic analogues, the sublexical frame answers to, or resists, the operations of grammatical advance. This happens via the kind of flicker effect able to conjure that Brooklyn ferry 'shore' as a strictly lexical vanishing point (how otherwise in a literary text?) within the ripple effect (recalling Tennyson's seaborne alphabetic ambiguities) of "furni*sh your*." One of the word's surest ways of resonant evocation is certainly to furnish its own alternatives on the run.

Before turning from Whitman's ferried aftertones to an explicit metaphor from railcar coupling, deployed to capture the entrainment of word forms in a novel by Richard Powers, we should consider once again how language can be enlisted with marked seriality in tracking the momentum of locomotion per se. Tracking has of course been our topic in part III as well: including the rush into invisibility by cinematic framelines in the spun run of motor image. Analogously, one may audit an inner sound track by which a word comes to realization—and goes over to the next in the line of its own nexus—in a way sometimes fully recognized only after the phonemic fact: phrasing as afterwording. So let's backtrack here to the evidence from Thomas Wolfe at the start of the part III, this time highlighting another cinematic sentence in Wolfe's prose that evokes the tracks of locomotion in its own verbal grooves. Vehicular momentum; inertial increments; entrained verbal force: that's what the gears of the last great iteration of the wheel—the spooled units of cinematic projection—have in common with the internal rotary drive of sentence formation. Whereas the shipboard hero in *Of Time and the River* is about to be launched forward into the next phase of his destiny at the rhapsodic close of Wolfe's novel, his journey began when leaving home by rail—or more to the point, when looking through the "screen" of his father's porch door at the distant signs of his pending locomotive release.

The description at this point, as opposed to the histrionic closing passage, is as succinct as it is complicated: "Down in the city's central web, the boy could distinguish faintly the line of the rails, and see the engine smoke above the railroad yards" (110). Yes, the 'engine's smoke,' a thing, an index of locomotion, but activated in its own spuming by the suppressed apostrophe of punctuation in any silent breathing of the words—whereby these machines of transport do indeed smoke, waiting to steam forth. Noun phrase is powered forward as verb, image as action, picture in motion. After a comma, the inferred presence of the vehicle stationside—this vision of the stationary itself, latent with possibility—gives way to the aura of transfiguring change: "and as he looked, he heard far off that haunting sound and prophecy of youth and of his life" (110). Here again a grammatical forking, and twice over, to match the alphabetic slippage of that elided possessive in 'engines smoke.' What that last sentence from Wolfe means, even though said otherwise, is that the hero heard the 'sounded prophecy of his young life.' Or words to that effect. Instead, and like that distended grammar of hendiadys in Whitman, each phrasing decouples modification into a separate categorical manifestation, eliciting cause and effect at the same plane of designation (the train's warning whistle as the sound of prophecy; youth as the source of life's fierce vitality). Grammar is heard inflating the moment with the syntactic aftertones of its own promise. And not just syntactic, but again cross-lexical, syllabic, phonemic, however faintly summoned. Which explains its withheld place in our discussion, awaiting until now the tracked soundings of this epilogue. For in its overt splitting and distention, the last phrase is also reverbed from one word to the next—by way of an internal slant rhyme—in the iambic grain of "and pro*phec*y of youth and o*f his* life." The almost overexplicit broken parallelism of the added "of his" has, therefore, more than sibilance in train, however ephemeral the aftertone. The potential foreseen is embedded by internalized echo in the very noun of its own anticipation. And hard on the heels of this effusion, we find the alliterative if illogical run of synecdoches—in what he "heard far off"—gathering (nearing?) toward their arrived collective name *train*: "—the bell, the wheel, the wailing whistle—and the train" (110), where even the em-dash punctuation is so loose as to read, graphically, more like an evoked mechanic coupling than the logical sorting of locomotive components. In the vocalic linkage of *ell/wheel/wail/whis*, and back to the long *a* of "train," one need only recall Dickens's phonemic gamut (from our last chapter) in the train's "shr*ill* y*ell* of ex*ul*tation" in order to sense bracketed here a century's imitative phonetics in figuring modern transport's linked couplings in the flashing past of their lateral motion.

Singing Time: "Not a Pitch but an Interval"

At a higher level of overview, technological time moves on, as does the writing meant to compass it. Well into the second industrial revolution—and the phonorobotics of language production—any such train-car figuration could only enter fiction by way of a retro trope. In Richard Powers's *Galatea 2.2*, for instance, about the language training (no pun intended, at least not at this point) of an AI computer system, metaphors return nonetheless, as we'll see, to the earlier engineering breakthrough of locomotion—and explicitly as a metaphor for incremental sentence structure and its own inertial thrust: the very syntax that computers must learn as a second, nonalgorithmic discourse. But between that novel and this writing, Powers has another book whose emphasis on the phonics of reading will help us in moving back into his Pygmalion story. In *The Time of Our Singing*, from 2003, Powers's plot is launched by the "close reading" of a musical passage—but one in which (after Pound again) melopoesis and logopoesis are inextricable.

To begin with, the opening description in Powers's novel reminds us that, beyond explicit grammatical formats, the factor of tense may sometimes be immanent in narrative, performed by the reading act itself (as maximized, for instance, by Whitman's proleptic vision in "Crossing Brooklyn Ferry") in some uneven mesh with the reminiscent discourse of story. Take, then, precisely as you take up with it through your own scanning eye, an effect achieved by Powers in what could be called the title scene of *The Time of Our Singing*. Story gives audition to a lost sound by having us lend, not our ears, but our silent voice to its evocation, its evocalization. "In some empty hall," opens the novel, "my brother is still singing."[4] Present participle, progressive tense, alongside the adverb of perpetuity in "still," but with an overtone of fixity as well as duration in that duplex monosyllable: that's the syntactic aggregate. "His voice hasn't dampened yet" (3)—been damped in the acoustic sense, buffered, muted. And the next "still" comes to govern a fuller biographical past, many singings in summary: "The rooms where he sang still hold an impression, their walls dimpled with his sound, awaiting some future phonograph capable of replaying them" (3). The dimples of imprint are, in fact, about to be retraced by our own present phono/graphy along the grooves, the laid bumpy tracks, of the writer's stylus in the transcription of one such song from the baroque repertoire.

John Dowland's sixteenth-century lyric is the quoted "text" from this archived recital, retrieved in two cited pairs of rhymed lines—and their silent recitation. In this respect they do locate the *time of our singing*—as we alone recover their semantic as well as syntactic rhythm, a rhythm complex enough to make the point of *subjective* activation (*our* singing) unmistakable. And the harder we listen to ourselves in what we're reading, the more fully language seems to participate directly in the tuneful ligatures of ephemeral permanence that is the song's burden. Even the nesting of Cather's closing lines near the end of Powers's *The Echo Maker* could infer, beyond citation, no more rigorous a secondary reading, no more thematized a verbal analysis. As if kin to the diction that has led up to it, "still" is a keynote in the lyric's own restless grammar:

> Time stands still with gazing on her face.
> Stand still and gaze for minutes, hours, and years to her give place.
> All other things shall change, but she remains the same,
> Till heavens changed have their course and time hath lost his name. (3)

After that semantically (if not phonetically) straightforward first line, the declarative present tense shifts to an imperative in the near-miss echo of the song's next line: "Stand still and gaze . . ."—gaze upon the face of desire. Love is commanded, in effect, to meet time on its own terms across the transferred verb "stand," first a metaphoric personification, then a literal injunction. But the very continuance of this second line plays with time in its own syntactic tempo: "Stand still and gaze for minutes, hours, and years . . ." This is what we think we've just read, in unpunctuated adverbial extension of the imperative predicate. But grammatical time hasn't—on its own linked terms—been standing still, since we've already embarked on a new clause without knowing it, sprung by the coordinating conjunction (rather than preposition) "for." Syntax flips on a dime, in the downbeat of temporality itself. As the full logic of the line unfurls, the effect seems, in musical terms, to have fallen somewhere between a cognitive "repeat" and a syntactic glissando, all dependent (as we read rather than listen) on the missing pause of a comma: "Stand still and gaze [,] for minutes, hours, and years"—all these measures of duration being merely relative—"to her give place." Which is to say, in this last inverted predicate, and beyond *emplacing* her changeless beauty: 'to her give way,' as captured in the line itself by enacted syntactic displacement.

The dialectic of change and fixity continues at the grammatical as well as thematic level. "All other things shall ch*ange*, but she rem*ains* the s*ame*." In redoubling the long *a(i)n* in an evocative syllabic prolongation (*ange* in its dominant internal maintenance by *ains*), so strong is the perdurance of the beloved that the future "shall" of mutability needs only to be countered by the present tense of "she remains"—followed, along this word chain, by its extra assonant prolongation into "same." After which the last line undergoes again a linguistic wavering in celebration of its opposite. An extreme—as if cosmically unnatural—inversion takes another corrective split second to catch (up with): "Till heavens changed"—not a complete clause yet, though the verb could rest there momentarily as an intransitive, even as the metrically requisite disyllable "changèd." But no, in fact, "changed have their course" (by inversion, before grammar instantaneously continues in implied parallelism) "and [till] time hath lost his name." At just the kind of switch point where, once again, the grammatical course of the sentence is itself adjusted, syntax sets the key signature for this time-based art of temporal transcendence. Its notice in poetry, as with the temporal ironies of grammar we began with in Whitman, bears immediately on the intensive reading of prose's own tense shift in the surrounding narrative text. With the term "verse" derived from the Latin for "furrow" (*versus*), and thus associated with a "turning" of the plow, and recalling in turn the figurative rows to hoe or harrow from the introduction, Dowland's lines—built on their own internal re-versals—calibrate the singing of time itself in the switchback ways of wording. And what better way to put it than that, caught in the throes of these self-revising grammatical verges and veers, it is the "frame" of reference, both broad-gauge and granular alike, that is under serial recalibration as we read? Time after time. Where words only "stand (s)till" propelled.

There is no need to guess, but less reason to doubt, how much of all this Powers's own verbal intuition had in mind with its inclusion. Novels citing poetry, or enclosing prose from other novels (*My Ántonia* in *The Echo Maker*), offer perforce an "episode of verbal attention" en abyme. Just as with embedded prose, so with inset poetry here, where the verbal principle exceeds the borrowed lyric instance. But not without keying the reader to the volatility of the circumambient prose by drilling down on shared modes of verbal dynamism. For the enlisted reader, still on the first page of a long novel, the point isn't just that a poem, a sampled sheet of lyric, incurs reading in line with the novel's already hinted temporal thematic (an acoustic space "*still* . . . dimpled with the sound"). The further inference—immanent in this particular case of one text reading, in effect, another—is that such recessive wording bears parsing, however intuitively, and with however many strategic slipups, in the necessitated present tense of our own prose-framed notice. This moment of literary "concentration"—this reading now of Dowland's lines—is also our own voicing of the song. So that the ultimate point—as borne out by the play of grammatical tense within and across the lines—is that the brother's past music, failing any other "future phonograph" to recover the impressed dimpling, is already revived, performed anew, in the present intensity of our own serial discernment: an "undampened" stream of intonation on our own immobile lips. The playback mechanism is us. We enunciate into the open the bracketing irony of letteral ephemera that has conveyed us, subliminally, from "Time stands s/till" through "Stand s/till" to "Till heavens changèd." If we're weighing the words here with interlocking precision, it is as if a primal step-time elision has not just sprung two alternatives from the opening sibilant matrix but has rendered a sense that in fact "Time stand(s) still" is no more, via its swiftly assimilated *s*, than a wish-fulfillment imperative to begin with. If we're really reading the lines supposedly traced in auditorium space, they do indeed sing their way through us as a first sounding in the novel's key of temporal irony.

This making over of sound into meaning in literary writing is also the intermittent topic of Powers's *Galatea 2.2*, driven by ruminations about artificial intelligence and phonorobotics, but returned in pertinence to fictional prose itself. In the buildup to its investigations of textual processing, the very nature of signification is reflected on by Powers's first-person narrator—apart from its more obvious vehicular forms, whether prose or film, and to whatever extent simulated by algorithmic computation. And what emerges, even from the feedback experiments of computer learning, is essentially a "dialectical montage" (Eisenstein) at the core of articulation itself. What the novelist hero is discovering, in using the programming skills of his onetime day job to aid in the application of cognitive neurology to computer language, is an insight that bridges fictional writing and computer code. In a decisive passage Powers sounds more like a French theorist than an American novelist. But what he really sounds like is a *writer*, neither pure nor simple. "Meaning was not a pitch but an interval. It sprang from the depth of disjunction, the distance between one circuit's center and the edge of another."[5] Or say, as the phrasing in its way just did by the interval rather than pitch of sibilance, 'one's circuit center' and another's. But, importantly, the semantics here are not alphabetically bound. Cinematic "meaning" could be said to operate on the same principle. What emerges from Powers's generalized formulation is the whole brunt of theoretical "différance," a sense of meaning not carried in the sounded phrase (or flashed image), not in some direct transmission of transparent vocal speech (or projected picture plane), but determined rather, whether sounded or not, by the traced—and itself signifying—gap between contributing units. Say celluloid cells and lexical phonemes alike. Again: "not a pitch but an interval." And in language the primary interval is phrasing's s/paced breach—sometimes become abrupt buckle—between words as well as letters.

This, in effect, is what Powers's narrator is recalling later from his first childhood reading experiences, where the rectangular chunks of wording on the children's book page were imagined by the young boy like entrained boxcars bonded more by ellipses than links, a nexus of gaps operating beneath the more or less continuous breath of his mother's reading aloud. As if building on this early experience, the novel's first-person prose keeps implicitly recurring to this ur-scene of reading in one strand—one track—of its developing irony. After growing into his role as a successful novelist, that is, the protagonist has reached an impasse in his midthirties. Frustrated by the withering of his invention, he has only the first line of a blocked novel: "Picture a train heading south" (25). And he orders us at one point, by apostrophe, to do more than that: to contemplate instead the words themselves—again in that mode of reader address often timed in literary rhetoric for some fresh attention to just such wording: "Picture these words"—the ones we are reading right there as well as those of the balked interior novel's own would-be headway under curtailment. We are then given this ekphrasis of their lineal status: "The letters tunnel astonishingly across the page" (55). Tunnel rather than stretch out or race? Tunnel through or under what? The letters themselves undergirding any further sense that might come of them?

In any case, odder yet, the narrator uses the rare noun form of "consist" for the set of train cars he is analogizing to lexical components (heavy "ah" in emphasis on the "con" [cahn] of its first syllable; *Merriam-Webster*, under noun: "makeup or composition [as of coal sizes or a railroad train] by classes, types, or grades and arrangement"). Powers must have recruited this unusual word, one imagines, in full cognizance that the very phrasing might read as a typo: "They form themselves into an extended consist of cars just pulling out" (55). But aside from the lurking threat of a distracting predication meant for 'consisting of cars,' the next sentence turns them allegorical: "The cars hold together by invisible coupling-gaps. When a boy, I counted those spaces as they clicked along on the tracks of type, under my mother's breath" (55)—again something like a tunneling of vehicular inscription beneath the flow of ambient phonic transmission.

In prose as in poetry, the effect in question, varying Powers's own aphorism, is often *pitched across intervals*. And it's hard to imagine an example more microphonic than a striking "interval" between words that, in his latest novel, *The Overstory*, he lets revert to a nonexistent "pitch" between paired monosyllables at the appositional crux of this breathless alliterative fragment: "The bl*oo*m still c*ou*rsing thr*ou*gh her, the p*u*re l*u*re, as if ridic*u*lous loveliness still had a job t*o* do this far past y*ou*th."[6] Amid the oohing (and indeed covert aahing) that is itself "coursing through" this erotic phrasal portrait, the electric spark of wording's sensuality, as well as its sense, depends in part on "the distance between one circuit's center and the edge of another"—where that edge remains almost tangibly fungible. Impelled further within the arc of alliteration, that is, by the vocalic deepening of "h*er*" into "p*u*re l*u*re," it's the not entirely unsaid "ah"- or "uh"-llure" that voices the silent *e* as an all but legible drawn breath.

A striking interval indeed—by being struck in both senses, excised and musically sounded at once, urged toward the more passive and idiomatic '(al)lure' rather than the deliberate "lure" of entrapped fascination. The true lure here, at this moment in *The Overstory*, is the undertext of wording's own gapped coupling in one of its recurrent forms, its secret sigh between sounded consonants. In an earlier book by Powers, *Orfeo*, the composer hero Peter Els not only falls prey to phrases like "much *else* that *Els* took for granted," but in his hermetic obsessions acts *elsewise* to his own best interests.[7] Not always, though. In joyously setting lines of Whitman's to music, he finds his favored dissonances only as "the phonemes and accents led him forward" (75), and later finds his own compositional logic implicitly spoken for via the syncopated silent *s* in an otherwise sibilant insularity of phonetic pressure articulating those "*islands* of *sil*ence" that "shaped the still surging ocean" of an internally rhyming "s*ound* ar*ound* them" (381).

Audial Tracks—and Backtracks

Few novels, in their preoccupation with verbal entrainment both in human reading and in artificial language intelligence, have been so fully if obliquely glossed as *Galatea 2.2*—though without its title even being mentioned—as has that book by its author's subsequent essay about his long-standing dictation practice, where a "digital prosthetic" seems elevated to a whole aesthetic. Powers's *New York Times Book Review* essay, "How to Speak a Book," offering certainly no advice to audiobook reciters, is not a user's manual for dummies either, some wry update of Pound's "How to Read." Only indirectly does its titular recipe have to do with subvocal reading. It details instead Powers's devotion to writing through voice dictation on a tablet PC "just a shade heavier than a hardcover"—and like a published book, "resting in my lap, almost forgettable."[8] The comparison is apt and tacitly definitive, with the textual product implicated from the first in the imagination of its compositional procedure. So the essay ends up being about reading after all, not in a closed circuit with authorial production, but in the feedback system of decipherment itself. Despite its guise as partisan pep talk, the essay is not ultimately about how we might train ourselves to speak a book, but about how we are always entrained by language to do so. Powers mentions having used a speech-recognition prosthesis "for years," perhaps predating the tablet format in its STT (speech-to-text) affordance. But whether or not these "years" stretch so far back as to include the composition of *Galatea 2.2* (1995), that is certainly a novel concerned with the increments of articulation programmed by such devices—and demonstrating, in the process, certain elusive turns in what we might call a TTS (text-to-speech) upload at the reading end.

In the brief *New York Times* piece, Powers is quick to historicize. Over the evolution of human literacy, "most reading was done out loud.

Augustine remarks with surprise that Bishop Ambrose could read without moving his tongue." Subvocalization was long in coming: "Our passage into silent text came late and slow, and poets have resisted it all the way." The "way" of wording itself, one might add—always cueing the inward tonalities of articulation. "Even novelists, working in a form so very written, have needed to write by voice." And what one ends up eventually reading isn't that voice, of course, but an impersonal voicing cognate with it. "Long after we've fully retooled for printed silence, we still feel residual meaning in the wake of how things sound." Call it textuality's millennial aftertoning. Powers explains further: "Speech and writing share some major neural circuitry, much of it auditory. All readers, even the fast ones, subvocalize." It is this neural circuitry that enters into the coils of the reader's playback mechanism. Powers's main stress, however, stays with his enunciation at the production end, here with an opening dead metaphor (emphasis added) tellingly derived from vinyl phonography: "When *in the groove*, my speech software is remarkably precise, far more accurate than most typists." In none of this is Powers directly issuing instructions, in the role of literary critic, for that silent reading that would elicit the "phonemes" he mentions as so crucial to the shape of phrase; he is, instead, as technological proselytizer, elucidating his place in a line of composition that includes Henry James's famous dictation of his late prose to a Remington-equipped typist. Powers is tacitly backdating the same voice-recognition technology that he satirized over a decade earlier in *Galatea 2.2*. But auto-dictation is only a halfway house, of course, as well he realizes, on the word's way to full reception as read event.

It is in just this respect that his proselytizing is anything but ironic. There is, however, a catch, since "no machine makes phonetic distinctions as fine as humans do," so that in the end "my software's recognition engine doesn't model meaning." Meaning is rooted instead in the differential precision of the structuring phonetic circuit. But once errors have been smoothed out, not typos but "speakos," as he calls them, the resultant laptop text has been imprinted with vocal contours that, although not closing the gap between author aloud and silent reader, do keep the lines of communication open—if only line by intoned line, rather than in some metaphysical pipeline. Again, there is no reading of voices in literature, only the reading that voices. So Powers's claim is finally a suitably modest, if infinitely suggestive, one: "Mostly," when dictating, "I'm just a little closer to what my cadences might mean, when replayed in the subvocal voices of some other auditioner." Not auditor, note, but a literate agent trying out for the role of attentive reader.

But back to the *Galatea* novel, where we left its Pygmalion figure laboring to inculcate the whole system of differential articulation into the storage coils, and activated synapses, of a robotic speaking machine. The novel's rumination on early language recognition, in that "coupling-gap" locomotive metaphor, is thus contextually braced by the cross-disciplinary ordeal in which the hero is involved, trying to turn a robot into a machine capable of sophisticated literary criticism. First, of course, the machine needs a fully stocked word bank, and with the initial device—and system—known as Implementation A, the research team "worked at the level not of phonemes but of whole words" (72). The second iteration of this programmable speaking machine, known as Imp B (with one forthcoming payoff, at least, for the nicked-off four syllables of its shorthand name), isn't able to assimilate its new, overeager hermeneutic preparation, stalling out mostly on the problem of metaphor: "Figuration was driving B as batty as a poet. It framed meaning too meagerly, extending semblance too far" (90). An overzealous "pitch" or stretch on metaphor's part, but only in the wrong sense, and an "interval" too wide for comprehension. But more specifically, too, it isn't so much the lexical or figural that is at stake in the following dismissive sentence, but the narrator's own contingent reversion to the phoneme as a postlexical aftertone. "Imp B always did rub me the wrong way" (90). The bumpy internal rhythm at *mp/b/ub/me* is enough to put us on alert that phonemes are rubbing words the wrong way as well. "Nothing violent," in the verbal case either. In effect: 'I just never cared for it, although I tried not to let that get in the way of our work' (90). Such is the sense, but the way of the actual wording is in fact otherwise, where "not to let that *imp*ede our work" installs "Imp B" wholesale at the accidental heart of that commitment like some kind of software glitch, rather than cross-word fluke, in the sentencing itself—a return of the repressed friction even in the narrator's supposed overcoming of it. In a maximized lexical economy, his "batty" play on words is exactly the "speako" AI robotics would be programmed to police against.

It is just this ultimate mystery of listening, the hear-say of more than is spelled out, that seems conjured in the novel's epigraph from Emily Dickinson. And so, in our book-long attunement to fictional prose in a transmedial poetics of the novel, we're back again, for comparison, in the mid-nineteenth century, Dickinson aligned with Dickens as well as with Whitman and Tennyson. In her three-stanza poem on the interlocking parameters of brain and world, we begin with the phrasing "The brain is wider than the sky": this because, via inversion, "The one the other will contain." This is meant not with the momentary suggestion of a radical subjectivity—where the one is the other, brain being all there is of world—but only with the suggestion of mind's being capable of compassing what lies outside it. By the third stanza, a final proposal has it that "the brain is just the weight of god"—bearing either a comparable gravity or being fully equivalent to divinity, 'just that and nothing more.' The conceit of weighted measure caps this trope, but with a riveting turn into the metaphorics of wording's own bodiless mass. For "heft them, pound for pound" and "they will differ, if they do / As syllable from sound." A difference without a distinction in this ratio and proportion? A logocentric vision of God breathing meaning into inert alphabetic matter? A textual claim about phonemic reading, near to Powers's own vested interests in subvocal prose? In any case, for a third time in our exhibits, first with Cather, then Dowland, now Dickinson, we have watched a Powers text throw into relief its own language by embedded instances of celebrated literary finesse in the ways of the word.

But what about Powers himself as character, so named in *Galatea 2.2*, in its role as stymied novelist? His whole problem seems like a double take—or a double-tracking. His inaugural sentence about locomotion is going nowhere. No story wants to unfold. Anxious as well as stalled, he has combed the web to make sure that no one has used before that would-be opener: "Picture a train heading south" (25; and a refrain throughout). Seems not. So that, if he has trouble getting his own narrative to leave the station, it's not that precedent has blocked the way. No need, for instance, to worry about, as eclipsing predecessor, any passages from Dickens to Thomas Wolfe or beyond, let alone an intermediate modernist like E. M. Forster.

But let us "picture" Forster's own famous train going north, rather than south—picture its language by another roundabout ekphrasis, that is—in the second chapter of *Howards End* (1910), launching a misbegotten journey by one Mrs. Munt, of all names, that actually uncouples the phonemes (even graphemes) of her surname—in *m*'s and *u*'s and *n*'s—across the prose vehicle of her progress. That alphabetic version of *nomen est omen* is incidental, maybe even accidental, and, to put it mildly, very easy to miss. What can't be mistaken is the flickering filmic series of Forster's three-word prepositional phrase, appended via its own train of aftertones: "The train sped northward, *under innumerable tunnels*." Holding to Powers's formula of direct reader address and optical uptake: "Picture" the *u*'s upside down, and the *m* split down the middle, and all of a sudden 'nnder innnnnerable tnnnels' becomes the very picture of a flicker effect in this cinematic lunge though the pulsing stroboscopic trench, not just of light and dark, but of serial alternation per se. The rebus dimensions of this aside, reading has once more ridden across a narrative transition in prose under the sign of logomotion—and here again in its thematized technological manifestation. But no real need to "picture" this finally, picto-graphically, since even the variant long and short *u*'s and lapping *l*'s of the phonemic pulse alone catch the audiovisual flutter of the barreling locomotive. Pictured here with those indicated "coupling-gaps" in em-dash form (recalled in Powers from the novelist-hero's childhood language acquisition), it is indeed the tracking of *un—num—le—unn—el* that is enough to capture the stroboscopic impulse of this journey—and this cinematic sentence—in the silent processing of its entrained dynamic. No "mother's breath" necessary to release the adult reader to the overridden gapes—or coupler links—between lexical carriers. No recitation, just phrasing. No voice, just voicing. As usual, the way of the word is to go with the uneven flow, negotiate the gaps—and lucky breaks—that render it sensible, hitch a ride in reading by tracking the actual hitches, syntactic, even phonemic, of phrasing under lateral way.

To sum up the variable terms of these chapters in the consideration of the single verbal term or word—and the ways of its wording—isn't as hard as the disparate evidence might suggest. Morphological form: phonemes making syllables making words. Semantic form: words making sense. In the generative process of wording per se—our recurrent third term—a certain morphing remains possible across words. Words are to wording as modules are to modulation, including the transitional force of their internal molecular motion at the alphabetic level. Putting aside debates about the literariness of language, there is no question that literary *reading* is an attunement to this, all this, as if from within. From the first chapter forward, when looking aside to the acquired English of Conrad,

An Epilogue on Aftertones 221

Nabokov, and Brodsky—in the syntactic wake of their skewed idiomatic compounds especially, as well as their calculated alphabetic skids—the point was a broader one about the foregrounded ways of wording. The real power of comparing writers whose prose arises from an internally "defamiliarized" skein of inherited rather than native wording is that we can almost hear them writing, not in a borrowed English cast against the grain, but dredged instead from the irrepressible depths of language itself.

Where the word's ways are sometimes waylayings: the bold interception of scheduled phrasal routes by a suddenly diverting beauty or ingenuity. Titling my sampling of this, as I've done, *The Ways of the Word* may have had the strategic advantage of a suggested scope, but the volume's topic has been, could only have been, *some* ways—some passage-ways, if you will—of language in action, wording as event. It isn't just that the avenues of literary phrasing are always predictably plural. More to the point: in the most exemplary sentences of prose fiction, such radical plurality is likely to inflect even the single sentence, its patterned strands of grammar bulging with self-adjusted undersong, strung out with ambivalence and internal detours, shadowed from within by afterthoughts deferred to our recognition. Yet this inherent verbal plurality is everywhere manifest—almost palpable—in the singularity of its deep means: always the felt subvocal materiality of language as medium.

Five brief chapters could only have hoped to pry loose, for inspection, for audition, a precious (let's trust) few instances in a cross section of these plural ways, these readerly means. The ways are always paved in advance by language. And it is always this, language as medium, prose in operation, that in great *writing* one is reading *through to* as well as *by means of*. In this zone of response, afterthoughts are simultaneous with possibility in a reading therefore never done. This is where the syntactic as well as graphonic force of verbal structure—from demanding grammatical spans all the way down to syllabic nuclei, their fissures, their fissions—are found to coincide in the expressive generation of prose's audiovisualized cinema, with all its rapid alternations, dissolves, and fluid residues. This is where the reader is often made privy—in private enunciation—to what I've gone so far, but on the best of literary evidence, as to call writing's frequent, in a word, "epiphony." Always *in* the word, yes, always inherent to wording—where such effects can only call themselves out, by way of self-revelation, when we're listening in with the right settings on our headphones.

So I return again to Powers, with his use not just of epigraphs left to our own analytic devices, but with those inset citations where the text we're reading may be said to decipher another text within it, again by deference to elicited interpretive energies of our own—though sharpened in focus by the metanarrative lens directed at the nested passage. The same is true of his own implanted wordplay, his own unflagged speed bumps or "Imp-B-ences": left to us not just for recognition, but for that kind of notice that comes from phonic enactment. This book began with recent evidence from early in his 2018 novel, *The Overstory*, a title coined in complement to the technical term "understory" for forest underbrush. Our evidence comes down to the wire now with climactic examples from that same novel in which the overarching thematic of arboreal empathy again sends us down into the weeds of reading. We remember how the etymological and phonetic entanglement of slurred human speech and the decoding of "booklike bark" had, in that opening example, set up an entire subplot for one character. It is again our weeding of surplus meaning from the intermittent thicket of letters that figures, in the ecocritical subtext of *The Overstory*, the "organic" mysteries of interconnection in certain late phonetic disclosures within Powers's own phrasal ecology. So that if "How to Speak a Book" wasn't actually a call to phonetic reading, it might well have been.

And sometimes, in deep league with theme, these fleeting inevitabilities of the lexicon in the speech effects of reading, these near accidents of design, are genuinely epiphonic. Two discrete instances near the end of *The Overstory* arc within or between single words in sparking verbal microplots that immediately scale up into alignment with the whole curve of the big story, with independent character strands thereby knotted up by separate wordplay over the matter of verbal decipherment itself. There is Ray, the bedridden victim of cerebral hemorrhage, who can barely grunt out his desire to play "Crss . . . wds" (371) with his wife, as in their old routine, and is then convulsed in frustration by not being able to articulate the answer except in scrawling out the alphabetic tendrils of a barely legible—but relieving—cross-syllabic "Releaf" (represented graphically rather than typographically on the page) in response to original newspaper prompt: "starts with an R. *Bud's comforting comeback*" (374).

This move from graphic decipherment, in the twisted filigree of a crippled hand, to its decoding as manifest phonic punning is reversed when another character more central to the plot of eco-terrorism (in defense of the giant redwoods) has been reduced, years later, to "scanning bar codes" (397) on boxed books—the doubly pulped fate (unsaid) of the arboreal—at the "enormous Fulfillment Center" of an (equally unsaid) Amazon of deforestation. The "product" there is "not so much books" as—so the sentence lisps out lazily in its own crss-wrd hiss—"convenien*ce. Ease* is the di*sease* and Nick is its vector" (397). Worlds apart from the "book-like bark" of botanical inscription and its devoted legibilities early in the plot, phonetic diagnosis here names an opposite syndrome, as national ailment, even before the noun of malady fully arrives. But that is an incidental slippage—a minor ironic sabotage by lexical contagion—compared to what we discover on the next page. In secret provocations apart from his day job, Nick's polemic vandalism is still bent on defacing public as well as private property with outsize tree paintings, whose "furrows of bark"—when *read*, as it were, up close—are said in this most recent case to resemble a "two-foot wide UPC bar code" (380). It's the "furrows" of the word that claim attention here: the double decryption of this *bark code* as undersung culmination to a novel-long *bark ode*.

Epiphony: an epiphenomenon of script in the aftertones of its reading, its suggestive vestiges of wording structurally reinvested on the run as glancing semantic touchtones. That's what we have been intermittently listening for. And as further befitting the open-eared scope of this epilogue—in its emphasis on a "technology" of phonemic recognition within a broader "ekphrastic" rendering of wording's variable ways—there is the added transmedial sense that the described hatchings of the computer graphic in that punning "code" from *The Overstory* are digitally read and then extrapolated to alphabetic play (in an association separate from the novel's own) by a distant but revealing analogy with how the wavelength etchings of film's standard optical soundtrack were for most of a century decoded (translated) in the double-tracked functions of celluloid projection and phonic amplification. But let's take one step back, via reprise, into an earlier century yet for a last classic example: this from an addendum (in print form itself) to that powerful evocation of the sunk Pequod in *Moby-Dick*. The climactic passage was detailed in our second chapter for its final foreclosure in invariant temporality—and its lift into a planetary cyclicity that, in its own right, throws all human environmentalism into something more like a cosmic perspective. Stressed there was the phonetic inflection of tense structure gathering toward the final image of a shrouding seascape that has "rolled . . . as it rolled" millennia on end. But that funereal image wasn't quite final. As with the present book, Melville's too has an epilogue, one begun in his case of aftermath by its own epigraph from Job, with its oddly jogged, adverbially overloaded, and ultimately ambiguous phrasing: "And I *only* am escaped *alone* to tell thee." Two exclusivities converge on our privilege in listening. "Call me Ishmael," the now surviving narrator had opened the novel, and again, at the end, he has "paged" the reader, by citational displacement, as the "thee" of what we can only think of as a discourse-rescuing sequel, however brief. This call comes via a grammar that, across the seemingly redundant indication of Job's singularity, has its own way of suggesting that 'I, solely, am escaped—and for the lone, the only and single, purpose of telling this tale.' By biblical precedent, verbal witness is the all or nothing of literary form.

And this afterpiece by Melville has its own signature aftertones, as fluid as the nautical closure they inflect. Our narrator, about whose imperiled person we'd almost forgotten in the phrasal histrionics of the sinking ship, had been left on the periphery of the narrative with the rest of the surviving crew in the passage previously examined—only now remarking, in retrospect, that he was there "floating on the margin of the ensuing scene, and in full sight of it." Even from that distance, however, when "the halfspent suction of the sunk ship reached me, I was then, but slowly, drawn towards the closing vortex." He speaks from the "margin" like the drama's own gloss. Coasting in on the sibilant alliteration of that "en*s*uing *s*cene, and in full *s*ight of it," the tongue twister "halfspent suction of the sunk ship"—the first noun turning on the German origin of an Indo-European imitative root related to "soak"—has produced a broader scope of imitative syntax propelled by "halfspent" breath (the epithet itself rushed forward hyphenless). In an ironic emphasis sprung by the very proximity of "suction" and "sunk," we encounter the etymological deep time of the word per se—and this in its additional anagrammatic reduction of *suc/n* into *sunk*, again cause to effect, on the thickened tongue of enunciation. With the narrator spiraling inward all the while, the inverted syntax spins on and out: "Round and round, then, and ever contracting towards the buttonlike black bubble at the axis of that slowly wheeling circle, like another Ixion I did revolve." Not only does that delayed predicate in "revolve" further imitate the cause-to-effect suction of the vortex and its resulting gravitational pull, but the openly onomatopoetic burbling ("the *b*utton-like *b*lack *bubb*le") is part of a causality so fateful that—perpendicular to the narrowing diameter of the whirling circle—the downward vertical "axis" seems declaring its death spiral under the coming phonetic spell of the "Ixion" archetype and its own first syllable.

On, down, and up again the narrator has gone. The plosive density of "black bubble" is only fully unleashed, next, when "gaining that vital centre, the black bubble upward burst" (even up-word, by inversion in the phantom wake of "bubble up—"). So that "now, liberated by reason of its cunning spring, and, owing to its great buoyancy, rising with great force, the coffin life-buoy shot lengthwise from the sea, fell over, and floated by my side." Enhancing the underlay of personification in "by reason of its cunning," the etymological relation of "buoy" to "buoyancy" is no sooner capitalized on than the nouns are turned verbal in the past-participial precondition of rescue, with no attempt at lexical variation for a material fact upon which the narrator's whole salvation rests—and is, as a result, verbally suspended: "Buoyed up by that for almost one whole day and night, I floated on a soft and dirgelike main"—dirge rather than surge, in concert with that previous "shroud." And in this case the placid if grave surface is marked as such by immediate assonance in the notation of suspended threat. "The unh*a*rming sh*a*rks, they glided by"—in idiometric deflection, we may well think, of "un*arm*ed"—"glided by," that is, "as if with padlocks on their mouths; the savage s*ea*-hawks sailed with sh*ea*thed b*ea*ks." Alliteration in its own right would seem part of the sheathing in which these tamed beaks are encased.

With the saving advent first spotted in the arriving next sentence, the aquatic analogy (dead metaphor) for aerial flight ("sailed") is turned to an actual nautical object, as focalized through the narrator's adrift vision: "On the second day, a *sail* drew near, nearer, and picked me up at last." After a paragraph of potent syntactic and syllabic enactment at the full reach of Melville's opulent rhetorical coloration, here instead, in a colloquial and mostly monosyllabic simplicity, is perhaps the most imitative wording of all: the tension of an ongoing tense in an elided—or, better, telescoped—concision of phrase. The narrator living to tell the tale, he has told it so much from the inside out that the POV of his prose has not simply fixated on "sail" as functional synecdoche for the potential rescuing vessel. Further, in this condensed suspense, prose has enacted the very hope of rescue in the step-time Fframe-advance of this telephoto shot. It has done so across the swift rippling melodrama of a mere comma splice in the breathless "near, nearer"—nothing less than the incremental time compression of the unspelled but simultaneously enunciated 'near 'n' nearer': normalized synonymous aftertone of the elision as written.

I like ending with the most famous prose passage in this entire book, returning to those last paragraphs of Melville's novel as one does, and must, with new ears always: aware of its "style" to begin with, of course, and scarcely exhausting its nuances under further episodes of attention: never in danger, that is, of over-reading it in reading it over again. In the splendor of Melville's dedicated lexicon and syntax, stretched over the passage's own conjured abyss from turmoil to subsidence, the echoism and onomatopoeia are (Pound one last time) melopoetic, certainly; the evoked suctional vortex and the sprung coffin dramatically phanopoetic as well. Both registers of the poetic, aural and visual, are then further instanced under compression in the phrasal zoom (or time-lapse) of that phonetically elongated second *n* of "near, nearer." But there too, as in the passage as a whole, a logopoetics is quite directly engaged: a prose poetics of phonemic juncture here, as before of etymology, of grammatical inversion, of syllabic insistence, and the rest. In all this *the ways of the word* invite access along the trail—and trailings—of undertow and aftertone at one level or another. I had suggested early in this endpiece, almost in dead metaphor, a sense of wording "floated on aftereffects syntactic and lexical alike." This is as much the case in the always rearward drift of *Gatsby*'s figurative river current as upon the tidal swells of Melville's real ocean. You're not encountering my next point for the first time here either, since it is an emphasis with which I began this whole study. Nor can it now seem like it was ever news, given the way several chapters since—of rich citation alone, commentary aside—can only have reminded you what it feels like to come upon, and somehow to grips with, a certain pressure of inspiration in language. But I do repeat. Density breeds intensity in the work of reading. To vary a play as well from Brodsky's *Watermark*, cited in the opening chapter, the episodes of attention in this book have, again and again, held up to the light of analysis the impress or watermark of stylistic impulse in the identifying weft of a text, marking not just the *ways*, but the *whys*, of words at work. In our earliest historical evidence, we heard Poe lamenting, from the thick of his own syllabic play, the present failure of understanding by the "general reader." In contrast, we've heard Whitman's phrasal and phonetic maneuvers speaking not just to, but confidently for, us. And more recently, we've heard Powers thinking to narrow the gap between wording and reception, author and "auditioner," by the digitally assisted act of what can best be called (after Roland Barthes in *The Pleasure of the Text*) the force of *writing aloud*.[9] But this, with Powers's voice-recognition software, is only the technological implementation of a broader phonetic principle. In an act of composition so closely aligned with its already inscribed apprehension, the fact of density, breeding intensity, transfers concentration. And, when it does, delivers writing at a new pitch of intricacy—and interest. Compound interest: ready for reinvestment in the next great page you *set to reading*. Not just set about engaging—but set to reading as if to the legible music of an activated inner ear, with its most elusive harmonies made from traces, aftertones, and, yes, passing epiphonic reveals. Whether the passage-ways of wording are markedly difficult or not, there's no listening too hard.

NOTES

Scanned

1. Richard Powers, *The Overstory* (New York: W. W. Norton, 2018), 119.

2. In contrast to this downplaying of linguistic and rhetorical terminology, my previous book, *The Value of Style in Fiction* (Cambridge: Cambridge University Press, 2018)—a broader and more historical survey of the genius of style in narrative writing, rather than the style of geniuses—was further designed as a primer in analytical strategies and vocabulary, the latter glossed in an "inventory" of "terms of engagement" for the reading of narrative prose.

3. I will be using single quotes in this way whenever the wording thus flagged is an imagined alternative to, or overtone of, the text as written.

For books out of copyright, quotations throughout (double checked with scholarly editions) are drawn from easily searchable e-texts (Project Gutenberg predominantly).

4. Garrett Stewart, *Reading Voices: Literature and the Phonotext* (Berkeley: University of California Press, 1990).

5. Toni Morrison, foreword to *The Bluest Eye* (New York: Vintage, 1993), x.

6. Toni Morrison, *Jazz* (New York: Penguin, 1992), 135.

7. Toni Morrison, *Beloved* (New York: Vintage, 1998), 285.

8. Sigrid Nunez, *The Friend* (New York: Penguin, 2018), 176.

9. Ezra Pound, "How to Read," in *Literary Essays of Ezra Pound*, ed. T. S. Eliot (New York: New Directions, 1968), 32.

1. Lexical Timelines, Phrasal Timings

1. Jeff Dolven, *Senses of Style: Poetry before Interpretation* (Chicago: University of Chicago Press, 2017), 88.

2. See (hear) "I" rather than "we," in the s/election slogan "I Like Ike"—the famous example in Roman Jakobson, "Linguistics and Poetics: Closing Statement," in *Style in Language*, ed. Thomas E. Sebeok (New York: Wiley, 1970), 358, where the vertical paradigm is contrasted with the horizontal axis of association and combination, so that the "poetic function," for prose as well as poetry, is defined as the mapping of likeness (alternate choices) onto a sequence (by way of stylistic bonus) that doesn't inherently require such patterned recurrence.

3. Zadie Smith, *NW* (London: Penguin, 2012), 42.

4. Ralph Ellison, *Invisible Man* (New York: Vintage, 1952), 19.

5. George Orwell, "Politics and the English Language" (1946), in *A Collection of Essays* (New York: Harvest, 1981), 157, 161.

6. Colson Whitehead, *Apex Hides the Hurt* (New York: Random House, 2006).

7. Giorgio Agamben, "On the Sayable and the Idea," in *What Is Philosophy?* trans. Lorenzo Chiesa (Stanford, CA: Stanford University Press, 2018), 35–90.

8. Alfred North Whitehead, *Process and Reality*, ed. David Ray Griffin and Donald W. Sherburne, corr. ed. (New York: Simon and Schuster, 2010), 264.

9. Toni Morrison, *A Mercy* (New York: Vintage, 2009), 161.

10. Don DeLillo, *Zero K* (New York: Scribner, 2016).

11. George Orwell, *1984* (1949; New York: Signet, 1950), 179.

12. Don DeLillo, "The Art of Fiction No. 135," interview by Adam Begley, *Paris Review*, no. 128 (Fall 1993), www.theparisreview.org/interviews/1887/don-dellilo-the-art-of-fiction-no-135-don-dellilo. For a fuller discussion of his phonetic aesthetic in this interview, see Stewart, *The Value of Style in Fiction*, 122–26.

13. It is just this typifying collaboration in Dickens's prose between syntactic forkings and the spreading out of syllabic slant rhymes that I trace back to the frustrations of phonetic stenography in his early stint as a parliamentary reporter in *The One, Other, and Only Dickens* (Ithaca, NY: Cornell University Press, 2018), an ordeal of inscriptive practice confirmed in yet more technical detail by the surprising simultaneous appearance of Hugo Bowles, *Dickens and the Stenographic Mind* (New York: Oxford University Press, 2018). In my emphasis, the medial vowels suppressed by the shorthand method Dickens was saddled with return from the repressed as the stylistic "other" of his narrative drive.

14. Vladimir Nabokov, *The Annotated Lolita*, ed. Alfred Appel Jr. (New York: Random House, 1991), 281.

15. Vladimir Nabokov, *The Real Life of Sebastian Knight* (New York: New Directions, 941), 172.

16. Joseph Brodsky, *Watermark: An Essay on Venice* (New York: Farrar, Straus and Giroux, 1992), 4.

2. The Tensed Word

1. Richard Powers, *The Echo Maker* (New York: Farrar, Straus and Giroux, 2006).

2. Martin Amis, *Time's Arrow* (New York: Harmony, 1991), 6.

3. Ian McEwan, *Nutshell* (New York: Anchor, 2017), 1.

4. Margaret Atwood, "Happy Endings," in *Murder in the Dark* (Toronto: New Canadian Library, 1997), 50.

5. Paul Auster, *Ghosts*, in *The New York Trilogy* (New York: Penguin, 1990), 161.

6. When the punned doubling of "assume" is followed in the next line of "Song of Myself" by the oddly noncolloquial "as good" in the double-valenced phrasing "every atom be-

longing to me as good belongs to you," a further, almost madcap, suspicion—prodded by that rogue "as"—can be kept no farther from mind than a footnote: namely, a fleeting sense that the transferential "assume," in its coercion of the readerly "you," is snapped loose by repetition into an alphabetic rebus of analogy in 'as u me': like unto like.

3. Reading-en-Scène

1. Michael Billington, review of *Gatz*, *The Guardian*, June 14, 2012, https://www.theguardian.com/stage/2012/jun/14/gatz-review.

2. John Beer, review of *Gatz*, *The Point*, Spring 2009, https://www.elevator.org/press_items/review-gatz/.

3. Ben Brantley, "Borne Back Ceaselessly into the Past," review of *Gatz*, *New York Times*, October 6, 2010, https://www.nytimes.com/2010/10/07/theater/reviews/07gatz.html.

4. F. Scott Fitzgerald, *Tender Is the Night* (New York: Scribner, 1935).

5. F. Scott Fitzgerald, *The Love of the Last Tycoon: A Western*, ed. Matthew J. Buccoli (Cambridge: Cambridge University Press, 1993).

6. Simon Levy, *The Last Tycoon* (New York: Dramatists' Play Service, 1998), 9.

7. With reference to the earlier work of Wheeler Winston Dixon in *The Cinematic Vision of F. Scott Fitzgerald* (Ann Arbor: UMI Research, 1986), the phrasing "melt away" is compared in passing by David Seed to a filmic "dissolve"—without connection to another and more explicit cinematic allusion also noted in the novel—in his comprehensive *Cinematic Fictions* (Liverpool: Liverpool University Press, 2009), 95. Seed identifies the "time-lapse" effect when Nick the narrator marvels at the the profusion of blooming leaves "just as things grow in fast movies" (91). Embedded just before—like a time bomb waiting to obliterate this sense of false promise, but going unmentioned by Seed—is a telling further detail, and its stylistic manifestation, that links this simile to the closing historical "dissolve" in that threnody for the original "fresh green breast" of arrival. For just before Nick marvels at the foliage as an objective correlative of his blooming hopes, this Long Island newcomer is able to give a stranger directions to West Egg, with the result that Nick feels arrived, in his own "freedom" of domain, as bold occupant of this new world, his euphoria couched in just the language of frontiersman screen heroism that will be ironized in the novel's final historical recession: Nick pluming himself here, in the confident push of appositional wording itself, on being "a guide, a pathfinder, an original settler."

4. Threading the Read

1. Stanley Cavell, *The World Viewed: Reflections on the Ontology of Film*, enl. ed. (Cambridge, MA: Harvard University Press, 1979), 142.

2. The backlog on this issue for American literary modernism is extensive. Following a thorough survey in his introduction of comparative media history regarding the influence of cinema on literature—beginning with Claude-Edmonde Magny's 1948 *The Age of the American Novel: The Film Aesthetic between the Two Wars*, trans. Eleanor Hochman (New York: Frederick Ungar, 1972), with her emphasis on Dos Passos, Hemingway, Steinbeck, and Faulkner—David Seed's *Cinematic Fictions*, the latest major work on this question, extends the film-"fiction" dialogue to poets like Stein and H.D., as well as, beyond Magny's touchstone American novelists, to further treatments of Fitzgerald and Dreiser down through Nathanael West. Seed's broad argument proceeds without emphasis on the microlevel of kinetic wording under inspection in this chapter and the next.

3. Terry Eagleton, *Humour* (New Haven: Yale University Press, 2019), 46.

4. Margaret Mitchell, *Gone With the Wind* (New York: Pocket Books, 2008), 500.

5. Friedrich Kittler, *Discourse Networks 1800/1900*, trans. Michael Meteer with Chris Cullens (Stanford, CA: Stanford University Press, 1980), 166.

6. Thomas Wolfe, *Of Time and the River* (New York: Scribner Classics, 1999).

7. Vladimir Nabokov, *The Annotated Lolita*, ed. Alfred Appel Jr. (New York: Vintage, 1991), 222.

8. Péter Táma, "The Attraction of Montages: Cinematic Writing Style in Nabokov's *Lolita*," *Nabokov Online Journal* 10/11 (2016/2017).

9. Heike Schaefer, *American Literature and Immediacy: Literary Innovation and the Emergence of Photography, Film, and Television* (Cambridge: Cambridge University Press, 2020), 184–210.

10. Robert Coover, "The Babysitter," in *Pricksongs and Descants* (New York: Grove Press, 1969), 208.

11. Robert Coover, *A Night at the Movies, or You Must Remember This* (Rochester, IL: Dalkey Archive Press Illinois State University, 1992), 22.

12. Salman Rushdie, *Midnight's Children* (1980; New York: Penguin, 1991), 189.

13. Salman Rushdie, *The Satanic Verses* (New York: Viking, 1998), 6.

14. Powers, *The Overstory*, 11.

15. Thomas Pynchon, *Gravity's Rainbow* (1973; New York: Penguin, 2006), 209.

16. Friderike Hirsch-Wright, "Favorite Sentence from the *Great Gatsby*," YouTube video, 24:28, https://www.youtube.com/watch?v=uxUYXt9yURA.

5. Fframe-Advance

1. Sergei Eisenstein, "Dickens, Griffith, and the Film Today," in *Film Form: Essays in Film Theory*, ed. and trans. Jay Leyda (New York: Harcourt, 1977), 195–256; Virginia Woolf, "The Cinema," *The Essays of Virginia Woolf*, vol. 4, *1925–1928*, ed. Andrew McNeillie (New York: Harcourt, 1994), 348–53.

2. Julian Murphet, *Multimedia Modernism* (New York: Cambridge University Press, 2009).

3. Garrett Stewart, *Framed Time: Toward a Postfilmic Cinema* (Chicago: University of Chicago Press, 2007), 34–38.

4. William Faulkner, *Absalom, Absalom!* (New York: Vintage International, 1990).

5. Don DeLillo, *Running Dog* (New York: Knopf, 1978), 234.

6. Don DeLillo, *Mau II* (New York: Penguin, 1991), 188.

7. Don DeLillo, *Underworld* (New York: Scribner, 1997), 415.

8. DeLillo, *Zero K*, 159.

9. Garrett Stewart, *Death Sentences: Styles of Dying in British Fiction* (Cambridge, MA: Harvard University Press, 1984); Stewart, "Deaths Seen," chap. 4 in *Between Film and Screen: Modernism's Photo Synthesis* (Chicago: University of Chicago Press, 1990), 151–88.

10. Jonathan Franzen, *Purity* (New York: Picador, 2015), 544.

Tracked

1. Gwendolyn Brooks, "The Mother," Poetry Foundation: https://www.poetryfoundation.org/poems/43309/the-mother-56d2220767a02

2. In another such cross-lexical rhyme on the word "love," not from the standard American songbook but from the current country canon, and with a comic strain more like Byron's than Irving Berlin's, there is the following lyric from the group Florida Georgia Line. The male persona endures in real narrative time a kind of prepositional comeuppance, having once

"talked" his girl "into" getting ready (the idiom repeated twice) for a night on the town—and now having urgent second thoughts. Remarking to his girl on the "fine little" dress she's "got on," he wants her to understand that, although "I love it"—fit and all, no doubt, as phonetically hinted—he suddenly wants, in rhyme with his desire, to "talk you out of it." In a song titled for those last five words in refrain, the fine unspoken "f-it" of that "little dress" has itself gone twice without saying in the capping rhyme. The word's ways are just that changeable, with a noun slipped on or off in the blink of a tuned ear.

3. Geoffrey G. O'Brien, "The Rhyme of the Left Margin," *Walt Whitman Quarterly Review* 30 (2013): 98.

4. Richard Powers, *The Time of Our Singing* (New York: Picador, 2003), 3.

5. Richard Powers, *Galatea 2.2* (New York: Picador, 1995), 154-55.

6. Powers, *The Overstory*, 245.

7. Richard Powers, *Orfeo* (New York: Picador, 2014), 94.

8. Richard Powers, "How to Speak a Book," *New York Times Book Review*, January 7, 2007, https://www.nytimes.com/2007/01/07/books/review/Powers2.t.html.

9. Roland Barthes, *The Pleasure of the Text*, trans. Richard Miller (New York: Hill and Wang, 1975), 66 (rephrased as "vocal writing," 67).

Index

absolute construction, 104, 143, 148, 153–54, 155, 156, 170, 174, 190–91
Agamben, Giorgio, 34
anagrammatic effects, 28, 33, 65, 163, 224
apostrophe (direct address) to the reader, 23, 78, 145–46, 214
apposition as verbal amplification, 38, 86, 104, 142, 157, 180, 185, 188, 189, 206, 215, 231n7
Astruc, Alexandre, 123
Atwood, Margaret, 72
audiobook, 95, 96, 197, 216

Barthes, Roland, *The Pleasure of the Text*, 227
Beer, John, 102
Bergman, Ingmar, jammed image in *Persona*, 148
Billington, Michael, 102
Brantley, Ben, 102
Brodsky, Joseph, 221; wordplay in *Watermark*, 54–57
Brooks, Gwendolen, 203

The Cabinet of Dr. Caligari, 161, 176, 183
caesura, 66, 69, 92, 169
Cather, Willa, *My Antonia* (embedded in Powers, *The Echo Maker*), 59–61, 202, 211, 219
Cavell, Stanley, 118, 130
Chaplin, Charles, 186
chiasm (phonetic and lexical): in Amis, 65, 69; in Auster, 73; in DeLillo, 44; in Dickens, 51; in Fitzgerald, 107; in Forster, 133; in Meredith, 49; in Morrison, 10; in Nabokov, 141; in Powers, 62; in Pynchon 153; in Tennyson, 171

cinematographic prose: double "Fframe" with both photograms and phonemes, 67–70. *See also* cross-fade, dissolve, Fframe-advance, flashback structure, flicker effects in prose and film, jump cut, loop effect, match cut, panning shot in film, suture, telephoto prose, wipe, zoom effects in prose
Citizen Kane, 155, 173
comma splice, 148, 150, 152, 159, 226; confused by students with absolute construction, 154–55
Conrad, Joseph, 85: anaphora in *Lord Jim*, 52–53; English as learned language, 54; Marlow as caretaker function, 85; syllabic contingency in *The Secret Agent*, 8; syllabic play in *Heart of Darkness*, 53–54. *See also* Coppola
Coover, Robert: "The Babysitter," 143–44; *A Night at the Movies*, 144–45, 156
Coppola, Francis Ford, *Apocalypse Now*, 54
cross-fade (in prose), 113, 119. *See also* dissolve
cross-lexical phonetic play, 7, 10, 11, 18, 200, 232n2; in Morrison, 10–11, as compared to Whitehead (Colson), 43, 48; in Nabokov, 54; in Powers, 62; in Pynchon, 153; in song lyrics, 204, 232n2; in Tennyson, 172; in Whitman, 83, 86, 206

Deleuze, Gilles, 130
DeLillo, Don: *Mau II*, 88; *Running Dog*, 186–81; as self-avowed "writer" of sentences and syllables, 45–47; *Underworld*, 188–90, 191; *Zero K*, 43, 45
Dickens, Charles, 50, 52; Cockney punning, 4; *David Copperfield*, 15, 63; *Oliver Twist*, 162; phonetic effect of locomotion in *Dombey and Son*, 162, 209; protocinematic effects, 127, 132, 160–62, 164, 165, 166, 168, 170, 172–73, 191–92. *See also* chiasm, Eisenstein, etymology, personification, syllepsis
différance, 214
dissolve (lap dissolve), 81, 145, 155, 161; in prose, 112, 127, 141, 145, 146, 153, 167
Dolven, Jeff: on style versus form, 31
Dos Passos, John, 119
Dowland, John, 211–13

Eagleton, Terry: on Hardy's "camera," 125, 126, 127, 240
Eisenstein, Sergei, 61, 196; on the cinematic Dickens, 162–63; dialectical montage, 166, 213; on Soviet montage, versus expressionism, 160–66. *See also* Griffith
ekphrastic effects, 20, 25, 179–80, 187, 201, 214, 219; methodological force in description of prose shape, 205
Eliot, George: grammar of premonition in *The Lifted Veil*, 63, 67, 70–76, 77, 78, 85
elision: grammatical, 153, 197; phonetic, 40, 42, 83, 169, 209, 213, 225, 226; photogrammatic, 136, 158, 165
ellipsis, 75, 136, 145
Ellison, Ralph: assonance and alliteration in *Invisible Man*, 33
Empson, William: double grammar, 93; hendiadys, 206
etymology: in Cather, 62; in DeLillo, 47; in Dickens, 51, 162; in Eliot, 75–76; in Faulkner, 180; in Fitzgerald, 94; Latin and Greek versus Germanic and Anglo-Saxon, 32, 69, 76, 79, 162–63, 164, 180; in Melville, 224, 225; in Poe, 29; in Powers, 3, 222; in Smith, 32; as stylistic feature in Emily Brontë, 15–16; in Whitehead (Colson), 40; in Whitman, 23

Faulkner, William: *Absalom, Absalom!*, 180–82; and film, 132, 137

Fframe-advance, 9, 67–70, 85–86, 118–20, 130, 136, 140, 148; aural correlate in Whitman, 84; in Coover, 187; in Franzen, 196; as freeze-Fframe, 126; in Melville, 226; and phonetic flicker effects, 23, 111, 113, 119, 122, 149, 152, 168, 172, 180, 188, 201, 208, 220

Fiennes, Ralph, 91

flashback structure, 17, 77, 93, 112, 167, 185, 191; and flash forward, 80

flicker effects in prose and film, 69. *See also* Fframe-advance

focalization, 67, 99, 105, 111, 131, 151, 171, 175, 193, 225; auditory in Faulkner, 179–83; in Woolf, 183–85

formalism: estrangement as benchmark, 50

fragment (syntactic), 10, 66, 75, 186, 215

frame narrative, 89, 96, 131. *See also* flashback structure

Franzen, Jonathan: cinematic death scene in *Purity*, 194–96; compared to Woolf, 194

free indirect discourse: embodied variant in *Gatz*, 97; optic equivalents, 131; in Orwell, 45; in Smith, 32; in Whitehead (Colson), 37; in Woolf, 178, 184

fricatives, 30, 39, 43, 134, 150, 152

Gatz (Elevator Repair Company), 23, 77, 93–95; critical response to, 102; dramatizing Fitzgerald's figurative style in *The Great Gatsby*, 103–5; escalating metadrama in, 96–98; e-text culture in, 95; narrator as "vocator," 98, 101, 104; performative variant of free indirect discourse, 97; "viewereader" of, 99

gerund, 71, 79, 181

Griffith, D. W.: debt to intercutting in Dickens, 161–62, 166, 173; film of Tennyson's *Enoch Arden*, 161, 165–67, 177; montage technique, 169, 171, 173, 176. *See also* Eisenstein, Murphet

Hemingway, Ernest, 192–93, 231n2

hendiadys, 67, 75, 87, 205, 209

homophone, 56; versus homonym, 92

idiometrics, 10, 11, 35, 43, 49, 50, 60, 85, 109, 152, 225

inverted wording, 60, 64–66, 78, 135, 172, 184, 212, 219, 224–25

Jakobson, Roman: "poetic function," 56, 204, 230n2

James, Henry: "cinematic" suture in *The Golden Bowl*, 173–75; dictating his late prose, 217; *The Turn of the Screw*, 16–17, 138

jump cut: in cinematic editing, 68; in prose, 69, 111, 143, 178, 191; in verse, 167

Kittler, Friedrich: on suppression of linguistic base in romantic poetry, 130, 207

Lawrence, D. H., *The Rainbow*, 151–53, 159

Lessing, Gotthold Ephraim, *Laocoön*, 156

Lindsay, Vachel: cinema as "sculpture in motion," 156

logomotion (on locomotive model), 162, 208, 220

logopoetics, 21–22, 164, 204, 226. *See also* Pound: melopoesis; phanopoeisis

loop effect: in Cather, 67–70, 202; syllabic equivalent, 41, 122, 124, 202, 206

Lyotard, Jean-François, 123

match cut, 82, 124; sound match, 112, 200

McEwan, Ian, *Nutshell*, 67

Melville, Herman, *Moby Dick*, 76–77, 223–26. *See also* etymology, personification

Meredith, George, *Diana of the Crossways*, 48–49

Mitchell, Margaret, *Gone with the Wind*, 126
Morrison, Toni: *Beloved*, 11; *The Bluest Eye*, 10; *Jazz*, 10–11; *A Mercy*, 43
Murphet, Julian: on imagism and the "media ecology," 164–69, 171, 173

Nabokov, Vladimir, 120, 221; cinematic effects in *Lolita*, 141–43, 146, 148, 153, 190; phonetic play in *Lolita*, 51, 54; syllepsis in *The Real Life of Sebastian Knight*, 52. *See also* chiasm
Nat King Cole, 204
Necker-like ambivalence, 205, 207
neologism, 1, 31, 37, 43
Nunez, Sigrid, 12

O'Brien, Geoffrey G., 206
onomatopoeia, 6, 20, 111, 145, 225, 226
Orwell, George: *1984*, 34, 36, 38, 39; "Politics and the English Language," 12, 33–36, 43, 47
oxymoron, 3, 38, 61

panning shot in film, 155; literary equivalent, 81, 134, 176, 186, 188; swish pan in prose, 58, 110, 111, 172, 178
parallelism in syntax, 51, 59, 80, 196; avoided, 196, 209, 212; in cinema, 196
participial grammar: alliterative form, 184; cinematic analogues, 143; future participle, 73; past in obsolete form, 151; past participle, as stylistic feature, 32, 110, 134, 148, 225; present, as progressive energy, 42, 60, 75, 78, 109, 142–43, 149, 150, 162, 163, 164, 210
pathetic fallacy, 107
personification, 211; in DeLillo, 47; in Dickens, 162–63; in Fitzgerald, 112; in James, 16; in Melville, 225; in Poe, 30; in Rushdie, 147; in Whitman, 206; in Woolf, 184

phenomenology of fiction, 19, 89, 94, 122, 130, 136. *See also* Poulet
phonetic features, 103; as epiphony, 2, 221, 223; as touchtones, 1. *See also* flicker effects
pleonasm, 55, 76
plosive enunciation, 35, 38, 45, 103, 108, 147, 162, 189, 225
Poe, Edgar Allan: on the hyper-"attentive" in "Berenice," 28–30, 227. *See also* etymology
portmanteau wording, 32, 38, 39, 41, 43, 62
Poulet, Georges, 101–2
Pound, Ezra: "dance of the intellect among words," 20–23, 47, 90; "How to Read," 20–22, 164; imagism, 20, 164–65, 167, 169; melopoesis, 21, 90, 204, 210; phanopoeisis, 20, 21, 120, 164; rejection of Tennysonian poetics, 166. *See also* logopoetics
Powers, Richard: *The Echo Maker*, 59–61, 211, 212; on electronic dictation and subvocal reading, 216–19, 227; *Galatea 2.0*, 210, 213, 216–19; *Orfeo*, 215–16; *The Overstory*, 3, 149, 215, 222–23; *The Time of Our Singing*, 211–13
prepositional grammar, 155; ambiguous for conjunction, 92, 211; comic variants, 232n2; in Dickens, 50–51, 62–63; in Fitzgerald, 100, 112–13; in Forster, 135, 220; in Morrison, 11; in Poe, 29; in Powers, 149–50
Pynchon, Thomas, *Gravity's Rainbow*, 153

rebus effect, 205, 220, 230–31n6
reflexive grammar, 16–17, 61, 152
reverse shot, 81, 144, 165, 171; narrative avoidance, 138, 140; prose equivalent, 174–75. *See also* suture
Rushdie, Salman: *Midnight's Children*, 145–46; *The Satanic Verses*, 146–48, 150, 151

Shakespeare, William: *Antony and Cleopatra* heard live, 91–92, 197; Empson on, 93, 206; *Othello*, 92; Woolf on, 176
sibilance, 18; in Conrad, 8; in DeLillo, 44, 188; in Dowland, 213; in Fitzgerald, 104; in Forster, 134; in Melville, 76, 224; in Powers, 214, 216; in Whitehead (Colson), 39–41; in Wolfe, 209
slant rhyme, 45, 51, 55, 62, 75, 86
Smith, Zadie, *NW*, 32, 33, 35, 50
Stein, Gertrude, 119
stroboscopic prose, 163, 220
suture, 165, 174, 177
syllepsis, 56, 94; in Brodksy, 54–55; in Coover, 144; in Dickens, 51, 54; in Franzen, 196; in Smith, 49–50; in Tennyson, 170
synecdoche, 172, 209
synesthesia, 93, 94, 126, 182, 194, 197

telephoto prose, 226
Tennyson, Alfred: musical sonority, 20, 120, 164; verse dynamics in *Enoch Arden*, 160, 168–71
tense, 23, 28, 57; in Atwood, 72; in Eliot, 70–71; in Melville, 76–77, 224; perfect tense, 59, 74, 76. *See also* participial grammar
time-based media, 5, 21, 22, 31, 67, 132, 156, 167, 197, 212; literature's difference from film via variable pace and instant replay, 69–70, 117–19, 121, 200–201
time-lapse in prose, 120, 141–44, 147, 149, 151, 190, 226, 231n7
transitive/intransitive grammar, 15, 52, 61, 80, 110, 148, 152, 170, 212
tropology (imagery versus image), 166, 176

Wharton, Edith, *The Age of Innocence*, 11
Whitehead, Alfred North, 41
Whitehead, Colson: *Apex Hides the Hurt*, 36–43, 49, 57, 78; *The Underground Railroad*, 36
Whitman, Walt: "Crossing Brooklyn Ferry," 23, 78, 79–83, 170, 205–6, 208, 210; "Song of Myself," 86
wipe (phonetic), 133; "ripple wipe," 171
Wolfe, Thomas: dated prose, 137; *Of Time and the River*, 138–40, 175, 208
Woolf, Virginia: "The Cinema," 176; *Mrs. Dalloway*, 9, 183–85, 194; *To the Lighthouse*, 177–79. *See also The Cabinet of Dr. Caligari*

zoom effects in prose, 112, 125, 138, 140, 146, 155, 184, 196

www.ingramcontent.com/pod-product-compliance
Lightning Source LLC
Chambersburg PA
CBHW031737230426
43669CB00007B/374